英語 L & R レベル別問題集

ENGLISH LISTENING & READING WORKBOOK —STEP BY STEP—

5

上級編
ADVANCED LEVEL

東進ハイスクール・東進衛星予備校 講師
安河内哲也
ハーバード大学 教育学修士
Andrew Robbins

はじめに
Preface

『英語 L&R レベル別問題集』の世界へようこそ。本書は，「共通テスト」や「4技能試験」の対策をする皆さんが，良質な問題演習を通じて「リーディング」「リスニング」の能力を無理なく段階別に高めていけるように作られた，新しい問題集シリーズです。

本シリーズの刊行にあたっては，英検®・TEAP などの資格・検定試験を参考に，共通テストや4技能試験に共通してよく出題される形式の問題を多数作成。それを国際標準である「CEFR」という指標に対応させてレベル別に編成することで，**自分に合ったレベルから始めて段階的に実力を伸ばしていける**問題集になっています。

アイテム（問題文）作成にあたっては，日米の専門家の力を借り，4技能試験の出題形式に準拠した英文を作成しました。リーディングのアイテムとしては，アカデミックおよび一般的な内容を題材とし，空所補充・内容一致問題を作成。リスニングのアイテムとしては，会話文・ナレーション問題など，汎用性の高い形式の問題を作成しました。内容についても，皆さんが「アカデミック」な刺激を受けることができるよう，興味深い題材を選定しています。

アイテム作成後には，独自に開発された「語彙分析ソフトウェア」を用いて，各アイテムに使用した語彙と過去の4技能試験で使用された語彙の整合性を総チェックし，CEFR-J[*]とも連動性を確保するよう徹底しました。

さて，これから英語の学習をするうえで，皆さんに1つ心得てほしいことがあります。それは，**4技能（リーディング，リスニング，ライティング，スピーキング）を組み合わせて学習する**ことです。本書では，リーディングのアイテムにおいても，音声を用意しています。リーディングと音声を融合させて学習することは，英文を英文のまま処理する能力を高め，同時にリスニング能力を高めることにもつながります。また，限られた時間の中で多くの情報を処理することが求められるこれからの大学入試では，「返り読み」をせず，チャンク（情報のまとまり）ごとに理解していくことも非常に重要になります。本書では，その練習ができるように，チャンクごとに英語と日本語を対にして掲載した「速読練習」のページと，チャンクごとに英文を読み上げた音声を用意しています。問題を解いたあとは，学んだ英文素材を「耳」で確認し，定着させましょう。

本書は，直近の大学入試対策はもちろん，将来社会に出たときにも役立つ本物の英語力が身につくよう，様々な工夫を詰め込んだ新しい問題集です。この本で英語力を高めた皆さんが，将来，世界を舞台に大活躍することを，心から応援しています。

2021年2月
安河内哲也

※CEFR-J…東京外国語大学の研究チームを中心に開発された，CEFR（ヨーロッパ言語共通参照枠）を日本のような環境に応用するための枠組み。CEFR に対応する語彙リストを一般に公表している。

本書の特長
Good Points of This Book

■1 新時代の英語入試に対応した 新しい問題集！

　本シリーズでは，共通テストや英検®・TEAP などの4技能試験を参考に，各種試験でよく出題される形式のリーディング・リスニング問題を多く収録しました。リーディングのアイテム（問題文）では，空所補充・内容一致問題の計 15 長文を用意。リスニングのアイテムとしては，会話文・ナレーション問題を計 40 題用意しました。

　問題集のアイテム作りにおいては，「TLU（Target Language Use）：目標使用言語領域」の設定が非常に重要です。例えば，TLU が「アカデミック」の場合は「大学生活で遭遇する語彙・場面・分野」が，「ジェネラル」の場合は「日常生活で遭遇する語彙・場面・分野」が，設問として出題されます。それぞれの試験の TLU は下図のように分類されます。本書では，TLU を「アカデミック」と「ジェネラル」の両方を含む範囲に設定してありますので，大学入試や英検をはじめとする4技能試験の出題分野を極めて効率的にカバーすることができます。

　英語では，共通テストや各種の4技能試験，さらに各大学の個別入試など，様々なレベル・形式の試験に対応する力が求められるようになりますが，汎用性の高い形式・分野の問題を多数収録した本書で演習を積むことで，どんな試験にも十分に対応できるリーディング・リスニングの根本的な力が必ず身につきます。1つ1つ段階的に，レベルを上げていきましょう。

▼各資格・検定試験の TLU と本書の範囲

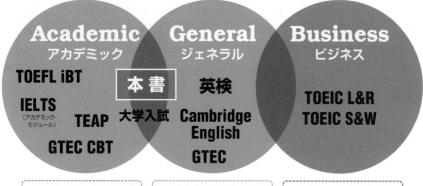

※「共通テスト」を含む大学入試のTLU は「アカデミック〜ジェネラル（一部）」の範囲です。

❷ 自分に合ったレベルから 段階的にレベルアップ！

この『英語 L&R レベル別問題集』は，「レベル① 超基礎編」から，「レベル⑥ 最上級編」までの全6冊からなるシリーズです。本シリーズは，国際的な英語力の指標である CEFR（ヨーロッパ言語共通参照枠）のレベルに準拠し，制作しています。下表のとおり，CEFR では，下から順番に A1 → A2 → B1 → B2 → C1 → C2 の6段階で語学力が示されています。そし

て，各4技能試験は，その試験のスコアやバンドと CEFR との準拠性を検証し，公表しています。本書「⑤ 上級編」は CEFR B2 レベルに準拠しており，これは英検準1級合格レベル（英検CSE スコア 2304-2599）にあたります。下表の➡の部分を基準に，自分が目指すレベルと本書のレベルを対比しながら，段階的に英語学習を進めていきましょう。

▼各資格・検定試験と CEFR との対照表 （出典：文部科学省HP〔平成30年3月〕）

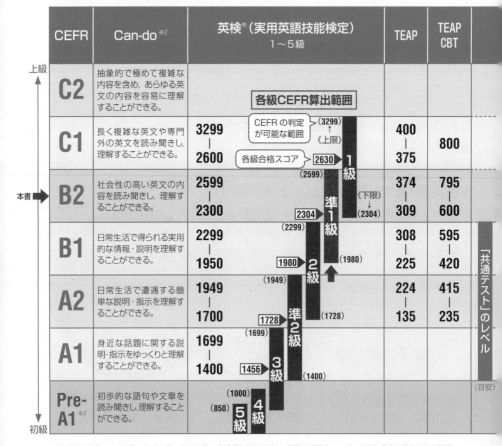

CEFR	Can-do※2	英検®（実用英語技能検定）1〜5級		TEAP	TEAP CBT
C2	抽象的で極めて複雑な内容を含め，あらゆる英文の内容を容易に理解することができる。	各級CEFR算出範囲			
C1	長く複雑な英文や専門外の英文を読み聞きし，理解することができる。	3299 − 2600（上限）〈3299〉	〈上限〉1級 各級合格スコア 2630	400 − 375	800
B2	社会性の高い英文の内容を読み聞きし，理解することができる。	2599 − 2300 （2599）2304	準1級 〈下限〉（2304）	374 − 309	795 − 600
B1	日常生活で得られる実用的な情報・説明を理解することができる。	2299 − 1950 （2299）1980	2級（1980）	308 − 225	595 − 420
A2	日常生活で遭遇する簡単な説明・指示を理解することができる。	1949 − 1700 （1949）1728	準2級（1728）	224 − 135	415 − 235
A1	身近な話題に関する説明・指示をゆっくりと理解することができる。	1699 − 1400 （1699）1456	3級（1400）		
Pre-A1※3	初歩的な語句や文章を読み聞きし，理解することができる。	（1000）（850）5級 4級			

上級 ↑ 本書➡ 初級 ↓

CEFR の判定が可能な範囲

「共通テスト」のレベル（目安）

※1…CSE は Common Scale for English の略。英検 CSE スコアは，英検の成績をユニバーサルな尺度で計るための指標。
※2…Can-do…実際の言語を使う場面で何がどの程度できるかを段階別に記述したもの。上表は「読むこと」「聞くこと」の一例。

■3 充実の音声で「リスニング」を 徹底強化できる！

　「共通テスト」で配点が倍増したように，「リスニング」の重要性は今後ますます高まります。本書では，リスニングの力を効率的に高められるよう，良質なリスニング問題を多数収録すると同時に，リーディング問題の英文音声も収録し，一度読んだ英文を使って復習とリスニング強化が同時にできるよう工夫しました。

　また，すべての音声は，同じ CEFR レベルにある4技能試験の音声と**同じ速度**（本書は英検準1級の音声と同じ速度）で収録しています。何度も音声を聞き，目標レベルの音声速度に慣れましょう。

【参考】「共通テスト」で高まるリスニングの重要性

比較項目	令和2年度 センター試験本試験	令和3年度 共通テスト本試験
試験時間	30分	30分
配点	50点	100点
問題数	4題 (25問)	6題 (37問)
問題ページ数	10 ページ	20 ページ
読み上げ語数	約1100語	約1500語
読み上げ回数	すべて2回	第1・2問：2回 第3・4・5・6問：1回

※試験時間は同じで，問題数が増え，読み上げ回数は減り，リーディングと同じく100点満点になっています。

	GTEC Advanced Basic Core CBT		ケンブリッジ 英検	IELTS	TOEFL iBT	TOEIC L&R/ TOEIC S&W ※4	本書のレベル ①〜⑥
C2		各試験CEFR 算出範囲	230 ｜ 200	9.0 ｜ 8.5			
C1	1400 ｜ 1350	(1400)	199 ｜ 180	8.0 ｜ 7.0	120 ｜ 95	1990 ｜ 1845	⑥ 最上級編
B2	1349 ｜ 1190	(1280)	179 ｜ 160	6.5 ｜ 5.5	94 ｜ 72	1840 ｜ 1560	⑤ 上級編
B1	1189 ｜ 960	(1080)	159 ｜ 140	5.0 ｜ 4.0	71 ｜ 42	1555 ｜ 1150	④ 中級編
A2	959 ｜ 690	(840)	139 ｜ 120			1145 ｜ 625	③ 標準編
A1	689 ｜ 270	(270)	119 ｜ 100			620 ｜ 320	② 初級編
Pre- A1							① 超基礎編

（GTEC欄内縦ラベル：Core　Basic　Advanced　CBT）

※3…CEFR の「Pre-A1」は，英検4級・5級の範囲を示すために便宜的に設置した本書独自のレベル表示で，実際にはありません。
※4…TOEIC L&R/TOEIC S&W は，S&W のスコアを 2.5 倍にして合算したスコアで判定する。

本書の対象・レベル

Target and Level of This Book

◀1▶ 本書の対象

☐ 英検「準1級」合格を目指す人
☐ TEAP「374点」取得を目指す人
☐ 大学入試で英語(リーディングやリスニング)を得点源にしたい人

◀2▶ 本書のレベル

　本書は,CEFR B2レベルを目指す皆さんを対象にしています。CEFR B2レベルは,英検では「準1級」合格レベルにあたります。リーディングやリスニングの応用的な力を鍛えたい人や,大学入試で英語を得点源にしたい人に最適です。

　リーディングでは,このレベルの英文を制限時間内に解く訓練をすることで,英検準1級レベルの長文を難なく読めるようになるでしょう。

　リスニングでは,音声を聞きながら要点をつかみとる練習(スキャニング),必要な情報を探し出す練習(スキミング)をしましょう。本書用のすべての音声(リーディングの音声を含む)は,英検準1級のリスニングの音声速度と同じになっています。繰り返し音声を聞くことで,目標とするレベルの速度に慣れ,リスニング力を高めていきましょう。

◀3▶ 本書と CEFR の準拠性

　前頁のとおり,各4技能試験はCEFRとの準拠性を検証・公表し,それにしたがって問題文の難易度を調整しています。CEFRにレベルを合わせる本書においても,収録するアイテムとCEFRの語彙的な準拠性を確立する必要があります。そこで,アイテムの作成にあたっては,一般に公開されているCEFR-Jの語彙データベースを活用して独自のソフトウェアを開発しました。このソフトウェアで英文をを読み込むと,1つ1つの単語に対し,その単語の難易度(CEFRのレベル,英検の級など)が色付きで表示されます。この表示結果と,過去の4技能試験における単語の頻度分析を照らし合わせ,アイテム中に使用している単語の難易度を調整しています。

　このような機械によるアルゴリズム分析は近年飛躍的に発展し,語彙のレベルや文の複雑さなどを客観的に把握できるようになりました。しかしながら,語彙分析における最大の課題は,文脈からの判断です。つまり,英文の「文脈」を適宜とらえて各単語の意味を機械が正確に判別することは,現在の技術では極めて困難なのです。本書のアイテム作成においては,そのような機械測定の限界を念頭に置いたうえで,熟練したプロのエディター,ネイティブのライターによる精査を徹底し,CEFRや4技能試験との準拠性を確立しました。

ハーバード大学 教育学修士
英文作成・監修　Andrew Robbins

本書の使い方

How to Use This Book

本書には，リーディングの問題を計 15 題（Lesson 01 ～ 15），リスニングの問題を計
40 題（Lesson 16 ～ 20）収録しました。本書の構成と使い方は極めてシンプルです。以
下のように，1 つずつ進めていきましょう。

リーディング（Lesson 01～15）

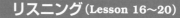

1 問題

← 問題文と設問を読み，解答の番号にマークをしましょう。

2 解答・解説

← 採点を行い，解説を読んで理解を深めましょう。

3 要点整理

← 音声を聞きながら，英文の空欄を埋め，段落ごとの要点を確認しましょう。

4 速読練習

← チャンクごとに区切られた音声を聞き，英文を語順のまま理解し，和訳できるようにしましょう。

リスニング（Lesson 16～20）

1 問題

← 音声を聞き，設問に答えます。解答の番号にマークをしましょう。

2 解答・解説

← 採点し，スクリプトを読んで，音声の内容を再度確認しましょう。

((📢 **本書の音声** 📢))

本書用の英文音声は，東進 WEB 書店の本
書ページから，無料でダウンロード［スト
リーミング］できます。

▼東進 WEB 書店
www.toshin.com/books

▼パスワード（ログイン時に要入力）
r27s12Mn

【収録音声】
◎ Lesson 01 ～ 15 リーディング
→英語長文音声（通常音声／チャンクごとに
英文和文を交互に読んだ音声）
◎ Lesson 16 ～ 20 リスニング
→問題・設問音声

もくじ・学習記録

Contents and Records of Study

英語 L&R レベル別問題集⑤ 上級編

＊問題を解いたあとは得点と日付を記入し，学習の記録・指針などにご活用ください。

Part 1
Lesson 01–05
Reading

空所補充問題
Fill-in-the-blank

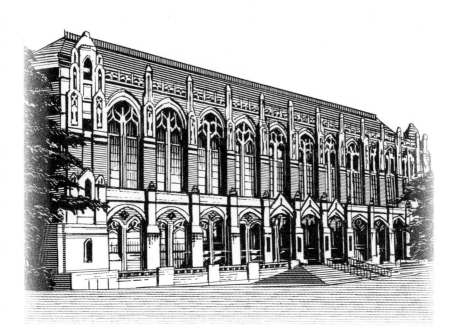

University of Washington

W 単 語 数 ▶ **286** 語

制限時間 ▶ **7** 分

✔ 目標得点 ▶ **20** /30点

DATE

▶次の英文を読み，その文意にそって（**1**）から（**3**）までの（　　）に入れるのに最も適切なものを **1**，**2**，**3**，**4** の中から１つ選び，その番号を所定欄にマークしなさい。

Blind Hiring

During the 1970s, most musicians in professional American orchestras were white males. The orchestras claimed they wanted to hire more women and racial minorities but that it was difficult to find musicians who were not white or male who were talented enough. (　　**1**　　), it was suggested that orchestras begin holding "blind auditions" in which the musicians sat behind screens so no one would know their race or sex. A few orchestras began trying it and even put carpets on the floor so people could not tell if the musician was a woman due to the sound of her high heels on the floor.

Thanks to blind auditions, the chances that a woman would be hired increased in some cases up to 46 percent. Because of this change, women and minorities realized they (　　**2**　　). As a result, more started applying, and the number of professional female and non-white musicians increased significantly.

Recently, some businesses have begun implementing this idea. A company called GapJumpers sends businesses profiles of job candidates without any details that would give hints about the applicants' age, sex, race, or other demographic information. There are also services that allow the candidate to sit behind a screen and have his or her voice disguised during the interview. These strategies enable companies to make decisions about who to hire without being influenced by prejudice. According to GapJumpers, putting together teams with people from different backgrounds can (**3**   ). This is because people from different backgrounds have different knowledge, experience, and ways of thinking. When a team takes advantage of these differences, it is able to come up with new and original ideas that help it to solve problems.

(**1**) **1** For example

  2 In other words

  3 In response to this

  4 On the other hand

(**2**) **1** could become more skillful

  2 would be treated more fairly

  3 played better than men

  4 had to change their playing style

(**3**) **1** cause communication problems

  2 help overcome racism

  3 create unhealthy competition

  4 improve their creativity

ANSWER		
(**1**) ① ② ③ ④	(**2**)	① ② ③ ④
(**3**) ① ② ③ ④		

Answers & Explanations ☞

Lesson 01
解答・解説
Answers & Explanations

□**（1）** **1** 例えば　　　　　　　　　　**2** 言い換えれば

③ これに応えて　　　　　　　**4** その一方で

解説▶（**1**）の前には解決すべき課題が，後ろにはその課題に対して提案された解決策が書かれている。したがって**3**を入れるのが文脈に合う。In response to this の this は，（**1**）を含む文の前の文で示された課題（オーケストラにとって十分な才能がある白人以外または男性以外の音楽家を見つけることは難しいこと）を指す。

重要語句 □ in response to 〜（熟 〜に応えて）

□**（2）** **1** 技能を高めることができる

② より公平にあつかわれるだろう

3 男性より上手に演奏する

4 自分の演奏スタイルを変えなければならない

解説▶（**2**）を含む文の前の文には，「ブラインド審査」によって女性が雇われるであろう機会が46％まで増加することもあったと述べられている。これによって女性や人種的マイノリティーはより公平にあつかわれることに期待をもてると考えられるので，**2**が正解。

□**（3）** **1** コミュニケーションの問題を引き起こす

2 人種差別に打ち勝つのに役立つ

3 不健全な競争を生み出す

④ 彼らの創造性を高める

解説▶最後の文の「**チームがこれらの違いをうまく利用すれば，問題を解決するのに役立つ新しく独創的な考えを思いつくことができる**」から，様々な経歴をもつ人々がチームをつくれば創造性が向上すると考えられる。したがって**4**が正解。

重要語句 □ overcome（動 〜に打ち勝つ）　□ racism（名 人種差別）

ANSWER		SCORE	CHECK YOUR LEVEL
（1） ① ② ③ ④	**（2）** ① ② ③ ④	／30点	0〜10点 ➡ *Work harder!*
			11〜20点 ➡ *OK!*
（3） ① ② ③ ④		（3問×各10点）	21〜30点 ➡ *Way to go!*

【和訳】

ブラインド採用

❶ 1970年代には，アメリカのプロのオーケストラのほとんどの音楽家が白人男性だった。より多くの女性や人種的マイノリティーたちを雇いたいが，十分な才能がある白人以外または男性以外の音楽家を見つけることは難しい，とオーケストラは主張した。これに応えて，人種や性別が誰にもわからないように，音楽家が仕切りの後ろに座る「ブラインド審査」をオーケストラが開催し始めることが提案された。少数のオーケストラはそれを試行し始め，床のハイヒールの音によって音楽家が女性かどうかわからないよう，床にカーペットまで敷いた。

❷ ブラインド審査のおかげで，女性が雇われるであろう機会は46%まで増加することもあった。この変化によって，女性やマイノリティーたちは自分たちがより公平にあつかわれるだろうと気づいた。その結果，より多くの人が応募し始め，女性や，白人以外のプロの音楽家の数はかなり増えた。

❸ 最近では，このアイデアを実行し始めている企業もある。ギャップジャンパーズという会社は，応募者の年齢，性別，人種やほかの人口統計情報などについての手がかりを与えそうな詳細を入れずに，求職者の職務経歴を送っている。応募者が仕切りの後ろに座り，面接の間その人の声を（機械で）変えることができるサービスもある。これらの方略によって，企業は先入観に左右されずに誰を雇うかを決めることができる。ギャップジャンパーズによれば，様々な経歴をもつ人々とチームを組むことで，創造性を高めることができる。これは，異なる経歴の人々が異なる知識，経験や考え方をもつからである。チームがこれらの違いをうまく利用すれば，問題を解決するのに役立つ新しく独創的な考えを思いつくことができるのだ。

重要語句リスト

❶
- [ ] blind　⑯ 先入観なしで行う，見ないで行う
- [ ] claim　⑲ ～を主張する
- [ ] racial minority　㊊ 人種的マイノリティー
- [ ] screen　㊊ 仕切り

❷
- [ ] apply　⑲ 応募する

❸
- [ ] job candidate　㊊ 求職者
- [ ] demographic information　㊊ 人口統計情報
- [ ] disguise　⑲ ～を（偽装して）隠す，～を変装させる
- [ ] strategy　㊊ 方略，策略
- [ ] prejudice　㊊ 先入観

Lesson 01
要点整理
Paragraph Summary

READING

■)) 音声 ▶**L&R_LV5_01-Q**

▶音声を聞きながら, ①〜④の空欄を埋め, 段落ごとの
要旨を確認しましょう(解答は下部にあります)。

Blind Hiring

❶ ◇ **professional American orchestras = white males**
  → want to hire more women and racial minorities
  → begin holding [① "b____ a_____"]

❷ ◇ **blind auditions**
  → women and minorities realized they will be treated more [② f_____]
  → the number of professional [③ f_____ and n_____] musicians increased significantly

❸ ◇ **businesses → implement this idea**
  • GapJumpers
  (1) sends businesses profiles of job candidates without any [④ d_____] about age, sex, race, or other demographic information
  (2) services that allow candidates to sit behind a screen and have his or her voice disguised
  → without being influenced by prejudice
  ◇ **putting together teams with people from different backgrounds**
  → come up with new and original ideas

【和訳】

ブラインド採用

❶ ◇ **アメリカのプロのオーケストラ ＝ 白人男性**

　　→ 女性や人種的マイノリティーたちをより雇いたい

　　→ 「ブラインド審査」を開催し始める

❷ ◇ **ブラインド審査**

　　→ 女性やマイノリティーたちは，自分たちがより公平にあつかわれるだ
　　　ろうと気づいた

　　→ 女性や，白人以外のプロの音楽家の数はかなり増えた

❸ ◇ **企業→ このアイデアを実行する**

　　• ギャップジャンパーズ

　　(1)年齢，性別，人種やほかの人口統計情報などについての詳細を入れず
　　　に，求職者の職務経歴を送る

　　(2)応募者が仕切りの後ろに座り，その人の声を（機械で）変えることが
　　　できるサービス

　　→ 先入観に左右されない

　◇ **様々な経歴をもつ人々とチームを組む**

　　→ 新しく独創的な考えを思いつく

Lesson 01
速読練習
Sight Translation

◀)) 英文音声 ▶ **L&R_LV5_01-ST**

英語	和訳
Blind Hiring	ブラインド採用
❶ During the 1970s,	1970年代には,
most musicians	ほとんどの音楽家が
in professional American orchestras	アメリカのプロのオーケストラの
were white males.	白人男性だった。
The orchestras claimed	オーケストラは主張した
they wanted to hire	雇いたいと
more women and racial minorities	より多くの女性や人種的マイノリティーたちを
but that it was difficult	しかし難しいと
to find musicians	音楽家を見つけることは
who were not white or male	白人以外または男性以外の
who were talented enough.	十分な才能がある。
In response to this,	これに応えて,
it was suggested	提案された
that orchestras begin holding	オーケストラが開催し始めることが
"blind auditions"	「ブラインド審査」を
in which the musicians sat	音楽家が座る
behind screens	仕切りの後ろに
so no one would know	誰にもわからないように
their race or sex.	彼らの人種や性別が。
A few orchestras began trying it	少数のオーケストラはそれを試行し始め
and even put carpets	カーペットまで敷いた
on the floor	床に
so people could not tell	人々がわからないように
if the musician was a woman	音楽家が女性かどうか
due to the sound	音によって
of her high heels on the floor.	床のハイヒールの。
❷ Thanks to blind auditions,	ブラインド審査のおかげで,
the chances	機会は
that a woman would be hired	女性が雇われるであろう
increased in some cases	増加することもあった
up to 46 percent.	46%まで。
Because of this change,	この変化によって,
women and minorities realized	女性やマイノリティーたちは気づいた
they would be treated	自分たちがあつかわれるだろうと
more fairly.	より公平に。

As a result,	その結果,
more started applying,	より多くの人が応募し始め,
and the number of professional female and non-white musicians	そして女性や,白人以外のプロの音楽家の数は
increased	増えた
significantly.	かなり。
❸ Recently,	最近では,
some businesses have begun implementing	実行し始めている企業もある
this idea.	このアイデアを。
A company called GapJumpers	ギャップジャンパーズという会社は
sends	送っている
businesses profiles of job candidates	求職者の職務経歴を
without any details	詳細を入れずに
that would give hints	手がかりを与えそうな
about the applicants' age, sex, race, or other demographic information.	応募者の年齢,性別,人種やほかの人口統計情報などについての。
There are also services	サービスもある
that allow the candidate to sit	応募者を座らせ
behind a screen	仕切りの後ろに
and have his or her voice disguised	その人の声を(機械で)変えることができる
during the interview.	面接の間。
These strategies enable companies to make decisions	これらの方略によって企業は決めることができる
about who to hire	誰を雇うかを
without being influenced	左右されずに
by prejudice.	先入観に。
According to GapJumpers,	ギャップジャンパーズによれば,
putting together teams with people	人々とチームを組むことで
from different backgrounds	様々な経歴をもつ
can improve their creativity.	創造性を高めることができる。
This is because	これは〜からである
people from different backgrounds have	異なる経歴の人々がもつ
different knowledge,	異なる知識や,
experience,	経験や,
and ways of thinking.	考え方を。
When a team takes advantage of these differences,	チームがこれらの違いをうまく利用すれば,
it is able to come up with	思いつくことができるのだ
new and original ideas	新しく独創的な考えを
that help it to solve problems.	問題を解決するのに役立つ。

END 　17

問題
Questions

▶次の英文を読み，その文意にそって (**1**) から (**3**) までの (　　) に入れるのに最も適切なものを **1**，**2**，**3**，**4** の中から 1 つ選び，その番号を所定欄にマークしなさい。

Boycotts

Since the 1990s, consumers have been using boycotts to protest against companies that exploit poor workers in developing countries to produce their goods. Millions of consumers refuse to purchase goods from big companies, and this puts great pressure on them due to falling sales. As a result of these boycotts, many companies have taken steps to ensure their factories are safe and that children are not working there. However, because such actions are not cheap, in recent years companies have (　**1**　).

One common way that companies do this is by purchasing their products from suppliers that they do not own. Complicated chains for producing and shipping products are set up, making it almost impossible for consumers to find out where products are made and who they are made by. (　**2**　), the companies are able to produce cheap products without having to worry about labor issues.

Some companies send inspectors to check that workers are treated well, but this can be extremely difficult. One reason is that (　**3**　). For example, when the inspectors arrive at a factory, the factory manager may play a song as a warning for the child workers to leave through the back door. Another way to

Lesson **02**

fool inspectors is by providing fake birth certificates to employees
who are legally too young to work. While boycotts have been
effective in improving working conditions in the past, it seems
that society may need to find new ways to improve conditions for
workers in developing countries.

(**1**) **1** tried to do more than that

      2 done the opposite of this

      3 explained the reason for this

      4 found ways to avoid this

(**2**) **1** By contrast

      2 In this way

      3 Ironically

      4 Nonetheless

(**3**) **1** the inspectors are dishonest

      2 the inspectors' visits are too short

      3 factories refuse the inspectors

      4 it is easy to trick inspectors

ANSWER		
(**1**) ① ② ③ ④	(**2**) ① ② ③ ④	
(**3**) ① ② ③ ④		

Answers & Explanations ☞

Lesson 02
解答・解説
Answers & Explanations

□**(1)**　**1**　それより多くのことをしようとした　**2**　これと逆のことをした
　　　　　3　この理由を説明した　　　　　　**④**　これを避ける方法を見つけた

解説▶（ 1 ）を含む文とその前文から，ボイコットを防ぐためには，工場が安全で，子供たちがそこで働いていないことを保証する必要があるが，企業にとってそのような行動を取ることは，高くつくことがわかる。続いて第 2 段落に着目してみると，企業が労働問題の責任から逃れるための（不正な）手段が具体的に説明されている。これらの情報から総合的に判断して，**4** が正解。

□**(2)**　**1**　対照的に　　　　　　　　　　**②**　このようにして
　　　　　3　皮肉にも　　　　　　　　　　**4**　それにもかかわらず

解説▶第 2 段落の最初の文で企業が労働問題の責任を逃れる一般的な方法が，第 2 文でその理由（背景）が述べられており，（ 2 ）の後ろでは，「企業は労働問題について心配する必要なく，安い製品を生産することができる」と述べられている。文章の内容から考えて，（ 2 ）を含む文の前と後ろをつなぐのに適しているのは「このようにして」。よって，**2** が正解。

□**(3)**　**1**　監視役は不正直である　　　　**2**　監視役の視察が短すぎる
　　　　　3　工場が監視役を拒む　　　　　**④**　監視役を欺くのが簡単だ

解説▶（ 3 ）には労働者がちゃんとあつかわれていることの確認は困難になりうる理由が入り，（ 3 ）を含む文の後ろの文では，工場に派遣される監視役を欺く方法が具体的に書かれている。したがって **4** が正解。監視役の視察にかける時間については本文中で触れられていないので，**2** は誤り。工場では，監視役を受け入れたうえで彼らを欺いているので，**3** も誤り。

重要語句　□ dishonest（㋭ 不正直な）　□ trick（㋰ ～を欺く）

ANSWER		SCORE	CHECK YOUR LEVEL
(1) ① ② ③ ④	**(2)** ① ② ③ ④	／30点	0〜10点 ➡ *Work harder!*
			11〜20点 ➡ *OK!*
(3) ① ② ③ ④		（3問×各10点）	21〜30点 ➡ *Way to go!*

【和訳】

ボイコット

❶ 消費者は 1990 年代からずっと，発展途上国の貧しい労働者を不当に使って商品を生産する企業に抗議するために，ボイコット（不買同盟）を利用している。何百万人もの消費者が大企業から商品を購入することを拒み，これは売り上げの減少によって企業に大きな圧力を与える。これらのボイコットの結果として，多くの企業は工場が安全で，子どもたちがそこで働いていないことを保証する対策を講じてきた。しかし，そのような行動は安くないので，近年，企業はこれを避ける方法を見つけた。

❷ 企業がこれを行う 1 つの一般的な方法は，自らが所有していない供給業者から自社の製品を購入することによってである。製品の生産と輸送には複雑な流れが構築されており，そのため製品がどこでつくられ，誰によってつくられているのかを消費者が知ることはほとんど不可能である。このようにして企業は労働問題について心配する必要なく，安い製品を生産することができる。

❸ 一部の企業は監視役を送り込んで労働者がちゃんとあつかわれていることを確認するが，これが極めて困難な場合もありうる。1 つの理由は，監視役を欺くのが簡単だということだ。例えば，監視役が工場に着くと，工場の管理者が，そこで働いている子どもたちに裏口から立ち去るよう警告として音楽を流すことがある。監視役を欺くための別の方法は，法律的に年齢が低すぎて働けない従業員に偽造した出生証明書を与えることによってだ。ボイコットはこれまで労働条件の改善に効果的だったが，社会は発展途上国の労働者の労働条件を改善するための新しい方法を見つける必要があるかもしれないようだ。

重要語句リスト

❶
- □ boycott　⊛ ボイコット，不買同盟
- □ protest against ～　⊛ ～に抗議する
- □ exploit　⊛ ～を不当に使う
- □ put pressure on ～　⊛ ～に圧力を与える
- □ take steps　⊛ 対策を講じる
- □ ensure　⊛ ～を保証する

❷
- □ supplier　⊛ 供給業者
- □ ship　⊛ ～を輸送する
- □ set up ～　⊛ ～を構築する

❸
- □ inspector　⊛ 監視役
- □ fool　⊛ ～を欺く
- □ birth certificate　⊛ 出生証明書

READING

Lesson 02
要点整理
Paragraph Summary

◀)) 音声 ▶ **L&R_LV5_02-Q**

▶音声を聞きながら，①〜⑤の空欄を埋め，段落ごとの
要旨を確認しましょう（解答は下部にあります）。

Boycotts

❶ ◇ **since the 1990s**

- consumers : using boycotts to [① p_ _ _ _ _ _] against companies
  that exploit poor workers

→ companies : have taken steps to ensure

  (1) their factories are safe

  (2) children are not working there

◇ **in recent years**

- companies : found ways to [② a_ _ _ _] taking steps

❷ ◇ **one common way that companies avoid taking steps**

= purchasing their products from suppliers that they do not own

→ making it impossible for consumers to find out where products are
  made and who they are made by

→ producing cheap products without having to worry about [③ l_ _ _ _
  i_ _ _ _ _]

❸ ◇ **checking that the workers are treated well can be difficult**

- reason = easy to [④ t_ _ _ _] inspectors

  (1) playing a song as a warning for the child workers to leave
    through the back door when the inspectors arrive at a factory

  (2) providing fake birth certificates to employees who are legally
    too young to work

  → need to find new ways to [⑤ i_ _ _ _ _ _] conditions for workers
    in developing countries

【解答】　① protest　② avoid　③ labor issues　④ trick　⑤ improve

【和訳】

ボイコット

❶ ◇ **1990 年代以降**

　　・ 消費者：貧しい労働者を不当に使う企業に抗議するためにボイコット

　　　　（不買同盟）を利用

　　→ 企業：保証する対策を講じた

　　　　(1) 工場が安全である

　　　　(2) 子どもたちがそこで働いていない

　　◇ **近年**

　　・ 企業：対策を講じることを避ける方法を見つけた

❷ ◇ **企業が対策を講じることを避ける 1 つの一般的な方法**

　　＝ 自らが所有していない供給業者から自社の製品を購入すること

　　→ 製品がどこでつくられ，誰によってつくられているのかを消費者が知

　　　ることを不可能にする

　　→ 労働問題について心配する必要なく，安い製品を生産する

❸ ◇ **労働者がちゃんとあつかわれていることを確認するのは困難になりうる**

　　・ 理由 ＝ 監視役を欺くのは簡単

　　　(1) 監視役が工場に着くと，働いている子どもたちに裏口から立ち去る

　　　　よう警告として音楽を流すこと

　　　(2) 法律的に年齢が低すぎて働けない従業員に偽造した出生証明書を与

　　　　えること

　　→ 発展途上国の労働者の労働条件を改善するための新しい方法を見つけ

　　　る必要がある

Lesson 02
速読練習
Sight Translation

 英文音声 ▶ **L&R_LV5_02-ST**

英語	和訳
Boycotts	ボイコット
❶ Since the 1990s,	1990年代からずっと,
consumers have been using	消費者は利用している
boycotts	ボイコット (不買同盟) を
to protest against companies	企業に抗議するために
that exploit poor workers	貧しい労働者を不当に使って
in developing countries	発展途上国の
to produce their goods.	商品を生産する。
Millions of consumers refuse	何百万人もの消費者が拒み
to purchase goods	商品を購入することを
from big companies,	大企業から,
and this puts great pressure on them	そしてこれは企業に大きな圧力を与える
due to falling sales.	売り上げの減少によって。
As a result of these boycotts,	これらのボイコットの結果として,
many companies have taken steps	多くの企業は対策を講じてきた
to ensure	保証するための
their factories are safe	工場が安全で
and that children are not working there.	かつ子どもたちがそこで働いていないことを。
However,	しかし,
because such actions are not cheap,	そのような行動は安くないので,
in recent years	近年
companies have found ways	企業は方法を見つけた
to avoid this.	これを避けるための。
❷ One common way	1つの一般的な方法は
that companies do this	企業がこれを行う
is by purchasing their products	自社の製品を購入することによってである
from suppliers	供給業者から
that they do not own.	自らが所有していない。
Complicated chains	複雑な流れが
for producing and shipping products	製品の生産と輸送には
are set up,	構築されており,
making it almost impossible	ほとんど不可能にしている
for consumers	消費者にとって
to find out	知ることを

where products are made	製品がどこでつくられ
and who they are made by.	誰によってつくられているのかを。
In this way,	このようにして,
the companies are able to produce	企業は生産できる
cheap products	安い製品を
without having to worry	心配することなく
about labor issues.	労働問題について。
❸ Some companies send inspectors	一部の企業は監視役を送り込む
to check	確認するために
that workers are treated well,	労働者がちゃんとあつかわれていることを,
but this can be extremely difficult.	しかしこれが極めて困難な場合もありうる。
One reason is that	1 つの理由は
it is easy	簡単だということだ
to trick inspectors.	監視役を欺くのが。
For example,	例えば,
when the inspectors arrive	監視役が着くと
at a factory,	工場に,
the factory manager may play a song	工場の管理者が音楽を流すことがある
as a warning	警告として
for the child workers	そこで働いている子どもたちに
to leave	立ち去るよう
through the back door.	裏口から。
Another way	別の方法は
to fool inspectors	監視役を欺くための
is by providing	与えることによってだ
fake birth certificates	偽造した出生証明書を
to employees	従業員に
who are legally too young to work.	法律的に年齢が低すぎて働けない。
While boycotts have been effective	ボイコットは効果的だったが
in improving working conditions	労働条件の改善に
in the past,	これまで,
it seems that society may need	社会は必要があるかもしれないようだ
to find new ways	新しい方法を見つける
to improve conditions for workers	労働者の労働条件を改善するための
in developing countries.	発展途上国の。

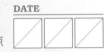

▶次の英文を読み，その文意にそって（**1**）から（**3**）までの（　　　）に入れるのに最も適切なものを **1**，**2**，**3**，**4** の中から１つ選び，その番号を所定欄にマークしなさい。

Electricity and the Brain

Can stimulating your brain with electricity make you smarter? Scientists have long known that a region of the brain called the medial prefrontal cortex acts as the "alarm bell of the brain." When people are surprised or make an error, it reacts and lets them know there is a problem. It (　　**1**　　) a part of the brain called the lateral prefrontal cortex. This part of the brain stores rules and goals. Recent experiments show that electricity can improve the communication between the two areas, allowing them to cooperate more efficiently and find mistakes. This allowed the participants in the experiments to perform better in various tasks.

In one experiment, people were asked to estimate when 1.7 seconds had elapsed and were given feedback on whether they were too fast, too slow, or right on time. When the researchers stimulated their brains with electricity, the people learned faster and made fewer errors, and when they did make mistakes, they were able to correct them more quickly. (　　**2**　　), when the researchers used electricity to interfere with the brain's natural signals, the participants performed worse.

The researchers believe that electricity could be effective in helping people with brain diseases, including Alzheimer's. Although such illnesses are usually treated with medicine, researchers believe that electricity may be more effective. Drugs, they say, are not ideal because they (**3**). Electrical stimulation, however, may be used to provide safer treatments since it can be applied to one precise location. Therefore, it is less likely to have as many side effects.

(**1**) **1** explains the function of **2** blocks signals from
     3 works together with **4** becomes larger than

(**2**) **1** On the other hand **2** Consequently
     3 In particular **4** In short

(**3**) **1** slowly lose their effect
     2 need to be taken more often
     3 affect large areas of the brain
     4 are less powerful

ANSWER		
(**1**) ① ② ③ ④	(**2**)	① ② ③ ④
(**3**) ① ② ③ ④		

Answers & Explanations ☞

Lesson 03
解答・解説
Answers & Explanations

□**(1)**　**1**　～の機能を説明する　　　　**2**　～からの信号を遮断する
　　　　　③　～と共に機能する　　　　　**4**　～よりも大きくなる

解説▶（ 1 ）には，前の it が指す the medial prefrontal cortex「内側前頭前皮質」と the lateral prefrontal cortex「外側前頭前皮質」との関係性を表す語句を入れる。（ 1 ）を含む文の後ろの内容から，2 つの領域は連携し，協力していることがわかるので，**3** が正解。

重要語句　□ function（图 機能）　□ block（働 ～を遮断する）

□**(2)**　**①**　その一方で　　　　　　　**2**　その結果
　　　　　3　特に　　　　　　　　　　**4**　要するに

解説▶（ 2 ）を含む文の前では，人が電気で脳を刺激された場合，学習速度が上がるなど実験における成績が改善したことが示されている。そして（ 2 ）を含む文の後ろには，人が電気を使って脳の自然信号を妨害された場合，成績が下がることが述べられている。これらの内容は対立関係にあるので，**1** が正解。

□**(3)**　**1**　効果をゆっくり失う　　　　**2**　より頻繁に飲む必要がある
　　　　　③　脳の広い範囲に影響を与える　**4**　効能があまり強力ではない

解説▶（ 3 ）の前後の「薬は……ため理想的ではない。しかし電気刺激は 1 つの正確な場所に適用されうるので，より安全な治療を提供するのに使われるかもしれない。よって，電気刺激は（薬と）同数の副作用をもつ可能性が低いのである」という文脈から考えて，薬は 1 つの場所に正確に適用することができないと考えられる。したがって **3** が正解。

ANSWER		SCORE	CHECK YOUR LEVEL
(1) ① ② ③ ④	**(2)** ① ② ③ ④	/30点 (3問×各10点)	'0～10点 ➡ *Work harder!* 11～20点 ➡ *OK!* 21～30点 ➡ *Way to go!*
(3) ① ② ③ ④			

【和訳】

電気と脳

❶ 脳を電気で刺激すると，あなたはより賢くなるだろうか？　内側前頭前皮質という脳の領域が「脳の警鐘」として働くことを，科学者はずっと前から知っていた。人々が驚いたりミスをしたりすると，それが反応して問題があると本人に知らせる。それは外側前頭前皮質という脳の一部と共に機能する。脳のこの部分は，規則と目標を蓄積する。最近の実験によれば，電気は2つの領域間の連携を高め，それらの領域がより効率的に協力してミスを見つけられる。これによって，実験の参加者たちは様々な作業をより上手に行うことができた。

❷ ある実験では，人々は 1.7 秒が経過した時点を推測するよう求められ，早すぎたか，遅すぎたか，あるいはちょうど時間どおりだったかについてフィードバックを受けた。研究者たちが電気で彼らの脳を刺激すると，人々の学習速度は上がり，ミスが少なくなり，ミスをしてもより素早く修正することができた。その一方で，研究者たちが電気を使って脳の自然信号を妨害すると，被験者たちの成績は下がった。

❸ 研究者たちは，電気がアルツハイマー病を含む脳の病気がある人々を助けるのに効果があるかもしれないと思っている。そのような病気はたいてい薬で治療されるが，電気の方がより効果的かもしれないと研究者たちは考えている。彼らによれば，薬は脳の広い範囲に影響を与えるため理想的ではない。しかし電気刺激は1つの正確な場所に適用されうるので，より安全な治療を提供するのに使われるかもしれない。よって，電気刺激は（薬と）同数の副作用をもつ可能性が低いのである。

重要語句リスト

❶

☐ stimulate	動	～を刺激する
☐ region	名	領域
☐ medial prefrontal cortex		
	名	内側前頭前皮質
☐ alarm bell	名	警鐘
☐ lateral prefrontal cortex		
	名	外側前頭前皮質
☐ participant	名	参加者

❷

☐ feedback	名	フィードバック，評価
☐ interfere with ～	熟	～を妨害する

❸

☐ Alzheimer's [= Alzheimer's disease]		
	名	アルツハイマー病
☐ ideal	形	理想的な
☐ electrical stimulation		
	名	電気刺激
☐ be applied to ～	熟	～に適用される
☐ side effect	名	副作用

要点整理
Paragraph Summary

▶音声を聞きながら、①～⑤の空欄を埋め、段落ごとの
要旨を確認しましょう（解答は下部にあります）。

Electricity and the Brain

❶ ◇ **stimulating your brain with electricity → make you smarter?**

◇ **scientists**

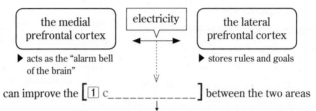

the medial prefrontal cortex

▶ acts as the "alarm bell of the brain"

electricity

the lateral prefrontal cortex

▶ stores rules and goals

can improve the [① c_____] between the two areas

↓

allows the participants in the experiments to perform better in various tasks

❷ ◇ **in one experiment**

• the researchers stimulated the brains with [② e_____]

→ the people　(1) learned faster

(2) made fewer errors

(3) corrected mistakes more quickly

• the researchers used electricity to [③ i_____] with the brain's natural signals

→ the participants performed worse

❸ ◇ **the researchers**

• electricity : help people with brain diseases

↔ such illnesses are usually treated with [④ m_____]

• electrical stimulation may be used to provide safer treatments

→ it is less likely to have as many [⑤ s___ e_____].

【解答】　① communication　② electricity　③ interfere　④ medicine　⑤ side effects

【和訳】

電気と脳

❶　◇ 脳を電気で刺激する→ あなたはより賢くなる？

　　◇ 科学者たち

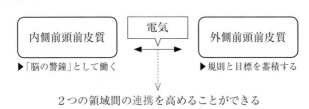

　　　内側前頭前皮質　　　　電気　　　　外側前頭前皮質

　　▶「脳の警鐘」として働く　　　　　　▶規則と目標を蓄積する

　　　　　　２つの領域間の連携を高めることができる

　　　実験の参加者たちが様々な作業をより上手に行えるようにする

❷　◇ ある実験で

　　• 研究者たちは，電気で脳を刺激した

　　→ 人々は，(1)学習速度が上がり

　　　　　　　(2)ミスが少なくなり

　　　　　　　(3)ミスをより素早く修正した

　　• 研究者たちが電気を使って脳の自然信号を妨害した

　　→ 被験者たちの成績は下がった

❸　◇ 研究者たち

　　• 電気：脳の病気がある人々を助ける

　　↔ そのような病気はたいてい薬で治療される

　　• 電気刺激はより安全な治療を提供するのに使われるかもしれない

　　→ （薬と）同数の副作用をもつ可能性が低い

Lesson 03
速読練習
Sight Translation

◀)) 英文音声 ▶ **L&R_LV5_03-ST**

英語	和訳
Electricity and the Brain	電気と脳
❶ Can stimulating your brain with electricity	脳を電気で刺激することは～できるか
make you smarter?	あなたをより賢くすることが。
Scientists have long known	科学者はずっと前から知っていた
that a region of the brain	脳の領域が
called the medial prefrontal cortex	内側前頭前皮質という
acts	はたらく
as the "alarm bell of the brain."	「脳の警鐘」として。
When people are surprised	人々が驚いたり
or make an error,	ミスをしたりすると,
it reacts	それが反応して
and lets them know	そして本人に知らせる
there is a problem.	問題があると。
It works together	それは共に機能する
with a part of the brain	脳の一部と
called the lateral prefrontal cortex.	外側前頭前皮質という。
This part of the brain stores	脳のこの部分は蓄積する
rules and goals.	規則と目標を。
Recent experiments show	最近の実験によれば
that electricity can improve the communication	電気は連携を高めることができる
between the two areas,	2つの領域間の,
allowing them to cooperate	それらの領域が協力できる
more efficiently	より効率的に
and find mistakes.	そしてミスを見つけられる。
This allowed the participants in the experiments	これによって実験の参加者たちはできた
to perform better	より上手に行うことが
in various tasks.	様々な作業を。
❷ In one experiment,	ある実験では,
people were asked to estimate	人々は推測するよう求められた
when 1.7 seconds had elapsed	1.7秒が経過した時点を
and were given feedback	そしてフィードバックを受けた
on whether they were too fast,	早すぎたかについて,
too slow,	遅すぎたか,

or right on time.	あるいはちょうど時間どおりだったか。
When the researchers stimulated their brains	研究者たちが彼らの脳を刺激すると
with electricity,	電気で,
the people learned faster	人々の学習速度は上がり
and made fewer errors,	ミスが少なくなり,
and when they did make mistakes,	そしてミスをしても,
they were able to correct them	修正することができた
more quickly.	より素早く。
On the other hand,	その一方で,
when the researchers used electricity	研究者たちが電気を使って
to interfere	妨害すると
with the brain's natural signals,	脳の自然信号を,
the participants performed worse.	被験者たちの成績は下がった。
❸ The researchers believe	研究者たちは信じている
that electricity could be effective	電気は効果があるかもしれないと
in helping people	人々を助けるのに
with brain diseases,	脳の病気がある,
including Alzheimer's.	アルツハイマー病を含む。
Although such illnesses are usually treated	そのような病気はたいてい治療されるが
with medicine,	薬で,
researchers believe	研究者たちは信じている
that electricity may be more effective.	電気の方がより効果的かもしれないと。
Drugs,	薬は,
they say,	彼らによれば,
are not ideal	理想的ではない
because they affect	それらは影響を与えるため
large areas of the brain.	脳の広い範囲に。
Electrical stimulation,	電気刺激は,
however,	しかし,
may be used	使われるかもしれない
to provide safer treatments	より安全な治療を提供するために
since it can be applied	適用されうるので
to one precise location.	1つの正確な場所に。
Therefore, it is less likely to have	よって, 電気刺激の方がもつ可能性が低いのである
as many side effects.	(薬と) 同数の副作用を。

END　33

READING

Lesson 04
問題
Questions

04

W 単語数 ▶ **276** 語
🕐 制限時間 ▶ **7** 分
☑ 目標得点 ▶ **20** /30点

DATE

▶次の英文を読み，その文意にそって（**1**）から（**3**）までの（　　　）に入れるのに最も適切なものを **1**，**2**，**3**，**4** の中から１つ選び，その番号を所定欄にマークしなさい。

Eli Whitney

Eli Whitney was an American inventor born in 1765. As a young man, he went to visit a cotton farm in Georgia. Whitney, who was good with machines, had an idea for (　　**1**　　). In those days, making things out of cotton required a huge amount of work because all the seeds had to be removed from it first. This process took many hours, and it was only possible to clean about half a kilogram of cotton a day. Whitney created a new machine called a cotton gin that removed the seeds automatically. Using this machine, workers were able to clean up to 10 times as much cotton as they had in the past.

Whitney's cotton gin (　　**2**　　). Prior to the invention of the cotton gin, new technology in England had been changing the way that clothes were made. Steam power and new machines were making it much faster to produce clothes for lower costs. All of this created a huge demand for cotton, and the cotton gin helped farmers in the Southern United States to meet England's demand. In 1791, when Whitney arrived in Georgia, these states exported just a few hundred bags of cotton. In 1810, they exported more than 17 million kilograms.

The cotton gin, although a work of genius, was actually simple to make, and soon many other companies began manufacturing cheaper imitations. Because of this, Whitney made only a little money from his invention. (　　**3**　　), some historians claim that when you consider everything he invested in developing it, he probably lost money. Still, the cotton gin remains one of the most important inventions of the 1800s.

(**1**) **1** improving cotton quality　**2** growing cotton faster
　　　3 increasing cotton production **4** making cotton softer

(**2**) **1** did not work well at first **2** sold best in England
　　　3 cost a lot to build　　　**4** came at the perfect time

(**3**) **1** Nevertheless　　　**2** In particular
　　　3 Besides　　　　　**4** In fact

ANSWER		
(1) ① ② ③ ④	(2)	① ② ③ ④
(3) ① ② ③ ④		

Answers & Explanations ☞

Lesson 04
解答・解説
Answers & Explanations

□**(1)**　**1**　綿の品質を改良する　　　　**2**　綿をより速く栽培する

　　　　③　綿の生産量を増やす　　　　**4**　綿をより柔らかくする

解説▶第1段落第4～5文より，綿から製品をつくる際に大きな労力が必要だった原因は，種を取り除く過程に時間がかかっていたからだとわかる。そして第1段落第6～7文に「ホイットニーは，種を自動的に取り除く綿繰り機という新しい機械をつくった」「この機械を使って，作業員たちは最大で以前の10倍ほどの綿の種を取り除くことができた」とあることから，彼のアイデアによって種を取り除くのにかかる時間が減少し，生産量が増えたことがわかる。よって，**3**が正解。

□**(2)**　**1**　最初はうまく動かなかった　　　　**2**　英国で最も売れた

　　　　3　つくるのに多くの費用がかかった　**④**　ちょうど良いときに現れた

解説▶第2段落第2文より，当時「**英国の新しい技術によって服のつくり方が変化**」していたことがわかる。そして第2段落第3～4文より，当時は，その新しい技術によってより安価に，はるかに速く服を製造できるようになり，綿の膨大な需要が生まれたタイミングだったことが読みとれる。ホイットニーの綿繰り機はそのタイミングで生まれたために広く普及したと考えられるので，**4**が正解。

重要語句　□ come at the perfect time（熟 ちょうど良いときにやってくる）

□**(3)**　**1**　それにもかかわらず　　　　**2**　特に

　　　　3　それに加えて　　　　　　　**④**　（いや）むしろ

解説▶（ 3 ）を含む文の前は「**ホイットニーは，自分の発明からわずかなお金しか得られなかった**」，（ 3 ）を含む文は「**その機械を開発するのに彼がつぎ込んだあらゆるものを考慮すると，彼はたぶん損をしただろう**」という内容である。ここから，ホイットニーは綿繰り機を発明したが，利益を得られなかったどころか実際は損をしたという文脈になることが予想できる。よって，**4**が正解。ここでのIn factは「（いや）むしろ」の意味。

ANSWER			SCORE	CHECK YOUR LEVEL
(1)	① ② ③ ④	**(2)**　① ② ③ ④	⁄30点	0～10点 ➡ *Work harder!* 11～20点 ➡ *OK!*
(3)	① ② ③ ④		（3問×各10点）	21～30点 ➡ *Way to go!*

【和訳】

イーライ・ホイットニー

❶ イーライ・ホイットニーは，1765年に生まれたアメリカの発明家だった。若いとき，彼はジョージアの綿花農場を訪ねた。機械のあつかいが得意だったホイットニーには，綿の生産量を増やすためのアイデアがあった。当時は，最初にすべての種を綿から取り除かなければならなかったので，綿から製品をつくるのには非常に大きな労力を必要とした。この過程には多くの時間がかかり，1日に約500gの綿しか種を取り除けなかった。ホイットニーは，種を自動的に取り除く綿繰り機という新しい機械をつくった。この機械を使って，作業員たちは最大で以前の10倍ほどの綿の種を取り除くことができた。

❷ ホイットニーの綿繰り機は，ちょうど良いときに現れた。綿繰り機の発明以前に，英国の新しい技術によって服のつくり方が変化していた。蒸気動力と新しい機械は，より安価に，服を製造するのをはるかに速くしていた。これらすべてが綿の膨大な需要を生み，綿繰り機は米国南部の農家が英国の需要を満たすのに役立った。1791年にホイットニーがジョージアに着いたとき，これらの州は数百袋の綿しか輸出していなかった。1810年には，それらは1700万キロを超える量を輸出していた。

❸ 綿繰り機は天才的発明だったが，実際にはつくりやすく，すぐにほかの多くの企業がより安価な模造品を製造し始めた。このためホイットニーは，自分の発明からわずかなお金しか得られなかった。（いや）むしろ，一部の歴史家は，その機械を開発するのに彼がつぎ込んだあらゆるものを考慮すると，彼はたぶん損をしただろうと主張している。それでも綿繰り機は，依然として1800年代の最も重要な発明の1つである。

❶

☐ cotton farm　⦿ 綿花農場
☐ remove　⦿ ～を取り除く
☐ cotton gin　⦿ 綿繰り機

❷

☐ steam power　⦿ 蒸気動力

❸

☐ manufacture　⦿ ～を製造する
☐ imitation　⦿ 模造品

要点整理
Paragraph Summary

🔊)) 音声 ▶ **L&R_LV5_04-Q**

▶ 音声を聞きながら、①〜⑤の空欄を埋め、段落ごとの
要旨を確認しましょう（解答は下部にあります）。

Eli Whitney

❶ ◇ **Eli Whitney = an American inventor born in 1765**

→ had an idea for increasing cotton production

◇ **in those days**

- making things out of cotton

  → required [① a h___ a_____ of w___], took many hours

◇ **a new machine that removed the seeds** [② a_____]

→ cleaned up to 10 times as much cotton as in the past

❷ ◇ **Whitney's cotton gin came at the perfect time**

- prior to the invention of the cotton gin

  (1) new [③ t_____]※1

+)(2) steam power and new machines※2

  _____

  created a huge demand for cotton

  ※1：changed the way that clothes were made

  ※2：made it much faster to produce clothes for lower costs

- in 1791 = exported just a few hundred bags of cotton

↔ in 1810 = exported more than 17 million kilograms

❸ ◇ **many other companies：manufactured similar, cheaper imitations**

→ Whitney made [④ o___ a l_____] money

◇ [⑤ T__ c_____ g__] remains one of the most important
inventions of the 1800s.

【解答】 ① a huge amount of work ② automatically ③ technology ④ only a little
⑤ The cotton gin

【和訳】

イーライ・ホイットニー

❶　◇ **イーライ・ホイットニー ＝ 1765 年に生まれたアメリカの発明家**

　　　→ 綿の生産量を増やすためのアイデアがあった

　◇ **当時**

　　• 綿から製品をつくること

　　　→ 非常に大きな労力，多くの時間を要した

　◇ **種を自動的に取り除く新しい機械**

　　→ 最大で以前の 10 倍ほどの綿の種を取り除くことができた

❷　◇ **ホイットニーの綿繰り機はちょうど良いときに現れた**

　　• 綿繰り機の発明以前

　　 (1) 新しい技術[※1]

　+) (2) 蒸気動力と新しい機械[※2]
　　─────────────────
　　　　綿の膨大な需要を生んだ

　　※1：服のつくり方が変化した

　　※2：より安価に，服を製造するのをはるかに速くした

　　• 1791 年 ＝ 数百袋の綿しか輸出していなかった

　↔ 1810 年 ＝ 1700 万キロを超える量を輸出していた

❸　◇ **ほかの多くの企業：似たようなより安価な模造品を製造した**

　　　→ ホイットニーは，わずかなお金しか得られなかった

　◇ **綿繰り機は依然として，1800 年代の最も重要な発明の 1 つである。**

READING

Lesson 04
速読練習
Sight Translation

 英文音声 ▶ L&R_LV5_04-ST

DATE

英語	和訳
Eli Whitney	**イーライ・ホイットニー**
❶ Eli Whitney	イーライ・ホイットニーは
was an American inventor	アメリカの発明家だった
born in 1765.	1765 年に生まれた。
As a young man,	若いとき,
he went to visit	彼は訪ねた
a cotton farm	綿花農場を
in Georgia.	ジョージアの。
Whitney,	ホイットニーは,
who was good with machines,	機械のあつかいが得意だった,
had an idea	アイデアをもっていた
for increasing cotton production.	綿の生産量を増やすための。
In those days,	当時は,
making things	製品をつくることは
out of cotton	綿から
required a huge amount of work	非常に大きな労力を必要とした
because all the seeds	なぜならすべての種は
had to be removed from it	綿から取り除かれなければならなかったので
first.	最初に。
This process took many hours,	この過程には多くの時間がかかり,
and it was only possible	〜しかできなかった
to clean about half a kilogram of cotton	約 500g の綿の種を取り除くこと
a day.	1 日に。
Whitney created	ホイットニーはつくった
a new machine	新しい機械を
called a cotton gin	綿繰り機という
that removed the seeds automatically.	種を自動的に取り除く。
Using this machine,	この機械を使って,
workers were able to clean	作業員たちは取り除くことができた
up to 10 times as much cotton	最大で 10 倍ほどの綿の種を
as they had in the past.	以前の。
❷ Whitney's cotton gin came	ホイットニーの綿繰り機は現れた
at the perfect time.	ちょうど良いときに。
Prior to the invention of the cotton gin,	綿繰り機の発明以前に,
new technology	新しい技術が
in England	英国の
had been changing the way	方法を変化させていた
that clothes were made.	服がつくられる。

Steam power and new machines	蒸気動力と新しい機械は
were making it much faster	はるかに速くしていた
to produce clothes	服を製造するのを
for lower costs.	より安価に。
All of this created	これらすべてが生んだ
a huge demand	膨大な需要を
for cotton,	綿の,
and the cotton gin helped	そして綿繰り機は助けた
farmers	農家が
in the Southern United States	米国南部の
to meet England's demand.	英国の需要を満たすのを。
In 1791,	1791年に,
when Whitney arrived	ホイットニーが着いたとき
in Georgia,	ジョージアに,
these states exported	これらの州は輸出していた
just a few hundred bags of cotton.	ほんの数百袋の綿だけを。
In 1810,	1810年には,
they exported	それらは輸出した
more than 17 million kilograms.	1700万キロを超える量を。
❸ The cotton gin,	綿繰り機は,
although a work of genius,	天才的発明だったが,
was actually simple to make,	実際にはつくりやすく,
and soon	そしてすぐに
many other companies began	ほかの多くの企業が始めた
manufacturing cheaper imitations.	より安価な模造品を製造することを。
Because of this,	このため,
Whitney made	ホイットニーは得た
only a little money	わずかなお金だけを
from his invention.	自分の発明から。
In fact,	(いや)むしろ,
some historians claim	一部の歴史家は主張している
that when you consider	考慮すると
everything	あらゆるものを
he invested in developing it,	彼がその機械を開発するのにつぎ込んだ,
he probably lost money.	彼はたぶん損をしただろうと。
Still,	それでも,
the cotton gin remains	綿繰り機は依然として～である
one of the most important inventions	最も重要な発明の1つ
of the 1800s.	1800年代の。

Lesson 04

READING

Lesson 05
問題
Questions

W 単 語 数 ▶ **270** 語
🕐 制限時間 ▶ **7** 分
☑ 目標得点 ▶ **20** /30点

DATE

▶次の英文を読み，その文意にそって（ **1** ）から（ **3** ）までの（　　）に入れるのに最も適切なものを **1**，**2**，**3**，**4** の中から１つ選び，その番号を所定欄にマークしなさい。

The Nixon-Kennedy Debates

In 1960, two future presidents, John F. Kennedy and Richard Nixon, faced off in America's first televised debate. Nixon was ill before the debate and was exhausted from his hectic campaign schedule, leaving him looking thin and pale. (　　**1**　　), Kennedy had taken the weekend off to prepare and was well-rested. Also, weeks of outdoor campaigning made him look healthy and tanned. It is often said that people who listened to the debate on the radio thought Nixon won, while the majority, who watched it on TV, felt Kennedy was the winner. Therefore, some say that Kennedy's win was a victory of charisma over content.

Recently, however, historians have been questioning this idea. Analysis of the survey in which radio listeners favored Nixon shows that they tended to live in the country, where there was much stronger support for Nixon, likely resulting in bias in the survey. People who watch the debate today also tend to believe that there was no significant difference in the quality and impact of what each candidate said. Historians therefore claim that the idea that Kennedy only won because of his charisma (　　**2**　　).

Regardless of who actually won, the debate changed American

politics forever. In fact, people often say the debate (**3**).
When Americans voted one month later, the race was extremely
close. Kennedy eked out a narrow victory in which the difference
in votes was just 0.1 percent. Just a few months before, Nixon
had been estimated to be ahead by 6 percent. The debate caused
politicians to realize the tremendous power of TV in shaping
popular opinion.

Lesson 05

(**1**)　**1**　For instance　　　　**2**　In exchange
　　　　3　Nonetheless　　　　**4**　In contrast

(**2**)　**1**　has almost been forgotten　**2**　worried many voters
　　　　3　is lacking in support　　　**4**　causes these complaints

(**3**)　**1**　had not been a fair one
　　　　2　actually helped Nixon
　　　　3　decided the election result
　　　　4　was less important than other factors

ANSWER								
(**1**)	①	②	③	④	(**2**)	①	②	③	④
(**3**)	①	②	③	④					

Answers & Explanations ☞

Lesson 05
解答・解説
Answers & Explanations

□（**1**）　**1**　例えば　　　　　　　　　　**2**　引き換えに

　　　　　3　それにもかかわらず　　　**④**　その一方

解説▶（**1**）の前は「ニクソンは討論の前には病気で，多忙な選挙運動の日程に疲れ果てていたので，やせて顔色が悪く見える状態だった」，後ろは「ケネディは週末に休みを取ったので休養十分で，また屋外での選挙運動によって，健康的で日焼けして見えた」という内容になっている。これらは対照的な内容なので，**4**が正解。

□（**2**）　**1**　ほとんど忘れられている　　　**2**　多くの有権者を心配させた

　　　　　③　裏づけを欠いている　　　　　**4**　これらの不満の原因となる

解説▶第2段落第2文では，「調査は偏向につながる可能性が高い」ことが指摘され，第2段落第3文では，今日討論を見る人々にも「それぞれの候補者の発言の質や影響に大きな違いはなかった」と考える傾向があることが述べられている。これによって，第1段落で述べられていた，ケネディはカリスマ性だけで勝利したという説の根拠が否定されているとわかるので，**3**が正解。

重要語句　□ voter（名 有権者）　□ lack in support（熟 裏づけを欠く）

□（**3**）　**1**　公平なものではなかった　　　**2**　実際にニクソンを助けた

　　　　　③　選挙結果を決定づけた　　　　　**4**　ほかの要因よりも重要度が低かった

解説▶第3段落第3〜5文から，元は優勢とされていたニクソンが，選挙でケネディに敗れたことがわかる。第3段落の最後の文の「その討論を通じて政治家たちは，世論を形成するテレビの途方もない威力を実感した」より，人々は，そのテレビ討論が選挙結果に大きく影響し，ケネディの逆転勝利につながったと感じたことが推測できる。したがって，**3**が正解。

ANSWER		SCORE	CHECK YOUR LEVEL
（**1**）　① ② ③ **④**	（**2**）　① ② **③** ④	／30点 （3問×各10点）	0〜10点 ➡ Work harder! 11〜20点 ➡ OK! 21〜30点 ➡ Way to go!
（**3**）　① ② **③** ④			

【和訳】
ニクソンとケネディの討論

❶ 1960 年，未来の大統領であるジョン・F・ケネディとリチャード・ニクソンの2人は，アメリカの最初のテレビ討論で対決した。ニクソンは討論の前には病気で，多忙な選挙運動の日程に疲れ果てていたので，やせて顔色が悪く見える状態だった。その一方，ケネディは，準備をするために週末に休みを取ったので休養は十分だった。また数週間にわたる屋外での選挙運動によって，彼は健康的で日焼けして見えた。ラジオで討論を聴いた人々はニクソンが勝ったと思ったが，大多数の人々は，それをテレビで見ていて，ケネディが勝者だと思ったとよく言われている。それゆえにケネディの勝利は，内容に対するカリスマ性の勝利だったと言う人もいる。

❷ しかし最近，歴史家たちはこの考えを疑っている。ラジオを聴いた人々がニクソンに好意を示したとする調査の分析によれば，ラジオを聴いた人々は田舎に住んでいる傾向があり，そこではニクソンへのずっと強い支持があったことから，その調査は偏向につながる可能性が高い。今日討論を見る人々にも，それぞれの候補者の発言の質や影響に大きな違いはなかったと考える傾向がある。したがって歴史家たちは，カリスマ性だけでケネディが勝ったという考えは裏づけを欠いていると主張している。

❸ 実際の勝者が誰であったにせよ，その討論はその後長い間アメリカの政治を変えた。実際に人々は，その討論が選挙結果を決定づけたとしばしば言う。アメリカ人が1ヵ月後に投票したとき，選挙は大接戦だった。ケネディはわずか 0.1％の票差でかろうじて勝った。ほんの2，3ヵ月前には，ニクソンが 6％優勢と予想されていた。その討論を通じて政治家たちは，世論を形成するテレビの途方もない威力を実感した。

重要語句リスト

❶
- ☐ face off　　（熟）対決する
- ☐ televised debate　（名）テレビ討論
- ☐ hectic　　（形）多忙な
- ☐ campaign　　（名）選挙運動
- ☐ well-rested　（形）十分に休息した
- ☐ tanned　　（形）日焼けした
- ☐ charisma　　（名）カリスマ性
- ☐ content　　（名）内容，中身

❷
- ☐ question　　（動）～を疑う
- ☐ bias　　（名）偏向，偏見

❸
- ☐ eke out a narrow victory
  　　　　　　（熟）僅差で勝つ

Lesson
05

READING

Lesson 05
要点整理
Paragraph Summary

◀)) 音声 ▶ **L&R_LV5_05-Q**

▶音声を聞きながら, ①～⑤の空欄を埋めるもしくは適語を選び, 段落ごとの要旨を確認しましょう(解答は下部にあります)。

The Nixon-Kennedy Debates

❶ ◇ **John F. Kennedy and Richard Nixon**

= faced off in America's first televised debate

Nixon	Kennedy
(1) was ill before the debate (2) was exhausted from his hectic campaign schedule	(1) had taken the weekend off to prepare and was well-rested (2) weeks of outdoor campaigning
→ looked thin and pale	→ looked healthy and tanned

◇ **it is often said**

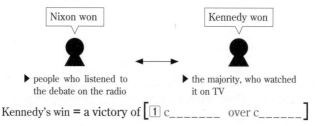

Nixon won	Kennedy won
▶ people who listened to the debate on the radio	▶ the majority, who watched it on TV

Kennedy's win = a victory of [① c_____ over c_____]

❷ ◇ **historians = question this idea**

(1) radio listeners = tended to live in the country, where there was much stronger support for [② Nixon / Kennedy]

(2) people who watch the debate today = there was no significant difference in the quality and [③ i_____] of what each candidate said

→ historians' claim : the idea that Kennedy only won because of his charisma is lacking in support

❸ ◇ **the [④ d_____] changed American politics**

• when Americans voted one month later, the race was extremely close

↔ a few months before, Nixon had been estimated to be ahead by 6 percent

→ the tremendous power of TV in shaping [⑤ p_____ o_____]

【解答】　① charisma over content　② Nixon　③ impact　④ debate　⑤ popular opinion

【和訳】

ニクソンとケネディの討論

❶ ◇ ジョン・F・ケネディとリチャード・ニクソン

= アメリカの最初のテレビ討論で対決した

ニクソン	ケネディ
(1)討論の前には病気だった (2)多忙な選挙運動の日程に疲れ果てていた	(1)準備をするために週末に休みを取り，休養は十分だった (2)数週間にわたる屋外での選挙運動
→ やせて顔色が悪く見えた	→ 健康的で日焼けして見えた

◇ よく言われていること

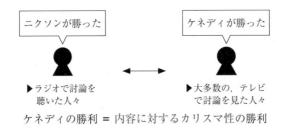

ニクソンが勝った

▶ラジオで討論を
聴いた人々

ケネディが勝った

▶大多数の，テレビ
で討論を見た人々

ケネディの勝利 = 内容に対するカリスマ性の勝利

❷ ◇ 歴史家たち = この考えを疑う

(1)ラジオを聴いた人々 = 田舎に住んでいる傾向があり，そこではニクソンへのずっと強い支持があった

(2)今日討論を見る人々 = それぞれの候補者の発言の質や影響に大きな違いはなかった

→ 歴史家たちの主張：ケネディがカリスマ性だけで勝利したという考えは，裏づけを欠いている

❸ ◇ 討論はアメリカの政治を変えた

• アメリカ人が1ヵ月後に投票したとき，選挙は大接戦だった

↔ 2，3ヵ月前には，ニクソンが6%優勢と予想されていた

→ 世論を形成するテレビの途方もない威力

Lesson 05
速読練習
Sight Translation

◀)) 英文音声 ▶ L&R_LV5_05-ST

DATE

英語	和訳
The Nixon-Kennedy Debates	ニクソンとケネディの討論
❶ In 1960,	1960 年,
two future presidents,	未来の大統領である 2 人は,
John F. Kennedy and Richard Nixon,	ジョン・F・ケネディとリチャード・ニクソンの,
faced off	対決した
in America's first televised debate.	アメリカの最初のテレビ討論で。
Nixon was ill	ニクソンは病気で
before the debate	討論の前には
and was exhausted	また疲れ果てていた
from his hectic campaign schedule,	多忙な選挙運動の日程に,
leaving him looking thin and pale.	やせて顔色が悪く見える状態だった。
In contrast,	その一方,
Kennedy had taken the weekend off	ケネディは週末に休みを取った
to prepare	準備をするために
and was well-rested.	そして休養は十分だった。
Also,	また,
weeks of outdoor campaigning	数週間にわたる屋外での選挙運動によって
made him look healthy and tanned.	彼は健康的で日焼けして見えた。
It is often said	よく言われている
that people who listened to the debate	討論を聴いた人々は
on the radio	ラジオで
thought	思った
Nixon won,	ニクソンが勝ったと,
while the majority,	一方で大多数の人は,
who watched it on TV,	それをテレビで見た,
felt	思った
Kennedy was the winner.	ケネディが勝者だと。
Therefore,	それゆえに,
some say	〜と言う人もいる
that Kennedy's win	ケネディの勝利は
was a victory of charisma	カリスマ性の勝利だったと
over content.	内容に対する。
❷ Recently,	最近,
however,	しかし,
historians have been questioning	歴史家たちは疑っている
this idea.	この考えを。
Analysis of the survey	調査の分析は

in which radio listeners favored Nixon	ラジオを聴いた人々がニクソンに好意をもったという
shows	示している
that they tended to live	彼らは住んでいる傾向にあり
in the country,	田舎に，
where there was much stronger support	そこではずっと強い支持があった
for Nixon,	ニクソンへの，
likely resulting in bias	偏向につながる可能性が高い
in the survey.	その調査は。
People who watch the debate today	今日討論を見る人々も
also tend to believe	また考える傾向がある
that there was no significant difference	大きな違いはなかったと
in the quality and impact	質と影響に
of what each candidate said.	それぞれの候補者の発言の。
Historians therefore claim	したがって歴史家たちは主張している
that the idea	考えは
that Kennedy only won	ケネディがただ勝ったという
because of his charisma	カリスマ性で
is lacking in support.	裏づけを欠いていると。
❸ Regardless of who actually won,	実際の勝者が誰であったにせよ，
the debate changed	その討論は変えた
American politics	アメリカの政治を
forever.	その後長い間。
In fact,	実際に，
people often say	人々はしばしば言う
the debate decided	その討論が決定づけたと
the election result.	選挙結果を。
When Americans voted	アメリカ人が投票したとき
one month later,	1ヵ月後に，
the race was extremely close.	選挙は大接戦だった。
Kennedy eked out	ケネディは苦労して手に入れた
a narrow victory	辛勝を
in which the difference in votes	票差で
was just 0.1 percent.	わずか0.1%の。
Just a few months before,	ほんの2，3ヵ月前には，
Nixon had been estimated	ニクソンが予想されていた
to be ahead	優勢と
by 6 percent.	6%。
The debate caused politicians to realize	その討論を通じて政治家たちは実感した
the tremendous power of TV	テレビの途方もない威力を
in shaping popular opinion.	世論を形成する。

END

Q 4技能のすべてに触れる機会を，日常生活の中でどのようにつくればよいでしょうか？

A 現代では，インターネットなどの通信技術の発達によって，英語に触れる機会を簡単につくることができます。

例えばNHKは，「**NHK World**」という番組を配信しています。これは，日本のニュースを世界に向けて多言語で配信するサービスで，パソコンやスマートフォンなどを使って，誰でも気軽に見ることができます。「日本のことを世界に発信しよう」という番組なので，生徒の皆さんにとって身近で興味深く，役に立つ内容も多いと思います。理解しやすいレベルの英語を用いた番組がたくさんあるので，ぜひ見たい番組を探してみましょう。日常的に生の英語に触れるには非常におすすめです。ネイティブスピーカーを対象とした海外のニュース番組に挑戦したい人もいるかもしれませんが，やはり非常に難しいものが多いので，それを理解するための架け橋として「NHK World」を利用するのもよいでしょう。

また SNS の発達により，世界の人たちに向けて，気軽に情報を発信することができるようになりました。**ぜひ SNS を使って，皆さんが日々撮っている写真を，英語の文を添えて発信してみましょう。**最初はうまく英文をつくることができないかもしれませんが，無料の添削サービスや，高精度の翻訳サービスも増えていますので，ぜひそれらを活用してみてください。最高の Writing 対策になると思います。自分が英語で何かを投稿すれば，英語のコメントが返ってくることもあると思いますから，それに対しても積極的に返信してみましょう。

皆さんの学校の英語の授業でも英語を話す機会が増えてきたのではないでしょうか。もし授業内で 3 分間 Discussion をするなどの機会があれば，その 3 分間を大切にして，たくさん英語を話してみましょう。**与えられた機会を最大限に活かす習慣**を身につけるのも大切です。

ほかにも，海外旅行，短期留学，オンライン英会話など，英語を使う経験を積むことができる機会は充実してきています。英語の勉強と日常生活を分けて考えるのではなく，融合させる形で，英語を使う機会をどんどん増やしていってくださいね。

Part 2
Lesson 06–10

Reading

内容一致問題
Reading Comprehension

Carnegie Mellon University

▶ 次の英文の内容に関して，（１）〜（４）の質問に対する最も適切な答え（または文を完成させるのに最も適切なもの）を **1**，**2**，**3**，**4** の中から１つ選びなさい。

Attachment Parenting

Before the 1960s, experts on child development held a negative view of parents showing affection toward their children, cautioning that frequent compliments or expressions of love could lead to psychological illnesses later in life. However, a series of experiments conducted by American psychologist Harry Harlow in the 1960s contradicted this view and revolutionized parenting. Before Harlow, it was theorized that infants formed an attachment to their parents due to the food that they provided. Harlow set out to test this belief by taking monkeys away from their birth mothers and raising them using two artificial "mothers." The first was made of wire and provided the young monkeys with milk, while the second was covered in soft material but provided no nutrition. It quickly became evident that the monkeys had become attached to the cloth mother rather than the wire one, offering strong evidence against the traditional explanation of attachment in infants.

Harlow's research also demonstrated that without normal levels of parental affection, monkeys were likely to develop physical and psychological problems. In the 1970s, the work of Harlow and others like him persuaded a doctor named William Sears that a technique called "attachment parenting" could not only prevent such effects but also have a positive influence. Mothers were encouraged to share beds with their babies, maintain physical contact with them throughout the day, and breastfeed them until a later age. His observations of members of modern hunter-gatherer societies showed that in pre-technological societies, it was normal for mothers to spend significant amounts of time right near their infants, and Harlow felt this was evidence that attachment parenting would produce children with improved health, confidence, and language ability.

Although attachment parenting has become popular, experts such as former Harvard Medical School instructor Amy Tuteur argue that attachment "is virtually guaranteed in all but the most extreme cases of abuse and neglect." Tuteur compares the way some people apply the principles of attachment parenting to how one might feed a baby. She says that someone who learns that a young baby only needs 400 calories a day to be healthy might decide to give their baby 2,000 calories to try to make them extra healthy. However, just like an excess of food would likely lead to obesity and other health problems, an excess of attachment could also lead to psychological problems.

Passionate supporters of attachment parenting have not helped the situation. Some have stated that failure to follow the principles of attachment parenting can lead to learning disabilities and even violence in children, even if the parents have not been abusive or neglectful. Others have expressed that the major commitment required by the technique along with its emphasis on frequent contact and breastfeeding make it difficult for women to have careers. Furthermore, such claims themselves have an impact, leading some parents to experience unnecessary guilt about factors beyond their control such as behavioral problems that are the result of genetic issues.

Questions ☞

(**1**) Harry Harlow's experiment on monkeys in the 1960s demonstrated that

    1 the way that young monkeys form attachments to their mothers differs significantly from the way that young humans do.

    2 the idea that infants become attached to their parents simply because they receive food from them is likely to be incorrect.

    3 after a certain age, it becomes impossible for a child to develop a deep emotional attachment to his or her mother.

    4 it is impossible for babies to become attached to their parents if they are not receiving a sufficient amount of nutrition.

(**2**) What did William Sears believe about attachment parenting?

    1 It could prevent many of the physical and psychological problems that appear in members of hunter-gatherer societies.

    2 Through the use of modern technology, it may be possible to increase the degree of attachment that children feel for their parents.

    3 Rather than increasing attachment, spending too much time with a baby can create serious problems.

    4 Having babies near their mothers for extended periods of time could have beneficial effects on the babies' mental and physical development.

(**3**) Amy Tuteur believes that some people who support attachment parenting

   1 have taken an important technique for raising healthy children and turned it into something that could be harmful to them.

   2 are endangering their children by forcing them to eat more calories than they need to grow up healthy.

   3 could encourage parents to abuse or neglect their children because attachment parenting is so strict.

   4 do not understand how difficult it can be to prevent a mother with mental problems from abusing or neglecting her baby.

(**4**) The author of the passage thinks that attachment parenting

   1 requires more research into the principles behind it so that it can become even more effective.

   2 requires a significant commitment but is certainly worth the effort if parents are willing to make one.

   3 can place undue pressure on parents by making them feel responsible for things that are not their fault.

   4 is generally more effective in influencing children's behavior than other techniques that have been developed by scientists.

ANSWER			
(**1**)	① ② ③ ④	(**2**)	① ② ③ ④
(**3**)	① ② ③ ④	(**4**)	① ② ③ ④

Answers & Explanations ☞

□**(1)** 1960 年代のハリー・ハーロウのサルに関する実験は……ことを示した。

   1 幼いサルが母親への愛着を形成する方法は，幼い人間がする方法とはかなり異なる

   ② 乳児が両親に愛着をもつのは単に彼らが両親から食べ物を受け取るからだという考えは間違っている可能性が高い

   3 一定の年齢を過ぎると，子どもは母親に深い情緒的な愛着を抱くことができなくなる

   4 十分な量の栄養を受けとっていなければ，赤ちゃんが親に愛着を抱くことは不可能である

[解説]▶第 1 段落第 3 文に，「**ハーロウの登場以前は，乳児は両親が与えた食べ物によって両親への愛着を形成することが理論化されていた**」とあり，第 1 段落の最後の文から，ハーロウの実験によってこの理論をくつがえすための強力な証拠が生み出されたことがわかる。したがって，**2** が正解。

□**(2)** ウィリアム・シアーズは愛情育児に関する何を信じていたか。

   1 狩猟採集社会の人々に現れる身体的および心理的問題の多くを防ぐかもしれない。

   2 現代の技術を使用することで，子どもたちが両親に対して感じる愛着の度合いを高めることができるかもしれない。

   3 愛着を強めることよりもむしろ赤ちゃんと長すぎる時間を過ごすことが深刻な問題を引き起こす可能性がある。

   ④ 赤ちゃんを母親の近くに長時間置くことは，赤ちゃんの心身の発達に有益な影響を与える可能性がある。

[解説]▶第 2 段落第 2 文に，「**ハーロウと彼のような人々の研究は，ウィリアム・シアーズという名の医師に，『愛情育児』と呼ばれる技術がそのような影響を防ぐだけでなく，前向きな影響ももつ可能性があることを確信させた**」とある。第 2 段落の最後の文より，この前向きな影響とは「健康や自信，言語能力が向上した子どもたちを生み出す」ことだとわかるので，**4** が正解。

[重要語句] □ degree of ～（熟 ～の程度）　□ beneficial（形 有益な）

□(**3**)　エイミー・チューターは，愛情育児を支持する一部の人々は……と考えている。

① 健康な子どもたちを育てるために重要な技術を利用して，それを子どもたちに有害になりうるものに変えてしまった

2 子どもたちが健康に成長するために必要なカロリーよりも多くのカロリーを無理やり摂取させることによって，子どもたちを危険にさらしている

3 愛情育児は非常に大変なので，親が子どもたちを虐待したり育児放棄したりすることを誘発しかねない

4 精神的な問題のある母親が赤ちゃんを虐待したり，育児放棄したりするのを防ぐのがどれほど難しいか理解していない

Lesson
06

解説▶第3段落の最後の2文より，エイミー・チューターは赤ちゃんに過剰なカロリーを摂取させることが健康上の問題につながるように，**過剰な愛情を与えることを問題だと考えている**ことがわかる。したがって，**1**が正解。

重要語句 □ endanger（動 ～を危険にさらす）

□(**4**)　この文章の作者は，愛情育児は……と考えている。

1 その効果をさらに高めるために，その背後にある原則をさらに研究する必要がある

2 かなりの献身を必要とするが，親が喜んでそれをするつもりであれば確かに努力する価値がある

③ 親のせいではないことに対して責任を感じさせることにより，親に過度のプレッシャーをかけてしまう可能性がある

4 一般に，科学者によって開発されたほかの手法よりも子どもたちの行動に影響を与えるのに効果的である

解説▶第4段落の最後の文に，「そのような主張自体が影響を与え，一部の両親に，遺伝的問題の結果である行動障害のような制御不能な要因について，不必要な罪悪感を感じさせることにつながっている」とある。「そのような主張」とは，第4段落第2～3文で述べられていて，第2文は愛情育児の原則に従えないことが子どもたちの学習障害や暴力につながりうるという主張を指すので，**3**が正解。

重要語句 □ worth（形 ～の価値がある）　□ undue（形 過度の）

ANSWER		SCORE	CHECK YOUR LEVEL
(**1**) ① **②** ③ ④ (**2**) ① ② ③ **④**		/40点 (4問×各10点)	0～20点 ➡ *Work harder!* 21～30点 ➡ *OK!* 31～40点 ➡ *Way to go!*
(**3**) **①** ② ③ ④ (**4**) ① ② **③** ④			

愛情育児

❶ 1960 年代以前，子どもの成長に関する専門家は，自分の子どもに愛情を示している親に対して否定的な意見をもっており，頻繁なほめ言葉や愛情表現が，のちの人生での心理的な病気につながる可能性があることを警告した。しかし，1960 年代にアメリカの心理学者ハリー・ハーロウによって行われた一連の実験は，この見方に反しており，子育てに革命をもたらした。ハーロウの登場以前は，乳児は両親が与えた食べ物によって両親への愛着を形成することが理論化されていた。ハーロウは，サルを彼らの産みの母から取り上げ，そのサルを 2 つの人工的な「母」を使って育てることで，この考えを確かめようとした。1 つ目はワイヤーでつくられ，幼いサルにミルクを与えるもので，対する 2 つ目は柔らかい素材で覆われているものの，栄養は与えないものだった。サルがワイヤーの母よりも布の母に愛着を示すようになったことがすぐに明らかになり，乳児の愛着についての伝統的な説明に反する強力な証拠を提供した。

❷ ハーロウの研究は，通常のレベルの親の愛情がなければ，サルが身体的および心理的な問題を起こしてしまう可能性が高いことも実証した。1970 年代，ハーロウと彼のような人々の研究は，ウィリアム・シアーズという名の医師に，「愛情育児」と呼ばれる技術がそのような影響を防ぐだけでなく，前向きな影響ももつ可能性があることを確信させた。母親たちは，赤ちゃんとベッドを共にし，1 日中彼らと身体的な触れ合いを継続し，後年まで母乳で育てることを勧められた。彼の現代の狩猟採集社会の人々の観察は，技術が未発達の社会において，母親が乳児のすぐ近くでかなり多くの時間を過ごすことは普通であったことを示し，そしてハーロウはこれが愛情育児が健康や自信，言語能力が向上した子どもたちを生み出す証拠であると感じた。

❸ 愛情育児が普及するようになったが，かつてのハーバード・メディカル・スクールの講師であるエイミー・チューターなどの専門家は，愛情は「虐待とネグレクトという最も極端な場合を除き，実質的に全体で保証されている」と主張している。チューターは，一部の人々が愛情育児の原則を適用する方法を，人々が赤ちゃんに食べ物を与える方法になぞらえる。彼女は，赤ちゃんが健康でいるために 1 日あたり 400 カロリーだけ必要とすると知っている誰かが，赤ちゃんを必要以上に健康にしようとして赤ちゃんに 2,000 カロリーを与えようと決めるかもしれないと言う。しかし，ちょうど過剰な食べ物が肥満やほかの健康問題につながりやすいように，過剰な愛着も心理的な問題につながりうる。

❹ 愛情育児の熱烈な支持者たちはその状況を改善してこなかった。たとえ両親が虐待やネグレクトをしなかったとしても，愛情育児の原則に従えないことが，子どもたちの学習障害や暴力にさえつながりうると述べている人もいた。頻繁な接触や授乳の重要視と併せて，その技術に必要とされている大きな献身は，女性が仕事を持つことを難しくすると言っている人もいる。さらに，そのような主張自体が影響を与え，一部の両親に，遺伝的問題の結果である行動障害のような制御不能な要因について，不必要な罪悪感を感じさせることにつながっている。

重要語句リスト

❶

☐ attachment	图 愛情	
☐ parenting	图 子育て	
☐ affection	图 愛情	
☐ caution	動 〜を警告する	
☐ compliment	图 ほめ言葉，賛辞	
☐ psychological	形 心理的な，精神の	
☐ psychologist	图 心理学者	
☐ contradict	動 〜を否定する，〜に反対する	
☐ revolutionize	動 〜に革命を起こす	
☐ infant	图 幼児，乳児	
☐ set out to *do*	熟 〜しようと試みる	
☐ artificial	形 人工的な	
☐ nutrition	图 栄養	

❷

☐ persuade 〜 that…	動 〜に…を確信させる
☐ not only…but (also) 〜	熟 …だけでなく〜も
☐ breastfeed	動 〜を母乳で育てる
☐ confidence	图 自信

❸

☐ virtually	副 実質的には，事実上
☐ abuse	图 虐待，悪用
☐ neglect	图 ネグレクト，育児放棄，無視
☐ compare 〜 to…	熟 〜を…になぞらえる
☐ obesity	图 肥満

❹

☐ disability	图 障害，ハンディキャップ，無能
☐ abusive	形 虐待的な，口汚い，悪用された
☐ neglectful	形 怠慢な，投げやりな
☐ commitment	图 献身，責任，委任
☐ emphasis	图 重点，強調
☐ breastfeeding	图 授乳，母乳で育てること

▶音声を聞きながら，①〜⑥の空欄を埋め，段落ごとの要旨を確認しましょう（解答は下部にあります）。

Attachment Parenting

❶ ◇ **before the 1960s**

- experts : held a [① n_____ v___] of parents showing affection toward their children

  ← frequent compliments or expressions of love could lead to [② p_____] illnesses later in life

◇ **in the 1960s**

- a series of experiments conducted by Harry Harlow contradicted this view

  <u>before Harlow</u>

  people thought infants formed an attachment to their parents due to food

  <u>Harlow's experiment</u>

  raising monkeys using two artificial "mothers"

  (1) made of wire + provides milk

  (2) covered in soft material + provides no nutrition

  → the monkeys became attached to the cloth mother

  = strong [③ e_____] against the traditional explanation of attachment in infants

❷ ◇ **Harlow's research**

- without parental affection → monkeys develop physical and psychological problems

- "attachment parenting" = share beds with babies, maintain physical contact, and breastfeed them

  → (1) [④ p_____] physical and psychological problems

  (2) have a positive influence

【解答】 ① negative view ② psychological ③ evidence ④ prevent

【和訳】

愛情育児

❶　◇ **1960 年代以前**

- 専門家：自分の子どもに愛情を示している親に対して否定的な意見をもった
   - ← 頻繁なほめ言葉や愛情表現が，のちの人生での心理的な病気につながる可能性がある

◇ **1960 年代**

- ハリー・ハーロウによって行われた一連の実験は，この見方に反していた
   ハーロウの登場以前
   人々は，乳児が食べ物によって両親への愛着を形成すると考えた
   ハーロウの実験
   サルを 2 つの人工的な「母」を使って育てる
   (1) ワイヤーでつくられる ＋ ミルクを与える
   (2) 柔らかい素材で覆われている ＋ 栄養は与えない
   → サルは布の母に愛着を示した
   ＝ 乳児の愛着についての伝統的な説明に反する強力な証拠

❷　◇ **ハーロウの研究**

- 親の愛情がない → サルが身体的および心理的な問題を起こす
- 「愛情育児」＝ 赤ちゃんとベッドを共にし，彼らと身体的な触れ合いを継続し，母乳で育てる
   → (1) 身体的および心理的な問題を防ぐ
   　　(2) 前向きな影響を与える

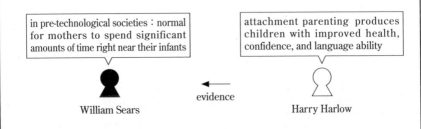

in pre-technological societies : normal for mothers to spend significant amounts of time right near their infants

William Sears

← evidence

attachment parenting produces children with improved health, confidence, and language ability

Harry Harlow

❸ ◇ **the way some people apply the principles of attachment parenting ≒ how one might feed a baby**

- how one might feed a baby

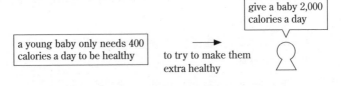

a young baby only needs 400 calories a day to be healthy

→ to try to make them extra healthy

give a baby 2,000 calories a day

→ obesity and other health problems

→ an [⑤ e_____] of attachment could also lead to psychological problems

❹ ◇ **some have stated that**

- failure to follow the principles of attachment parenting

  → can lead to learning disabilities and even violence in children

◇ **others have expressed that**

- the major commitment required by the technique

  → make it difficult for women to have careers

◇ **such claims themselves have an impact**

- some parents experience unnecessary [⑥ g____] about factors beyond their control

【解答】 ⑤ excess ⑥ guilt

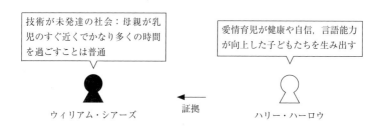

技術が未発達の社会：母親が乳児のすぐ近くでかなり多くの時間を過ごすことは普通

愛情育児が健康や自信，言語能力が向上した子どもたちを生み出す

ウィリアム・シアーズ　←証拠　ハリー・ハーロウ

Lesson
06

❸　◇ 一部の人々が愛情育児の原則を適用する方法 ≒ 赤ちゃんに食べ物を与える方法

- 赤ちゃんに食べ物を与える方法

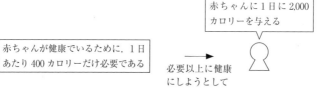

赤ちゃんに 1 日に 2,000 カロリーを与える

赤ちゃんが健康でいるために，1 日あたり 400 カロリーだけ必要である

必要以上に健康にしようとして

→ 肥満やそのほかの健康上の問題

→ 過剰な愛着も心理的な問題につながりうる

❹　◇ 一部の人々は述べている

- 愛情育児の原則に従えないこと

    → 子どもたちの学習障害や暴力にさえつながりうる

◇ ほかの人々は言っている

- その技術に必要とされている大きな献身

    → 女性が仕事を持つことを難しくする

◇ そのような主張自体が影響を与える

- 一部の両親は制御不能な要因について，不必要な罪悪感を感じる

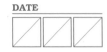 英文音声 ▶ L&R_LV5_06-ST

英語	和訳
Attachment Parenting	愛情育児
① Before the 1960s,	1960 年代以前，
experts on child development	子どもの成長に関する専門家は
held a negative view	否定的な意見をもっており
of parents	親に対して
showing affection toward their children,	自分の子どもに愛情を示している，
cautioning	警告した
that frequent compliments or expressions of love	頻繁なほめ言葉や愛情表現が
could lead to psychological illnesses	心理的な病気につながる可能性があると
later in life.	のちの人生で。
However,	しかし，
a series of experiments	一連の実験は
conducted by American psychologist Harry Harlow	アメリカの心理学者ハリー・ハーロウによって行われた
in the 1960s	1960 年代に
contradicted this view	この見方に反しており
and revolutionized parenting.	そして子育てに革命をもたらした。
Before Harlow,	ハーロウの登場以前は，
it was theorized	理論化されていた
that infants formed an attachment	乳児は愛着を形成することが
to their parents	両親への
due to the food	食べ物によって
that they provided.	両親が与えた。
Harlow set out to test this belief	ハーロウはこの考えを確かめようとした
by taking monkeys away	サルを取り上げることで
from their birth mothers	彼らの産みの母から
and raising them	そしてそのサルを育てることで
using two artificial "mothers."	2 つの人工的な「母」を使って。
The first was made of wire	1 つ目はワイヤーでつくられ
and provided the young monkeys with milk,	そして幼いサルにミルクを与えるもので，
while the second was covered in soft material	対する 2 つ目は柔らかい素材で覆われているものの

but provided no nutrition.	栄養は与えなかった。
It quickly became evident	すぐに明らかになった
that the monkeys had become attached	サルが愛着を示すようになったことが
to the cloth mother	布の母に
rather than the wire one,	ワイヤーの母よりも,
offering strong evidence	強力な証拠を提供した
against the traditional explanation	伝統的な説明に反する
of attachment in infants.	乳児の愛着についての。
❷ Harlow's research also demonstrated	ハーロウの研究は, また実証した
that without normal levels of parental affection,	通常のレベルの親の愛情がなければ,
monkeys were likely to develop	サルが起こしてしまう可能性が高いことも
physical and psychological problems.	身体的および心理的な問題を。
In the 1970s,	1970年代,
the work of Harlow and others like him	ハーロウと彼のような人々の研究は
persuaded a doctor	医師を確信させた
named William Sears	ウィリアム・シアーズという名の
that a technique	技術が
called "attachment parenting"	「愛情育児」と呼ばれる
could not only prevent such effects	そのような影響を防ぐだけでなく
but also have a positive influence.	前向きな影響も与える可能性があることを。
Mothers were encouraged	母親たちは勧められた
to share beds with their babies,	赤ちゃんとベッドを共にし,
maintain physical contact with them	彼らと身体的な触れ合いを継続し,
throughout the day,	1日中,
and breastfeed them	そして母乳で育てることを
until a later age.	後年まで。
His observations	彼の観察は
of members of modern hunter-gatherer societies	現代の狩猟採集社会の人々の
showed	示していた
that in pre-technological societies,	技術が未発達の社会において,
it was normal	普通であったと
for mothers	母親が
to spend significant amounts of time	かなり多くの時間を過ごすことは
right near their infants,	乳児のすぐ近くで,
and Harlow felt	そしてハーロウは感じた

this was evidence	これが証拠であると
that attachment parenting would produce children	愛情育児が子どもたちを生み出すことの
with improved health, confidence, and language ability.	健康や自信，言語能力が向上した。
❸ Although attachment parenting has become popular,	愛情育児が普及するようになったが，
experts	専門家は
such as former Harvard Medical School	かつてのハーバード・メディカル・スクール
instructor Amy Tuteur	の講師であるエイミー・チューターなどの
argue	主張している
that attachment "is virtually guaranteed in all	愛情は「実質的に保証されている 全体で
but the most extreme cases	最も極端な場合を除き
of abuse and neglect."	虐待とネグレクトという」と。
Tuteur compares	チューターはなぞらえる
the way	方法を
some people apply	一部の人々が適用する
the principles of attachment parenting	愛情育児の原則を
to how one might feed a baby.	人々が赤ちゃんに食べ物を与える方法に。
She says	彼女は言う
that someone who learns	知っている誰かが
that a young baby only needs 400	赤ちゃんが 1 日あたり 400 カロリーだけ
calories a day	必要とすると
to be healthy	健康でいるために
might decide	決めるかもしれないと
to give their baby 2,000 calories	赤ちゃんに 2,000 カロリーを与えることを
to try to make them extra healthy.	赤ちゃんを必要以上に健康にしようとして。
However,	しかし，
just like an excess of food would likely lead	ちょうど過剰な食べ物がつながりやすいように
to obesity and other health problems,	肥満やほかの健康問題に，
an excess of attachment	過剰な愛着も
could also lead	またつながりうる
to psychological problems.	心理的な問題に。
❹ Passionate supporters of attachment parenting	愛情育児の熱烈な支持者たちは

have not helped	改善してこなかった
the situation.	その状況を。
Some have stated	述べている人もいた
that failure to follow	従えないことが
the principles of attachment parenting	愛情育児の原則に
can lead	つながりうると
to learning disabilities and even violence	子どもたちの学習障害や暴力にさえ，
in children,	
even if the parents	たとえ両親が
have not been abusive or neglectful.	虐待やネグレクトをしなかったとしても。
Others have expressed	言っている人もいる
that the major commitment	大きな献身は
required by the technique	その技術に必要とされている
along with its emphasis	重要視と併せて
on frequent contact and breastfeeding	頻繁な接触や授乳の
make it difficult	難しくすると
for women	女性にとって
to have careers.	仕事を持つことを。
Furthermore,	さらに，
such claims themselves	そのような主張自体が
have an impact,	影響を与え，
leading some parents	一部の両親にもたらしている
to experience unnecessary guilt	不必要な罪悪感を感じさせることを
about factors	要因について
beyond their control	制御不能な
such as behavioral problems	行動障害のような
that are the result	結果である
of genetic issues.	遺伝的問題の。

READING

Lesson 07
問題
Questions

07

W 単 語 数 ▶ **523** 語

🕐 制限時間 ▶ **12** 分

✔ 目標得点 ▶ **30** /40点

DATE

▶次の英文の内容に関して，(1)〜(4)の質問に対する最も適切な答え（または文を完成させるのに最も適切なもの）を **1**，**2**，**3**，**4** の中から 1 つ選びなさい。

The End of Moore's Law

In 1965, a computer scientist named Gordon Moore created Moore's Law, which states that the speed of computers will double roughly every two years. The primary way that engineers have continued to increase the speed of computers is by putting more transistors into computer chips. Transistors are tiny switches that regulate the flow of electricity to allow the chips to make calculations, and having more transistors increases a computer's power. For years, thanks to a scientific principle known as Dennard scaling, the amount of power necessary for the transistors to operate remained the same, even when there were many of them placed in a small space. Now, however, Dennard scaling has reached its limit, and the increased number of transistors has caused the amount of power they require to rise, leading to problems such as overheating. Moreover, the higher voltages required by newer chips have also increased power use. These two factors have presented an enormous challenge for engineers attempting to increase processing power. In fact, most experts are now predicting the end of Moore's law within a few years.

The impact cannot be understated. While Moore's Law was originally just an observation, it's been used to guide long-term research and development planning in the semiconductor industry. The end of Moore's Law can be compared to the current state of the oil industry. Oil companies have found that easily available oil is running out, requiring them to search deep below the Earth's surface or in isolated areas to find more. Similarly, processor speed improvements may come to require substantial financial investments as gains become increasingly difficult to achieve. Whether chip makers will be able to gain enough profit from their investments to make further research into new chip-making technologies has therefore become a major issue.

Even if Moore's Law does come to an end, it doesn't necessarily mean that software programs will not be able to run more quickly. After all, the way software is developed also has an impact on speed. For better or for worse, many software projects prioritize business goals over code efficiency. That's why some programs contain thousands if not millions of lines of unnecessary code. If development teams were given the freedom to invest more time and energy in organization and planning, the software programs they produced would not only run more efficiently, but they would also contain fewer bugs.

Another solution may lie in creating more-specialized chips, such as GPUs and TPUs. GPUs are built to be extremely efficient at performing calculations needed to produce images, and TPUs are designed specifically for artificial intelligence. They could both be much faster and more energy efficient than the general-purpose chips in common use today. However, there are considerable costs associated with their development. Additionally, experts such as Princeton University's David Wentzlaff argue that although rapid gains have been seen from the use of specialized chips, these will soon level off and become subject to the same problems that have affected ordinary computer chips. Others, however, argue that even if that is the case, by that time other not yet developed techniques will exist to ensure that rapid progress continues.

Lesson
07

Questions ☞

(**1**)　In recent years, Dennard scaling has

    1　no longer proven true when it comes to limiting the amount of electricity required by some computer chips.

    2　been used by scientists to increase the amount of power available to transistors used for making calculations in computers.

    3　helped scientists to raise and lower the voltage in transistors so that less power is consumed overall.

    4　caused the voltages that pass through transistors to rise and fall, causing them to wear out much more quickly than in the past.

(**2**)　The computer chip manufacturing industry is currently facing uncertainty about

    1　whether or not it will be worth the money companies will need to spend on developing chips with faster processors.

    2　the way that the recent increases in oil prices will affect the costs of producing computer chips.

    3　the negative environmental effects that could be caused by the new production techniques used to increase processor speeds.

    4　whether it can efficiently collect material to build chips because it is often located deep under the Earth's surface.

(3) What point does the author make about modern software and the end of Moore's Law?

 1 Because of improvements that have recently occurred in software development, there is a chance Moore's Law will not have to end.

 2 When Moore's Law ends, it will become necessary to update software much more frequently than it is now.

 3 If software were to be written more carefully, the end of Moore's Law would not be such a serious problem.

 4 Since companies have been hiring fewer software developers and more hardware engineers, computer chips will improve despite the end of Moore's Law.

(4) What is one reason some experts are pessimistic about specialized computer chips?

 1 Although they are very useful in the field of artificial intelligence, they are not as efficient at the calculations needed for computer graphics.

 2 It is unlikely that it will be possible for them to continue to improve processor speeds in the future.

 3 Despite being much easier to design, the cost of their production will be much higher than the cost of regular chips.

 4 They require so much more energy than ordinary chips do that it may be impossible for engineers to create them.

ANSWER			
(1) ① ② ③ ④		**(2)** ① ② ③ ④	
(3) ① ② ③ ④		**(4)** ① ② ③ ④	

Answers & Explanations ☞

Lesson 07
解答・解説
Answers & Explanations

☐ **(1)** 　近年，デナード則は……

① 一部のコンピューターチップで必要とされる電気の量を制限する段階になると，もはや当てはまらないと証明された。

2 コンピューターが計算をするのに使われるトランジスタが利用可能な電力量を増やすために科学者によって使用されている。

3 全体としてより少ない電力の消費で済むように，科学者がトランジスタの電圧を上げたり下げたりするのに役立った。

4 トランジスタにかかる電圧が上がったり下がったりすることの原因となり，昔よりもそれらがはるかに速く摩耗する原因になった。

解説▶第１段落第４〜６文より，**デナード則はかつては効果的であったが，もはや限界に達し，必要とされる電力量が増えている**ことがわかる。したがって，**1** が正解。

重要語句 ☐ wear out（熟 摩耗する）

☐ **(2)** 　コンピューターチップの製造業は現在……についての疑念に直面している。

① より速い処理装置のチップに，企業がそれを開発するために必要とするであろう資金分の価値があるかどうか

2 最近の石油の値段の上昇がコンピューターチップを生産するのにかかる費用にどのように影響するか

3 処理装置の速度を上げるために使われている新しい生産技術によって生じている可能性のある環境への悪影響

4 チップをつくるための材料はしばしば地表の下深くにあるため，効率良くそれを集められるかどうか

解説▶第２段落の最後の２文に，「**処理装置の速度の向上はかなりの財政投資を必要とするようになるかもしれない**」「**チップメーカーが，新しいチップをつくる技術へのさらなる研究をするための投資から十分な利益を得られるかどうかは，それゆえ大きな問題になっている**」とあり，コンピューターチップを製造している企業は，新たに開発するチップに，開発費用に見合う価値があるかどうかについて疑念をもっていることがわかる。したがって，**1** が正解。

☐ **(3)** 　筆者は現代のソフトウェアとムーアの法則の終わりについてどんな点を指摘しているか。

1 ソフトウェアの進歩の中で最近起きた改良によって，ムーアの法則が終わらなくてもよい可能性がある。

2 ムーアの法則が終わるとき，今よりもはるかに高い頻度でソフトウェアを更新する必要が出てくる。

③ もしソフトウェアがより注意深く書かれれば，ムーアの法則の終わりはそこまで深刻な問題ではない。

4 企業がより少ないソフトウェア開発者を雇い，ハードウェアエンジニアをより多く雇っているため，ムーアの法則の終わりに関係なくコンピューターチップは改良されるだろう。

Lesson 07

解説▶第3段落の最後の3文より，現在のソフトウェアは，コードの効率性よりも事業目標を優先するがゆえに不必要なコードを多く含んでいるが，**もし開発チームが組織化や計画により多くの時間やエネルギーをつぎ込む自由を与えられたら，より効率的に動作し，バグも少なくなる**と考えられていることがわかる。コードが整理されれば，ムーアの法則の終わりによる大きな問題はないと考えられる。したがって，**3** が正解。

□ **(4)** 一部の専門家が特殊化されたコンピューターチップに対して悲観的である理由の1つは何か。

1 人工知能の分野では非常に便利ではあるが，コンピューターグラフィックに必要な計算にはそれほど効果的ではない。

② 将来，処理装置の速度が向上し続けることができる可能性は低い。

3 設計しやすくなったにも関わらず，これらの製造にかかる費用は通常のチップにかかる費用よりもはるかに高い。

4 これらには普通のチップよりも多くのエネルギーが必要であり，エンジニアがつくるのは不可能かもしれない。

解説▶第4段落第5文に，「**専門家は，特殊化したチップの使用によって急速な進歩が見られるが，これらはすぐに横ばいになり，通常のコンピューターチップに影響を与えたのと同じ問題にさらされると主張する**」とある。これより，一部の専門家は，特殊化したチップを開発しても，電力量が増える問題にさらされ，進歩は続かないだろうと考えていることがわかる。したがって，**2** が正解。第4段落第4文より，開発には多額の費用が発生するとわかるが，設計しやすいかどうかはわからないため，**3** は誤り。

ANSWER		SCORE	CHECK YOUR LEVEL
(1) ① ② ③ ④	**(2)** ① ② ③ ④	／40点	0〜20点 ➡ Work harder! 21〜30点 ➡ OK!
(3) ① ② ③ ④	**(4)** ① ② ③ ④	(4問×各10点)	31〜40点 ➡ Way to go!

ムーアの法則の終わり

❶ 1965年にゴードン・ムーアという名のコンピューター科学者が，コンピューターの速度がおおむね2年ごとに2倍になるというムーアの法則を生み出した。エンジニアたちがコンピューターの速度を増加させ続けた最初の方法は，より多くのトランジスタをコンピューターチップに入れること（によって）だった。トランジスタは電流を調節して，チップに計算を可能にするとても小さなスイッチで，トランジスタをより多く持つことがコンピューターの処理能力を高める。長年にわたって，デナード則として知られている科学原理のおかげで，それらの多くが小さな場所に配置されているときでも，トランジスタが作動するのに必要な電力量には変化がなかった。しかしながら今，デナード則はその限界に達し，増加したトランジスタの数がそれらの必要とする電力量を増やし，オーバーヒートなどの問題につながっている。さらに新たなチップによって必要とされるより高い電圧もまた，電力利用を増やしている。これら2つの要因は，処理能力を増やそうと試みるエンジニアたちにとてつもない難題を提起している。実際，今，ほとんどの専門家たちは，あと数年のうちのムーア法則の終わりを予測している。

❷ その影響は軽視できない。ムーアの法則はもともと1つの見解にすぎなかったが，それは半導体産業における長期的研究や開発計画を導くのに使われてきた。ムーアの法則の終わりは，現在の石油産業の状況と比較されうる。石油会社は，簡単に手に入る石油がなくなってきており，さらに（石油を）見つけるためには，地表の下の深いところ，または孤立した地域を探す必要があることに気がついた。同様に，進歩を達成することがますます難しくなるにつれて，処理装置の速度の向上はかなりの財政投資を必要とするようになるかもしれない。チップメーカーが，新しいチップをつくる技術へのさらなる研究をするための投資から十分な利益を得られるかどうかは，それゆえ大きな問題になっている。

❸ たとえムーアの法則が終わるとしても，それは必ずしもソフトウェア・プログラムがより速く動作できないことを意味するわけではない。結局，ソフトウェアが発展する方法は，速度にも影響をもたらす。良くも悪くも，多くのソフトウェア事業はコードの効率性よりも事業目標を優先する。それが一部のプログラムが何百万行とは言わないまでも何千行もの不必要なコードを含む理由だ。もし，開発チームが組織化や計画により多くの時間やエネルギーをつぎ込む自由を与えられたら，彼らがつくるソフトウェア・プログラムは，より効率的に動作するだけではなく，より少ないバグを含むようにもなるだろう。

❹ もう1つの解決策は，GPUやTPUなどのより特殊化したチップを開発することにあるかもしれない。GPUは画像を作成するために必要な計算を実行するのに，極めて効率的になるようつくられており，TPUは人工知能用に特化してつくられたものである。それらはどちらも今日よく使われている多目的用のチップよりもはるかに速く，エネルギー効率が良くなりうる。しかしそれらの開発に関連するかなりの費用が発生する。そのうえ，プリンストン大学のデイビッド・ウェンザルフなどの専門家は，特殊化したチップの使用によって急速な進歩が見られるが，これらはすぐに横ばいになり，通常のコンピューターチップに影響を与えたのと同じ問題にさらされると主張する。しかし，たとえそれが事実だとしてもその頃までには，ほかのまだ開発されていない技術が存在し，それが急速な進歩が続くことを確実にするだろうとほかの専門家は主張している。

重要語句リスト

❶

☐ transistor	名 トランジスタ
☐ regulate	動 〜を調節する，整える
☐ Dennard scaling	名 デナード則
☐ voltage	名 電圧
☐ present	動 〜を提供する，提出する
☐ predict	動 〜を予測する

❷

☐ understate	動 〜を軽視する
☐ observation	名 （観察に基づく）見解，所見
☐ semiconductor	名 半導体
☐ industry	名 産業，工業，製造業
☐ isolated	形 孤立した，隔離された
☐ processor	名 処理装置
☐ investment	名 投資

❸

☐ for better or for worse	
	熟 良くも悪くも
☐ prioritize	動 〜を優先する
☐ if not	熟 〜とは言わないまでも

❹

☐ perform	動 〜を行う，実行する
☐ specifically	副 特に，特別に
☐ artificial intelligence	
	名 人工知能
☐ associated with 〜	
	熟 〜と関連する
☐ level off	熟 横ばい状態になる
☐ become subject to 〜	
	熟 〜にさらされる，〜を被る
☐ ensure	動 〜を確実にする，保証する

Lesson
07

要点整理
Paragraph Summary

▶音声を聞きながら，①〜⑥の空欄を埋め，段落ごとの
要旨を確認しましょう（解答は下部にあります）。

The End of Moore's Law

❶ ◇ **Moore's Law**

= the speed of computers will [① d_ _ _ _ _] roughly every two years

for years

a scientific principle known as Dennard scaling

→ the amount of power necessary for transistors [② r_ _ _ _ _ _ _ the s_ _ _]

now

Dennard scaling has reached its limit

(1) the increased number of transistors

→ problems such as overheating

(2) the higher voltages required by newer chips

→ have increased power use

• these two factors → an enormous challenge for engineers

❷ ◇ **the impact of the end of Moore's Law cannot be understated**

• the end of Moore's Law can be compared to the current state of the oil industry

oil companies	chip makers
• easily available oil is running out	• the end of Moore's Law
→ requires searching deep below the Earth's surface or in isolated areas	→ requires substantial financial investments for processor speed improvements

→ whether chip makers will be able to gain [③ e_ _ _ _ _ p_ _ _ _ _] from their investments = a major issue

【解答】 ① double ② remained the same ③ enough profit

【和訳】

ムーアの法則の終わり

❶　◇ ムーアの法則

　　　＝ コンピューターの速度がおおむね２年ごとに２倍になる

　　長年

　　デナード則として知られている科学原理

　　→ トランジスタが必要とする電力量には変化がなかった

　　今

　　デナード則はその限界に達した

　　(1)トランジスタの数の増加

　　→ オーバーヒートなどの問題

　　(2)新たなチップによって必要とされるより高い電圧

　　→ 電力利用を増やした

　　・ これら２つの要因 → エンジニアたちにとってのとてつもない難題

❷　◇ ムーアの法則の終わりの影響は軽視できない

　　・ ムーアの法則の終わりは，現在の石油産業の状況と比較されうる

石油会社	チップメーカー
・ 簡単に手に入る石油がなくなってきている	・ ムーアの法則の終わり
→ 地表の下の深いところ，または孤立した地域を探す必要がある	→ 処理装置の速度の向上にかなりの財政投資を必要とする

　　→ チップメーカーが投資に対して十分な利益を得られるかどうか

　　　＝ 大きな問題

❸ ◇ the end of Moore's law ≠ software programs will not be able to run more quickly
- many software projects [④ p_____] business goals over code efficiency
→ some programs contain thousands if not millions of lines of unnecessary code
- If development teams were given the freedom to invest more time and energy in organization and planning
→ the software programs they produced would not only run more efficiently, but they would also contain [⑤ f____] bugs

❹ ◇ another solution
= creating more-specialized chips, such as GPUs and TPUs
- GPUs : built to be extremely efficient at performing calculations needed to produce images
- TPUs : designed specifically for [⑥ a_____ i_____]

good	• faster and more energy efficient
bad	• considerable costs associated with their development • rapid gains will soon level off and become subject to the same problems as ordinary computer chips

↕

- other experts
other not yet developed techniques will ensure that rapid progress continues

【解答】　④ prioritize　⑤ fewer　⑥ artificial intelligence

❸　◇ **ムーアの法則の終わり ≠ ソフトウェア・プログラムはより速く動作できないだろう**

　　• 多くのソフトウェア事業はコードの効率性よりも事業目標を優先する

　　→ 一部のプログラムは何百万行とは言わないまでも何千行もの不必要なコードを含む

　　• もし，開発チームが組織化や計画により多くの時間やエネルギーをつぎ込む自由を与えられたら

　　→ 彼らがつくるソフトウェア・プログラムは，より効率的に動作するだけではなく，より少ないバグを含むようにもなるだろう

Lesson
07

❹　◇ **もう1つの解決策**

　　　= GPU や TPU などのより特殊化したチップを開発すること

　　• GPU：画像を作成するために必要な計算を実行するのに，極めて効率的になるようにつくられている

　　• TPU：人工知能用に特化してつくられている

良い点	• より速く，エネルギー効率が良い
悪い点	• それらの開発に関連するかなりの費用 • 急速な進歩はすぐに横ばいになり，通常のコンピューターチップと同じ問題にさらされる

　　　　↕

　　• ほかの専門家

　　　ほかのまだ開発されていない技術は急速な進歩が続くことを確実にする

Lesson 07
速読練習
Sight Translation

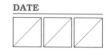

◀)) 英文音声 ▶ **L&R_LV5_07-ST**

英語	和訳
The End of Moore's Law	ムーアの法則の終わり
❶ In 1965,	1965年に,
a computer scientist named Gordon Moore	ゴードン・ムーアという名のコンピューター科学者が
created Moore's Law,	ムーアの法則を生み出した,
which states	～という
that the speed of computers	コンピューターの速度が
will double	2倍になる
roughly every two years.	おおむね2年ごとに。
The primary way	最初の方法は
that engineers have continued	エンジニアたちが続けた
to increase the speed of computers	コンピューターの速度を増加させることを
is by putting more transistors	より多くのトランジスタを入れることによってだ
into computer chips.	コンピューターチップに。
Transistors are tiny switches	トランジスタはとても小さなスイッチである
that regulate the flow of electricity	電流を調節し
to allow the chips to make calculations,	チップが計算するのを可能にする,
and having more transistors	そしてトランジスタをより多く持つことが
increases a computer's power.	コンピューターの処理能力を高める。
For years,	長年にわたって,
thanks to a scientific principle	科学原理のおかげで
known as Dennard scaling,	デナード則として知られている,
the amount of power necessary	必要な電力量は
for the transistors to operate	トランジスタが作動するのに
remained the same,	変化がなかった,
even when there were many of them placed	それらの多くが配置されているときでも
in a small space.	小さな場所に。
Now, however,	しかしながら, 今,
Dennard scaling has reached its limit,	デナード則はその限界に達し,
and the increased number of transistors	増加したトランジスタの数が
has caused the amount of power they require to rise,	それらの必要とする電力量を増やし,
leading to problems	問題につながっている
such as overheating.	オーバーヒートなどの。
Moreover,	さらに,

the higher voltages	より高い電圧
required by newer chips	新たなチップによって必要とされる
have also increased power use.	もまた，電力利用を増やしている。
These two factors	これら2つの要因は
have presented an enormous challenge	とてつもない難題を提起している
for engineers	エンジニアたちに
attempting to increase processing power.	処理能力を増やそうと試みる
In fact,	実際，
most experts are now predicting	今，ほとんどの専門家たちは予測している
the end of Moore's law	ムーアの法則の終わりを
within a few years.	数年のうちの。
❷ The impact	その影響は
cannot be understated.	軽視できない。
While Moore's Law was	ムーアの法則は〜だが
originally just an observation,	もともと1つの見解にすぎなかった，
it's been used	それは使われてきた
to guide	導くのに
long-term research and development planning	長期的研究や開発計画を
in the semiconductor industry.	半導体産業における。
The end of Moore's Law	ムーアの法則の終わりは
can be compared	比較されうる
to the current state	現在の状況と
of the oil industry.	石油産業の。
Oil companies have found	石油会社は気がついた
that easily available oil	簡単に手に入る石油が
is running out,	なくなってきており，
requiring them to search	探す必要があることに
deep below the Earth's surface	地表の下の深いところ
or in isolated areas	または孤立した地域を
to find more.	さらに（石油を）見つけるためには。
Similarly,	同様に，
processor speed improvements	処理装置の速度の向上は
may come to require	必要とするようになるかもしれない
substantial financial investments	かなりの財政投資を
as gains become increasingly difficult to achieve.	進歩を達成することがますます難しくなるにつれて。
Whether chip makers	チップメーカーが〜かどうかは
will be able to get enough profit	十分な利益を得ることができる

Lesson
07

from their investments	投資から
to make further research	さらなる研究をするための
into new chip-making technologies	新しいチップをつくる技術への
has therefore become a major issue.	それゆえ大きな問題になっている。
❸ Even if Moore's Law	たとえムーアの法則が
does come to an end,	終わるとしても,
it doesn't necessarily mean	それは必ずしも意味するわけではない
that software programs	ソフトウェア・プログラムが
will not be able to run	動作できないことを
more quickly.	より速く。
After all,	結局,
the way software is developed	ソフトウェアが発展する方法は
also has an impact	影響ももたらす
on speed.	速度に。
For better or for worse,	良くも悪くも,
many software projects	多くのソフトウェア事業は
prioritize business goals	事業目標を優先する
over code efficiency.	コードの効率性よりも。
That's why	それが理由だ
some programs contain	一部のプログラムが含む
thousands if not millions of lines	何百万行とは言わないまでも何千行もの
of unnecessary code.	不必要なコードを。
If development teams were given	もし開発チームが与えられたら,
the freedom	自由を
to invest more time and energy	より多くの時間やエネルギーをつぎ込む
in organization and planning,	組織化や計画に,
the software programs	ソフトウェア・プログラムは
they produced	彼らがつくる
would not only run	動作するだけではなく
more efficiently,	より効率的に,
but they would also contain	含むようにもなるだろう
fewer bugs.	より少ないバグを。
❹ Another solution may lie	もう1つの解決策はあるかもしれない
in creating more-specialized chips,	より特殊化したチップを開発することに,
such as GPUs and TPUs.	GPUやTPUなどの。
GPUs are built	GPUはつくられた
to be extremely efficient	極めて効率的になるよう
at performing calculations	計算を実行するのに
needed to produce images,	画像を作成するのに必要な,

and TPUs are designed specifically	そして TPU は特化してつくられたものである
for artificial intelligence.	人工知能のために。
They could both be much faster	それらはどちらもはるかに速く
and more energy efficient	そしてよりエネルギー効率が良くなりうる
than the general-purpose chips	多目的用のチップよりも
in common use	よく使われている
today.	今日。
However,	しかし,
there are considerable costs	かなりの費用が発生する
associated with their development.	それらの開発に関連する。
Additionally,	そのうえ,
experts	専門家は
such as Princeton University's David Wentzlaff	プリンストン大学のデイビッド・ウェンザルフなどの
argue	主張する
that although rapid gains have been seen	急速な進歩が見られるが
from the use	使用によって
of specialized chips,	特殊化したチップの,
these will soon level off	これらはすぐに横ばいになり
and become subject	そしてさらされる
to the same problems	同じ問題に
that have affected ordinary computer chips.	通常のコンピューターチップに影響を与えたのと。
Others,	ほかの専門家は,
however,	しかし,
argue	主張する
that even if that is the case,	たとえそれが事実だとしても,
by that time	その頃までには
other not yet developed techniques	ほかのまだ開発されていない技術が
will exist	存在するだろう
to ensure	確実にすると
that rapid progress continues.	急速な進歩が続くことを。

Lesson

07

READING

Lesson 08

問題
Questions

W 単語数 ▶ **529** 語

制限時間 ▶ **12** 分

☑ 目標得点 ▶ **30** /40点

DATE

▶次の英文の内容に関して，(1) ～ (4) の質問に対する最も適切な答え（または文を完成させるのに最も適切なもの）を **1**，**2**，**3**，**4** の中から１つ選びなさい。

Popular Initiatives in Switzerland

In normal elections, voters select people whose job is to represent them in a diet, parliament, or congress. However, in addition to electing representatives, the European nation of Switzerland also holds what are called "popular initiatives." This system allows any proposed law that receives more than 100,000 signatures in 18 months to be brought before the people so that every adult in the country can vote on whether they want it to become law or not. Since 1848, there have been some 200 of these votes with decisions on everything from tax reform to environmentally friendly housing. While just a handful of them have become law, they often bring attention to important but little known issues, such as the needs of disabled people. In addition, the system itself frequently attracts international attention due to its potential as a novel method of expressing the will of the general public.

Political experts are particularly interested in popular initiatives because of their relationship with a movement known as "populism." Populist leaders appeal to public anger and dissatisfaction concerning issues such as government corruption or policies that are believed to favor elites instead of the lower and middle classes. They present themselves as outsiders who are the voice of average citizens. Surveys show, however, that Switzerland has been relatively unaffected by the anger that drives this phenomenon. One citizen suggested this could be because people "have at least the feeling that you vote for your destiny, that you can have influence."

Critics of the system, however, point out various dangers. One example they criticize is a 2016 popular initiative that attempted to change tax laws. It was raised because some citizens believed it to be unfair that married couples had to pay more tax than unmarried couples with similar incomes. The proposal was passed, with 50.8 percent of people for the proposal and 49.2 percent against. However, a court decided that inaccurate statistics presented by the government had influenced people's votes, so the law was overturned. There are fears that such deceptive practices are common in popular initiatives making them potentially dangerous in a democratic nation.

Lesson
08

Other unfortunate initiatives have been voted on in recent years. One attempted to force foreigners who committed serious crimes to leave the country, while another tried to limit the ways that Islamic religious buildings could be built. The restrictions on religious buildings actually became law, raising serious concerns that it was a violation of people's religious freedom. It has traditionally been believed that the people would always decide in favor of human rights, so it was thought that popular initiatives were a viable way of protecting them. The recent voting results, however, disprove this idea, so legal restrictions on popular initiatives are increasingly being seen as necessary. One such proposal calls for a review of any popular initiative by the court system to ensure that it is not in conflict with international laws designed to protect human rights. If this simple and commonsense measure were used, it would help to ensure that popular initiatives live up to their potential as a tool for ensuring fairness and the rights of individuals rather than becoming a threat to them.

Questions ☞

(**1**) What is one thing that the first paragraph says about popular initiatives?

    1 They have often been used in cases where elected officials had been shown to be failing to make necessary changes.

    2 Because they have been used for such a long time, politicians say the system is badly in need of improvement.

    3 They are likely to replace the usual system of electing representatives that is found in most countries.

    4 Although they are rarely successful, they are an interesting way to learn the general public's stance on various issues.

(**2**) The statement by the Swiss citizen supports the idea that

    1 Swiss elites are more likely to be involved with popular initiatives than people who do other types of work are.

    2 populism has been less popular in Switzerland because people there are less likely to feel that they need to elect leaders who represent ordinary people.

    3 Swiss people are much more likely to believe that everyone has a different destiny than people in other countries do.

    4 Swiss people tend to distrust outsiders more than people who live in countries with more corruption do.

(**3**) Critics of popular initiatives believe that

    1 government statistics about popular initiative results mislead many people into believing that most proposals that are voted on are unlikely to pass.

    2 courts have misused their power several times when they reversed decisions that were clearly popular with the majority of Swiss people.

    3 if people based their votes on mistaken information, it could lead to poor decisions that are harmful to society.

    4 since the votes in most popular initiatives tend to be extremely close, a way should be found to produce more definite results.

(**4**) What is the author's conclusion about popular initiatives and human rights in Switzerland?

    1 Although popular initiatives are important for democracy, more needs to be done to ensure that they do not violate human rights.

    2 Recent voting patterns in popular initiatives show that awareness of the importance of human rights is increasing.

    3 Popular initiatives are more effective than the legal system in making sure that human rights are protected.

    4 Procedures for voting in popular initiatives need to be simplified to make sure that human rights are protected.

ANSWER		
(**1**) ① ② ③ ④	(**2**) ① ② ③ ④	
(**3**) ① ② ③ ④	(**4**) ① ② ③ ④	

Answers & Explanations ☞

青文字＝設問・選択肢の和訳　　赤文字＝正解

☐ **(1)** 第 1 段落でイニシアチブについて述べられていることの 1 つは何か。

    1 選出議員が必要な変化を起こせていないことが明らかになった場合にたびたび使われてきた。

    2 実に長い間使われてきたため，政治家たちはこの制度は大いに改良する必要があると言っている。

    3 ほとんどの国で見られる通常の代議士を選出する制度に取って代わりそうだ。

    ④ めったに成功しないが，様々な問題についての一般市民の立場を学ぶ興味深い方法だ。

解説▶第 1 段落の最後の 2 文より，イニシアチブによって法律になるものは一握りだが，あまり知られていない問題に注目が集まることや，一般市民の願望を伝える新しい種類の方法としての可能性によって国際的関心をひきつけていることがわかる。したがって，**4** が正解。

重要語句 ☐ official（⑧ 役人，公務員）

☐ **(2)** スイス住民による発言は……という考えを支持する。

    1 スイスの上流階級は，ほかの種類の職業の人よりもイニシアチブに携わる傾向がある

    ② スイスでポピュリズムがあまりはやらないのは，そこに住む人々は庶民（一般大衆）を代表するリーダーを選ぶ必要があると思う傾向が弱いためである

    3 スイス人はほかの国の人々よりも，皆が異なる宿命をもっていると考える傾向がはるかに高い

    4 スイス人はより多くの汚職がある国々に住んでいる人々よりも，部外者に対して不信感を抱く傾向がある

解説▶第 2 段落の最後の文では，スイスがポピュリズムを活発にする怒りに，比較的影響を受けていない理由として，「人々が（イニシアチブを通して）『少なくとも，自分の運命に投票して自分が影響力をもちうるという思いを抱いている』からかもしれない」と，ある市民の声を例に挙げて示している。したがってスイス人は自分たちのリーダーを選ばずとも自分自身が政治に影響をもたらすことができるだろうと考えていることがわかるため，**2** が正解。

□**(3)** イニシアチブの批評家は……と考えている。

　　　1 イニシアチブの結果についての政府の統計は，多くの人に対して，投票を受けたほとんどの提案は通る可能性が低いという誤解をまねく

　　　2 裁判所は，大多数のスイス人に明らかに評判がよかった判決をひっくり返したとき，何度か権力を濫用してきた

　　　③ もし人々が間違った情報をもとに投票した場合，社会にとって害のある不適切な決断につながる可能性がある

　　　4 ほとんどのイニシアチブの投票は非常に僅差になる傾向があるため，より明確な結果を生む方法を探すべきである

解説▶第3段落では，批評家が指摘するイニシアチブの危険性について，1つの例を挙げながら説明している。その例は，政府による不正確な情報が投票者に影響を与えたと考えられ，一度通った提案が裁判所によってひっくり返されたという内容である。したがって，**3** が正解。

□**(4)** スイスのイニシアチブと人権についての筆者の結論は何か。

　　　① 民主主義にとってイニシアチブは重要であるが，人権を侵害しないことを確かにするためにさらなる行動が必要である。

　　　2 最近のイニシアチブの投票パターンは，人権の重要性についての認識が強まっていることを示している。

　　　3 イニシアチブは法制度よりも，確実に人権を守ることに効果的だ。

　　　4 確実に人権を守るためには，イニシアチブの投票手順を簡素化する必要がある。

解説▶第4段落の前半では，イニシアチブはかつて人権を守る方法だと考えられていたが，実際は宗教建築の制限などが提案され，宗教［信教］の自由が侵害される危険性があることが述べられている。それに対して筆者はイニシアチブに法的制限が必要であることや，イニシアチブと人権を守るためにある国際法との間に矛盾がないかの再検討が必要だという提案を紹介している。したがって，**1** が正解。

重要語句 □ awareness（图 認識）

ANSWER		SCORE	CHECK YOUR LEVEL
(1) ① ② ③ ❹	**(2)** ① ② ③ ④	／40点	0～20点 ➡ *Work harder!*
			21～30点 ➡ *OK!*
(3) ① ② ③ ④	**(4)** ① ② ③ ④	（4問×各10点）	31～40点 ➡ *Way to go!*

【和訳】
スイスのイニシアチブ

❶ 通常の選挙では，投票者は国会や議会で自分たちの代表を務める人々を選ぶ。しかし，ヨーロッパの国であるスイスでは，代表者を選ぶのに加えて「イニシアチブ（国民発議・国民請願）」と呼ばれるものも行う。この制度は 18 ヵ月間に 100,000 を超える署名を集めたあらゆる法案が人々の前に持ち出されることを認めるので，国内の成人たちは皆，それを法律にしたいかどうかについて投票することができる。1848 年以来，これらの投票は約 200 ほど存在し，税制改革から環境に優しい住宅についてまで，あらゆるものについての決定がなされた。それらのほんの一握りは法律になった一方で，それらは身体障害者の要求など，重要であるがほとんど知られていない問題に対して，たびたび関心を呼び起こしている。さらにこの制度自体が，一般市民の願望を示す新しい種類の方法としての可能性によって，しばしば国際的関心をひきつけている。

❷ 政治専門家は「ポピュリズム」として知られる運動との関連性によって，特にイニシアチブに興味がある。ポピュリズムの指導者は，政府の汚職や，下層もしくは中間層ではなく上流階層を特別あつかいしていると思われる政策などの問題について民衆の怒りや不満に訴える。彼らは，一般的な市民の代弁者である部外者として自らを売り込む。しかし調査によると，スイスはこの現象（ポピュリズム）を活発にする怒りによって，比較的影響を受けていない。ある市民は，これは人々が「少なくとも，自分の運命に投票して自分が影響力をもちうるという思いを抱いている」からかもしれないと示唆した。

❸ しかし，この制度の批評家は様々な危険性を指摘する。彼らが批判する 1 つの例は，税法を変えようと試みた 2016 年のイニシアチブである。それは結婚している夫婦が同じような所得をもつ未婚のカップルより多くの税を支払わなければいけ

ないのは不公平だと考えた市民がいたので起こった。その提案は 50.8% の人々の賛成と 49.2% の反対で，可決された。しかし裁判所は，政府によって示された不正確な統計が人々の投票に影響を及ぼしたと判断し，その法律はひっくり返された。イニシアチブにはそのような詐欺的手法がよくあるという懸念があり，それによってイニシアチブは民主主義国における潜在的な危険になっている。

❹ ほかの不適切なイニシアチブがここ数年のうちに決を採られた。1 つは重罪を犯した外国人に国外退去するよう強いようとし，一方でもう 1 つはイスラム教の宗教建築が建築される可能性のある方法を制限しようとした。宗教建築の制限は実際に法律となり，それは人々の宗教［信教］の自由の侵害であるという深刻な懸念を提起した。人々は常に人権を支持して判断すると伝統的に信じられてきたため，イニシアチブはそれらを守る実行可能な方法だと考えられていた。しかし，最近の投票結果はこの考えが間違っていたことを証明しており，それでイニシアチブに対しての法的制限がますます必要だと見られている。そのような提案の 1 つでは，人権を守るためにつくられた国際法と矛盾しないよう保証するために，裁判制度であらゆるイニシアチブを再検討することを要求している。もしこの単純かつ常識的な手段が用いられれば，イニシアチブは個人の脅威となるのではなく，公平と個人の権利を確保するためのツールとしての力を発揮することを確実にする助けとなるだろう。

重要語句リスト

❶

☐ initiative	图 イニシアチブ, 国民発議, 国民請願	
☐ diet	图 国会	
☐ parliament	图 国会, 議会	
☐ congress	图 国会, 議会	
☐ propose	動 ～を提案する	
☐ signature	图 署名, サイン	
☐ disabled	形 身体障害のある	
☐ potential	图 可能性, 将来性	
☐ will	图 願望, 意向	

❷

☐ corruption	图 汚職, 不正行為
☐ present oneself	熟 自らを売り込む
☐ destiny	图 運命, 宿命

❸

☐ criticize	動 ～を批判する
☐ proposal	图 提案, 計画案
☐ inaccurate	形 不正確な, ずさんな
☐ statistics	图 統計
☐ overturn	動 ～をひっくり返す, くつがえす
☐ deceptive practice	图 詐欺的手法
☐ potentially	動 潜在的に
☐ democratic	形 民主主義の

❹

☐ commit	動 (犯罪など) を犯す
☐ religious	形 宗教の, 宗教に関する
☐ restriction	图 制限, 規制
☐ violation	图 (権利などの) 侵害
☐ in favor of ～	熟 ～を支持して
☐ disprove	動 ～が誤りであることを証明する
☐ in conflict with ～	熟 ～と矛盾して
☐ commonsense	形 常識的な
☐ live up to ～	熟 ～に応える, ～にかなう

Lesson 08

READING

要点整理
Paragraph Summary

▶音声を聞きながら、①〜⑤の空欄を埋め、段落ごとの
要旨を確認しましょう（解答は下部にあります）。

Popular Initiatives in Switzerland

❶ ◇ **Switzerland**

- normal elections **+** "popular initiatives"[※1]

  ※1 popular initiatives：allow any proposed law that receives more than 100,000 signatures in 18 months to be brought before every adult in the country

- The system attracts international attention due to its potential as a novel method of expressing the will of the $\big[$① g_ _ _ _ _ _ p_ _ _ _ _$\big]$.

❷ ◇ **populist leaders appeal to public dissatisfaction over issues**[※2]

  ※2 issues：government corruption or policies that are believed to favor elites

- ↔ Switzerland：unaffected by the anger that drives populism

- ← have the feeling that you vote for your destiny, that you can have influence

❸ ◇ **critics of the system point out** $\big[$② v_ _ _ _ _ _ d_ _ _ _ _ _$\big]$

- one example：a popular initiative that attempted to change tax laws

> inaccurate statistics presented by the government had influenced people's votes

the proposal was passed ⟶ ♟ ⟶ the law was overturned

a court

- → there are fears that such deceptive practices are common in popular initiatives

- → make them potentially dangerous in a $\big[$③ d_ _ _ _ _ _ _ _$\big]$ nation

【解答】 ① general public ② various dangers ③ democratic

【和訳】

スイスのイニシアチブ

❶　◇ スイス

- 通常の選挙 ＋「イニシアチブ（国民発議・国民請願）[1]」

※1 イニシアチブ：18ヵ月間に 100,000 を超える署名を集めたあらゆる法案が国内のすべての成人たちの前に持ち出されることを認める

- その制度は，一般市民の願望を示す新しい種類の方法としての可能性によって，国際的関心をひきつけている。

❷　◇ **ポピュリズムの指導者は問題[2]に対して民衆の不満に訴える**

※2 問題：政府の汚職や，上流階層を特別あつかいしていると思われる政策

　↔ スイス：ポピュリズムを活発にする怒りによって，影響を受けていない

　← 自分の運命に投票する，また自分が影響力をもちうるという思いを抱く

❸　◇ **批評家は様々な危険性を指摘する**

- 1つの例：税法を変えようと試みたイニシアチブ

政府によって示された不正確な統計が
人々の投票に影響を及ぼした

提案は可決された　⟶　法律はひっくり返された

裁判所

→ イニシアチブにはそのような詐欺的手法がよくあるという懸念がある

→ イニシアチブを民主主義国における潜在的な危険にしている

❹ ◇ other unfortunate initiatives

(1) attempted to force foreigners who committed serious crimes to leave the country

(2) limited the ways that Islamic religious buildings could be built

→ serious concerns that it was a violation of people's religious freedom

→ legal restrictions on popular initiatives are increasingly being seen as necessary

• one such proposal = a [④ r_____] of any popular initiative to ensure that it is not in conflict with international laws

→ popular initiatives = a tool for ensuring [⑤ f_____ and the r_____] of individuals

【解答】 ④ review ⑤ fairness and the rights

❹　◇ ほかの不適切なイニシアチブ

(1) 重罪を犯した外国人を国外退去させようと試みた

(2) イスラム教の宗教建築が建築される可能性のある方法を制限した

　　→ 人々の宗教［信教］の自由の侵害であるという深刻な懸念

→ イニシアチブに対しての法的制限がますます必要だと見られている

・ ある提案 ＝ 国際法と矛盾しないよう保証するためのあらゆるイニシアチ

　　　　　　ブの再検討

→ イニシアチブ ＝ 公平と個人の権利を確保するためのツール

Lesson 08
速読練習
Sight Translation

◀)) 英文音声 ▶ **L&R_LV5_08-ST**

英語	和訳
Popular Initiatives in Switzerland	スイスのイニシアチブ
❶ In normal elections,	通常の選挙では,
voters select	投票者は選ぶ
people	人々を
whose job is to represent them	自分たちの代表を務める
in a diet, parliament, or congress.	国会や議会で。
However,	しかし,
in addition to electing representatives,	代表者を選ぶのに加えて,
the European nation of Switzerland	ヨーロッパの国であるスイスでは
also holds what are called "popular initiatives."	「イニシアチブ（国民発議・国民請願）」と呼ばれるものも行う。
This system allows	この制度は認める
any proposed law	あらゆる法案が
that receives more than 100,000 signatures	100,000 を超える署名を集める
in 18 months	18 ヵ月間に
to be brought	持ち出されることを
before the people	人々の前に
so that every adult in the country can vote	だから国内の成人たちは皆投票できる
on whether they want it to become law or not.	それを法律にしたいかどうかについて。
Since 1848,	1848 年以来,
there have been some 200	約 200 ほど存在し
of these votes	これらの投票は
with decisions	決定がなされた
on everything	あらゆるものについての
from tax reform to environmentally friendly housing.	税制改革から環境に優しい住宅まで。
While just a handful of them	それらのほんの一握りは〜である一方で
have become law,	法律になった,
they often bring attention	それらはたびたび関心を呼び起こしている
to important but little known issues,	重要であるがほとんど知られていない問題に,
such as the needs of disabled people.	身体障害者の要求などの。

In addition,	さらに,
the system itself frequently attracts	この制度自体がしばしば国際的関心をひき
international attention	つけている
due to its potential	可能性によって
as a novel method	新しい種類の方法としての
of expressing the will	願望を示す
of the general public.	一般市民の。
❷ Political experts are particularly interested	政治専門家は特に興味がある
in popular initiatives	イニシアチブに
because of their relationship	関連性によって
with a movement	運動との
known as "populism."	「ポピュリズム」として知られる。
Populist leaders appeal	ポピュリズムの指導者は訴える
to public anger and dissatisfaction	民衆の怒りや不満に
concerning issues	問題について
such as government corruption	政府の汚職などの
or policies	また政策などの
that are believed to favor elites	上流階層を特別あつかいしていると思われる
instead of the lower and middle classes.	下層もしくは中間層ではなく。
They present themselves	彼らは自らを売り込む
as outsiders	部外者として
who are the voice of average citizens.	一般的な市民の代弁者である。
Surveys show,	調査は示す,
however,	しかし,
that Switzerland has been relatively unaffected	スイスは比較的影響を受けていないことを
by the anger	怒りによって
that drives this phenomenon.	この現象を活発にする。
One citizen suggested	ある市民は示唆した
this could be because people	これは人々が〜からもしれないと
"have at least the feeling	「少なくとも思いを抱いている
that you vote for your destiny,	自分の運命に投票し,
that you can have influence."	自分が影響力をもちうるという」。
❸ Critics of the system,	この制度の批評家は,
however,	しかし,

point out various dangers.	様々な危険性を指摘する。
One example	1つの例は
they criticize	彼らが批判する
is a 2016 popular initiative	2016年のイニシアチブである
that attempted to change tax laws.	税法を変えようと試みた。
It was raised	それは起こった
because some citizens believed it	それを考えた市民がいたので
to be unfair	不公平だと
that married couples had to pay more tax	結婚している夫婦がより多くの税を支払わなければいけないのは
than unmarried couples	未婚のカップルより
with similar incomes.	同じような所得をもつ。
The proposal was passed,	その提案は可決された,
with 50.8 percent of people for the proposal	50.8%の人々の提案に対する賛成と
and 49.2 percent against.	49.2%の反対で。
However,	しかし,
a court decided	裁判所は判断した
that inaccurate statistics presented by the government	政府によって示された不正確な統計が
had influenced people's votes,	人々の投票に影響を及ぼしたと,
so the law was overturned.	だからその法律はひっくり返された。
There are fears	懸念があり,
that such deceptive practices are common	そのような詐欺的手法がよくあるという
in popular initiatives	イニシアチブには
making them potentially dangerous	潜在的な危険になっている
in a democratic nation.	民主主義国における。
❹ Other unfortunate initiatives	ほかの不適切なイニシアチブが
have been voted on	決を採られた
in recent years.	ここ数年のうちに。
One attempted	1つは試みた
to force foreigners	外国人に強いることを
who committed serious crimes	重罪を犯した
to leave the country,	国外退去するよう,
while another tried	一方でもう1つは試みた
to limit the ways	方法を制限することを

that Islamic religious buildings	イスラム教の宗教建築が
could be built.	建築される可能性のある。
The restrictions on religious buildings	宗教建築の制限は
actually became law,	実際に法律となり,
raising serious concerns	深刻な懸念を提起した
that it was a violation	それは侵害であるという
of people's religious freedom.	人々の宗教 [信教] の自由の。
It has traditionally been believed	伝統的に信じられてきた
that the people would always decide	人々は常に判断すると
in favor of human rights,	人権を支持して,
so it was thought	だから考えられていた
that popular initiatives were a viable way	イニシアチブは実行可能な方法だと
of protecting them.	それらを守る。
The recent voting results,	最近の投票結果は,
however,	しかし,
disprove this idea,	この考えが間違っていたことを証明しており,
so legal restrictions on popular initiatives	それでイニシアチブに対しての法的制限が
are increasingly being seen	ますます見られている
as necessary.	必要だと。
One such proposal calls for	そのような提案の 1 つでは要求している
a review of any popular initiative	あらゆるイニシアチブの再検討を
by the court system	裁判制度による
to ensure	保証するために
that it is not in conflict	それが矛盾しないことを
with international laws	国際法と
designed to protect human rights.	人権を守るためにつくられた。
If this simple and commonsense measure were used,	もしこの単純かつ常識的な手段が用いられれば,
it would help to ensure	確実にする助けとなるだろう
that popular initiatives live up to their potential	イニシアチブが力を発揮することを
as a tool	ツールとしての
for ensuring fairness and the rights of individuals	公平と個人の権利を確保するための
rather than becoming a threat to them.	個人の脅威となるのではなくむしろ。

Lesson

08

Lesson 09
問題
Questions

W 単語数 ▶ **517** 語
🕐 制限時間 ▶ **12** 分
☑ 目標得点 ▶ **30** /40点

DATE

▶次の英文の内容に関して, (1)～(4) の質問に対する最も適切な答え (または文を完成させるのに最も適切なもの) を **1**, **2**, **3**, **4** の中から 1 つ選びなさい。

The Cape Honey Bee

In most places around the world, bee colonies contain a single queen bee, the only female that will lay eggs. The other females act as worker bees, collecting pollen from plants, while the male drones help the queen bee produce eggs. But in South Africa, the Cape honey bee does things a little differently. Queen bees in all bee colonies are extremely dominant, and they normally emit a chemical substance that causes the female worker bees to be infertile. But on occasions where she is away from the hive, it is not uncommon for a worker bee from a Cape honey bee colony to take advantage of her absence and begin to lay eggs.

This behavior has long been considered extremely mysterious. Although a bee hive is made up of thousands of individual bees, in many ways it resembles a single creature with large numbers of bees supporting a single fertile queen bee. Worker bees typically cannot produce young, sacrificing the ability to give birth for the benefit of the hive as a whole. Female Cape honey bees, however, not only produce young of their own, but also travel to other colonies, lay eggs in them, and steal the honey produced there, abandoning their relatives in their home colony.

In order to find out why this happens, researchers compared the Cape honey bee with the African honey bee, the species whose colonies they typically invade. After analyzing the entire genome of individual bees from both subspecies of honey bee, the scientists discovered that the Cape honey bee's behavior is the result of a mutation in a single gene. For such a genetic change to happen and become common in a type of bee, it must give the bee some sort of advantage in nature. Scientists speculate that the mutation is a backup mechanism in case something unfortunate happens to the queen bee. Since she is the only fertile individual, her death would be fatal to the colony were it not for the unique ability of the Cape honey bee workers.

Cape honey bees have had a significant effect on populations of the African honey bee. They were considered threatened in the 1990s, and researchers who studied the bees believed that it would be beneficial to introduce them to new habitats. A number of studies were conducted to see what effect they would have on African honey bees, whose territory they were to be moved into, and all evidence made researchers optimistic that there would be no significant conflict between the two types of bee. They were unaware, of course, that Cape honey bees were capable of invading the other species' colonies. This proved disastrous for the African honey bee, particularly because the Cape honey bee is able to produce chemicals that make it impossible to detect when they are laying eggs in their stolen homes. It was not until 2003 that German researcher C. W. W. Pirk discovered that they were endangering the African honey bee. Today, researchers fear that if the Cape honey bee continues to thrive, it could be a threat to bee populations around the world.

Lesson 09

Questions ☞

(1) How are female Cape honey bee workers different from other types of female bees?

   1 They are much less likely to leave the hive when the queen bee tries to act in a way that shows her dominance.

   2 As a result of being able to collect more pollen than other types of bees can, they are able to produce a much greater number of eggs.

   3 Because their social structure causes them to cooperate more closely with the queen bee, there are fewer conflicts regarding the laying of eggs.

   4 In certain circumstances, they can perform an act that is usually exclusive to a colony's queen bee.

(2) What is mysterious about the behavior of Cape honey bees?

   1 How the queen bees in their colonies produce far more young than the queen bees in other types of bee colonies do.

   2 Why they act in a self-interested manner instead of behaving in a way that benefits the other bees in their colony.

   3 How the queen bees in their colonies are able to travel much longer distances than the worker bees are able to.

   4 Why such an extremely large percentage of the worker bees in their colonies are unable to produce any young bees.

(**3**) The mutation that affects Cape honey bees may be helpful because

    1 it allows the colony to survive in situations where there has been a serious misfortune that could threaten its future.

    2 it helps to lessen the effects of a gene mutation that causes them to behave like members of another subspecies of honey bee.

    3 it allows their queen bees to survive an illness that often kills the queen bees in other types of bee colonies.

    4 it makes them genetically similar to another type of bee whose queen bees tend to be more fertile than the Cape honey bees are.

(**4**) What mistake did researchers make in the 1990s?

    1 They were too optimistic about their ability to transport the bees without them escaping into another species' territory.

    2 They did not realize that the chemicals that Cape honey bees produce make it impossible for other bee species to lay eggs.

    3 They failed to predict that Cape honey bees had the ability to take over the colonies of other types of bees.

    4 They did not realize that Cape honey bees tended to lay a far greater number of eggs than bees of other species did.

Lesson
09

ANSWER		
(**1**) ① ② ③ ④	(**2**) ① ② ③ ④	
(**3**) ① ② ③ ④	(**4**) ① ② ③ ④	

Answers & Explanations ☞

Lesson 09
解答・解説
Answers & Explanations

青文字＝設問・選択肢の和訳　赤文字＝正解

□**(1)**　メスのケープミツバチの働きバチは，ほかの種類のメスバチとどう違うのか。

  1 女王バチが自分の支配を示すようにふるまおうとするとき，巣を離れる可能性がはるかに低い。

  2 ほかの種類のハチよりも多くの花粉を集めることができるため，はるかに多くの卵をつくることができる。

  3 彼らの社会構造によって女王バチとより密接に協力するため，産卵に関する対立がより少ない。

  ④ ある特定の状況では，普通はコロニーの女王バチだけに限定される行為をすることがある。

解説▶第1段落の最初の文に「**産卵する唯一のメスである1匹の女王バチ**」とあり，通常は働きバチが卵を産むことはないことがわかる。そして第1段落の最後の文より，ケープミツバチの場合，**女王バチが巣を離れているという状況では働きバチも産卵することがある**とわかる。したがって，**4**が正解。

□**(2)**　ケープミツバチの行動に関する不可解なことは何か。

  1 それらのコロニーの女王バチが，ほかの種類のハチのコロニーの女王バチよりもはるかに多くの子どもをつくる方法。

  ② コロニーにいるほかのハチに利益をもたらすように行動するのではなく，利己的な態度で行動する理由。

  3 コロニーの女王バチが，働きバチよりもはるかに長い距離を移動できる方法。

  4 コロニーのそのような非常に大きな割合の働きバチが，全く子どもをつくれない理由。

解説▶第2段落の最初の文に「この行動様式は長い間非常に不可解だと考えられてきた」とあるので，このあとの記述に注目する。すると，第2段落第3文に「**働きバチは通常，子どもをつくることができず，群れ全体の利益のために出産する能力を犠牲にする**」とある。対して，第2段落の最後の文より，**ケープミツバチのメスは自分の子どもをつくるうえ，ほかのコロニーへも移動し，そこで子どもをつくるが，彼らのホームコロニーに自分たちの身内を置き去りにする**ことがあるとわかる。したがって，**2**が正解。

重要語句　□ self-interested manner（⑫ 利己的な態度）

□(**3**)　ケープミツバチに影響を与える突然変異は，……ため有益かもしれない。

① コロニーの未来を脅かす可能性のある深刻な不幸がある状況で，コロニーが生き残ることを可能にする

2 ほかのミツバチの亜種の一員かのようにふるまう原因となる遺伝子の突然変異の影響を軽減するのに役立つ

3 ほかの種類のハチのコロニーの女王バチをよく殺す病気から，ケープミツバチの女王バチが生き残ることを可能にする

4 女王バチがケープミツバチよりも繁殖力の高い傾向があるほかの種類のハチに，遺伝子学的に似せる

[解説]▶第3段落の最後の2文より，研究者たちは，女王バチ以外のメスバチも生殖能力をもつことが，**女王バチが死んでしまったときにコロニーが生き残る**ことに**役立つだろ**うと推測していることがわかる。したがって，**1**が正解。

[重要語句]　□ misfortune（⑧ 不運，逆境）　□ genetically（⑩ 遺伝子学的に，遺伝的に）

□(**4**)　1990年代に研究者たちが犯した間違いは何か。

1 彼らは，ほかの種の縄張りに逃げ込むことがないようにハチを輸送する能力について楽観的すぎた。

2 彼らは，ケープミツバチが生産する化学物質によって，ほかの種のハチが卵を産めなくなることを認識していなかった。

③ 彼らは，ケープミツバチがほかの種類のハチのコロニーを奪う能力をもつと予測することに失敗した。

4 彼らは，ケープミツバチがほかの種のハチよりもはるかに多くの卵を産む傾向にあることを認識していなかった。

[解説]▶第4段落第3文より，研究者は多数の研究を行った結果，ケープミツバチとアフリカミツバチの間に重大な対立は存在しないだろうと楽観的になっていたことがわかる。しかし，第4段落第4文の「**彼らはケープミツバチがほかの種のコロニーに攻め入ることができることを知らなかった**」より，その判断は間違っていたことが読み取れる。したがって，**3**が正解。

ANSWER		SCORE	CHECK YOUR LEVEL
(**1**) ① ② ③ ④ (**2**) ① ② ③ ④		/40点 (4問×各10点)	0〜20点 ➡ *Work harder!* 21〜30点 ➡ *OK!*
(**3**) ① ② ③ ④ (**4**) ① ② ③ ④			31〜40点 ➡ *Way to go!*

ケープミツバチ

❶ 世界中のほとんどの場所で，ハチのコロニー（群れ）は，産卵する唯一のメスである1匹の女王バチを含む。ほかのメスは働きバチとして活動し，植物から花粉を集め，一方でオスバチは女王バチが卵を産むのを助ける。しかし南アフリカでは，ケープミツバチが少し違うことをする。すべてのハチのコロニーの女王バチは非常に支配的であり，通常はメスの働きバチを生殖能力のない状態にする化学物質を放出する。しかし女王バチが巣から離れている場合，ケープミツバチのコロニーの働きバチが，彼女の不在を利用して産卵を始めることは珍しくない。

❷ この行動様式は長い間非常に不可解だと考えられてきた。ハチの群れは何千もの個々のハチで構成されているが，多くの点で多数のハチが1匹の生殖能力のある女王バチを支えている単一の生き物のようだ。働きバチは通常，子どもをつくることができず，群れ全体の利益のために出産する能力を犠牲にする。しかし，メスのケープミツバチは，自分自身の子どもをつくるだけではなく，ほかのコロニーにも移動し，産卵し，そこでつくられたハチミツを盗み，彼らのホームコロニーに自分たちの身内を置き去りにするのである。

❸ このようなことがなぜ起こるのかを解明するために，研究者たちはケープミツバチを，それらが典型的に侵入するコロニーにいる種であるアフリカミツバチと比較した。科学者たちは，両種のミツバチの亜種から個々のハチのゲノム全体を分析したあと，ケープミツバチの行動様式が1つの遺伝子の突然変異の結果であることを発見した。そのような遺伝的変化が起こり，ある種類のハチで一般的になるためには，本質的にハチに何らかの利点を与えなければならない。突然変異は女王バチに不幸なことが起こった場合の予備機構であると科学者たちは推測している。女王バチは唯一の生殖能力のある個体であるため，ケープミツバ

チの働きバチのまたとない能力がなければ，女王バチの死がコロニーにとって致命的となってしまうだろう。

❹ ケープミツバチは，アフリカミツバチの個体数に大きな影響を与えてきた。ケープミツバチは1990年代に絶滅のおそれがあると考えられており，ハチを研究していた研究者たちは，ケープミツバチに新しい生息地を紹介することが有益だろうと考えていた。ケープミツバチが，これらの移り住むことになっている生息地を縄張りとしていたアフリカミツバチにどのような影響を与えるかを調べるために，多数の研究が行われ，そしてすべての証拠により，研究者たちは2種類のハチの間で重大な対立はないだろうと楽観的になった。もちろん，彼らはケープミツバチがほかの種のコロニーに攻め入ることができることを知らなかった。特にケープミツバチは，いつ彼らの盗まれた巣で卵を産んでいるのかをわからなくする化学物質を生産できるため，これはアフリカミツバチにとって悲惨なことだと判明した。2003年になって初めて，ドイツの研究者 C. W. W. パークは，ケープミツバチがアフリカミツバチを危険にさらしていることを発見した。今日，研究者たちは，ケープミツバチが繁殖し続けると，世界中のハチの個体数にとって脅威になってしまうのではないかとおそれている。

重要語句リスト

❶

☐ colony	⑧ 群落，群棲
☐ pollen	⑧ 花粉
☐ male drone	⑧ オスバチ
☐ dominant	⑯ 支配的な，有力な
☐ infertile	⑯ 生殖能力のない，不妊の
☐ hive	⑧ ミツバチの巣，ミツバチの群れ
☐ take advantage of ～	
	⑲ ～を利用する

❷

☐ resemble	⑩ ～のようである，～と似ている
☐ fertile	⑯ 生殖能力のある
☐ sacrifice	⑩ ～を犠牲にする，投げうつ
☐ abandon	⑩ ～を置き去りにする，捨てる

❸

☐ invade	⑩ ～に侵入する，侵略する
☐ subspecies	⑧ 亜種
☐ mutation	⑧ 突然変異
☐ gene	⑧ 遺伝子
☐ speculate	⑩ ～と推測する
☐ fatal	⑯ 命取りになる，致命的な
☐ were it not for ～	⑲ もし～がなかったら

❹

☐ beneficial	⑯ 有益な，助けになる
☐ optimistic	⑯ 楽天的な，楽観主義の
☐ disastrous	⑯ 悲惨な，損害の大きい
☐ detect	⑩ ～に気づく，～を見つける

Lesson
09

READING

Lesson 09
要点整理
Paragraph Summary

◀)) 音声 ▶ **L&R_LV5_09-Q**

▶音声を聞きながら、① ~ ⑤の空欄を埋め、段落ごとの要旨を確認しましょう（解答は下部にあります）。

The Cape Honey Bee

❶ ◇ **bee colonies**

= **a single queen bee, female worker bees and male drones**

↔ South Africa's Cape honey bee :

does things a little [① d_____]

normal honey bee	Cape honey bee
• queen bees in all bee colonies are dominant → normally emit a chemical substance that causes the female worker bees to be infertile	• the female worker bees begin to [② l_ e___] on occasions where the queen bee is away from the hive

❷ ◇ **this behavior has long been considered extremely mysterious**

• a bee hive : made up of thousands of individual bees

↔ resembles a single creature

normal honey bee	Cape honey bee
• worker bees sacrifice the ability to give birth for the benefit of the hive as a whole	• female bees produce young, travel to other colonies, lay eggs in them, and steal the honey, abandoning their relatives in their home colony

❸ ◇ **a comparison between the Cape honey bee and the African honey bee**

• the Cape honey bee's behavior :

the result of a [③ m_____] in a single gene

→ the mutation = a [④ b_____] mechanism in case something

unfortunate happens to the queen bee

【解答】　① differently　② lay eggs　③ mutation　④ backup

【和訳】

ケープミツバチ

❶　◇ ハチのコロニー

　　＝ 1匹の女王バチ，メスの働きバチ，オスバチ

　　↔ 南アフリカのケープミツバチ：

　　　少し違うことをする

通常のミツバチ	ケープミツバチ
• すべてのハチのコロニーの女王バチは支配的 → 通常はメスの働きバチを生殖能力のない状態にする化学物質を放出する	• 女王バチが巣から離れている場合，メスの働きバチが，産卵を始める

❷　◇ この行動様式は長い間非常に不可解だと考えられてきた

　　• ハチの群れ：何千もの個々のハチで構成されている

　　　　　　↔ 単一の生き物のようだ

通常のミツバチ	ケープミツバチ
• 働きバチは群れ全体の利益のために出産する能力を犠牲にする	• メスバチは子どもをつくり，ほかのコロニーに移動し，そこで産卵し，ハチミツを盗み，彼らのホームコロニーに自分たちの身内を置き去りにする

❸　◇ ケープミツバチとアフリカミツバチの比較

　　• ケープミツバチの行動：

　　　1つの遺伝子の突然変異の結果

　　→ 突然変異 ＝ 女王バチに不幸なことが起こった場合の予備機構

Lesson
09

❹ ◇ **a significant effect on populations of the African honey bee**

in the past

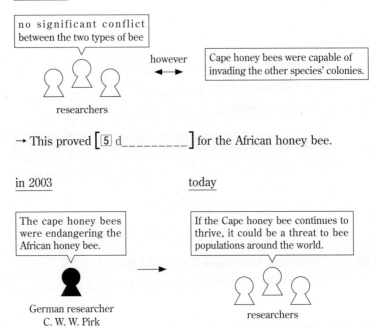

no significant conflict between the two types of bee

researchers

however

Cape honey bees were capable of invading the other species' colonies.

→ This proved [[5] d_____] for the African honey bee.

in 2003

The cape honey bees were endangering the African honey bee.

German researcher
C. W. W. Pirk

today

If the Cape honey bee continues to thrive, it could be a threat to bee populations around the world.

researchers

【解答】　[5] disastrous

❹　◇ アフリカミツバチの個体数への大きな影響

過去

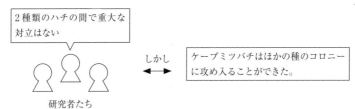

2種類のハチの間で重大な
対立はない

研究者たち

しかし

ケープミツバチはほかの種のコロニー
に攻め入ることができた。

→ これはアフリカミツバチにとって悲惨なことだと判明した。

2003 年

今日

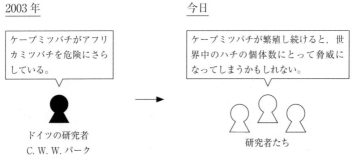

ケープミツバチがアフリ
カミツバチを危険にさら
している。

ドイツの研究者
C. W. W. パーク

ケープミツバチが繁殖し続けると，世
界中のハチの個体数にとって脅威に
なってしまうかもしれない。

研究者たち

Lesson 09
速読練習
Sight Translation

🔊) 英文音声 ▶ L&R_LV5_09-ST

英語	和訳
The Cape Honey Bee	ケープミツバチ
❶ In most places around the world,	世界中のほとんどの場所で,
bee colonies contain	ハチのコロニー (群れ) は, 含む
a single queen bee,	1匹の女王バチを,
the only female	唯一のメスである
that will lay eggs.	産卵する。
The other females	ほかのメスは
act as worker bees,	働きバチとして活動し,
collecting pollen from plants,	植物から花粉を集め,
while the male drones	一方でオスバチは
help the queen bee produce eggs.	女王バチが卵を産むのを助ける。
But in South Africa,	しかし南アフリカでは,
the Cape honey bee	ケープミツバチが
does things a little differently.	少し違うことをする。
Queen bees in all bee colonies	すべてのハチのコロニーの女王バチは
are extremely dominant,	非常に支配的であり,
and they normally emit	そして通常は放出する
a chemical substance	化学物質を
that causes the female worker bees to be infertile.	メスの働きバチを生殖能力のない状態にする。
But on occasions where she is away	しかし彼女が離れている場合は
from the hive,	巣から,
it is not uncommon	珍しくない
for a worker bee	働きバチが
from a Cape honey bee colony	ケープミツバチのコロニーの
to take advantage of her absence	彼女の不在を利用して
and begin to lay eggs.	そして産卵を始めることは。
❷ This behavior has long been considered	この行動様式は長い間考えられてきた
extremely mysterious.	非常に不可解だと。
Although a bee hive is made up	ハチの群れは構成されているが
of thousands of individual bees,	何千もの個々のハチで,
in many ways	多くの点で

it resembles a single creature	単一の生き物のようだ
with large numbers of bees	多数のハチが
supporting a single fertile queen bee.	1匹の生殖能力のある女王バチを支えている。
Worker bees typically	働きバチは通常
cannot produce young,	子どもをつくることができず,
sacrificing the ability	能力を犠牲にする
to give birth	出産する
for the benefit of the hive as a whole.	群れ全体の利益のために。
Female Cape honey bees,	メスのケープミツバチは,
however,	しかし,
not only produce young	子どもをつくるだけではなく
of their own,	自分自身の,
but also travel to other colonies,	ほかのコロニーにも移動し,
lay eggs in them,	そこで産卵し,
and steal the honey	そしてハチミツを盗み
produced there,	そこでつくられた,
abandoning their relatives	自分たちの身内を置き去りにする
in their home colony.	彼らのホームコロニーに。
❸ In order to find out	解明するために
why this happens,	これがなぜ起こるのかを,
researchers compared the Cape honey bee	研究者たちはケープミツバチを比較した
with the African honey bee,	アフリカミツバチと,
the species	種の
whose colonies they typically invade.	それらが典型的に侵入するコロニーにいる。
After analyzing the entire genome	ゲノム全体を分析したあと
of individual bees	個々のハチの
from both subspecies of honey bee,	両種のミツバチの亜種から,
the scientists discovered	科学者たちは発見した
that the Cape honey bee's behavior	ケープミツバチの行動様式が
is the result	結果であることを
of a mutation in a single gene.	1つの遺伝子の突然変異の。
For such a genetic change	そのような遺伝的変化が
to happen	起こり
and become common	そして一般的になるためには,
in a type of bee,	ある種類のハチで,

Lesson **09**

it must give the bee	それがハチに与えなければならない
some sort of advantage	何らかの利点を
in nature.	本質的に。
Scientists speculate	科学者たちは推測している
that the mutation is a backup mechanism	突然変異が予備機構であると
in case something unfortunate happens	不幸なことが起こった場合の
to the queen bee.	女王バチに。
Since she is the only fertile individual,	女王バチは唯一の生殖能力のある個体であるため,
her death would be fatal	女王バチの死が致命的となるだろう
to the colony	コロニーにとって
were it not for the unique ability	またとない能力がなければ
of the Cape honey bee workers.	ケープミツバチの働きバチの。
❹ Cape honey bees have had	ケープミツバチは与えてきた
a significant effect	大きな影響を
on populations of the African honey bee.	アフリカミツバチの個体数に。
They were considered threatened	彼らは絶滅のおそれがあると考えられており
in the 1990s,	1990 年代に,
and researchers	そして研究者たちは
who studied the bees	ハチを研究していた
believed	考えていた
that it would be beneficial	有益だろうと
to introduce them to new habitats.	彼らに新しい生息地を紹介することが。
A number of studies were conducted	多数の研究が行われ
to see	調べるために
what effect they would have	どのような影響を与えるかを
on African honey bees,	アフリカミツバチに対して,
whose territory they were to be moved into,	それらの移り住むことになっている生息地を縄張りとしていた,
and all evidence made researchers optimistic	そしてすべての証拠が研究者たちを楽観的にさせた
that there would be no significant conflict	重大な対立はないだろうと
between the two types of bee.	2種類のハチの間で。

They were unaware,	彼らは知らなかった,
of course,	もちろん,
that Cape honey bees were capable	ケープミツバチには能力があると
of invading the other species' colonies.	ほかの種のコロニーに攻め入る。
This proved disastrous	これは悲惨なことだと判明した
for the African honey bee,	アフリカミツバチにとって,
particularly because the Cape honey bee is able to produce	特にケープミツバチは生産できるため
chemicals	化学物質を
that make it impossible to detect	わからなくする
when they are laying eggs	いつ彼らが卵を産んでいるのかを
in their stolen homes.	彼らの盗まれた巣で。
It was not until 2003	2003年になって初めて
that German researcher C. W. W. Pirk discovered	ドイツの研究者 C. W. W. パークは発見した
that they were endangering the African honey bee.	彼らがアフリカミツバチを危険にさらしていることを。
Today,	今日,
researchers fear	研究者たちはおそれている
that if the Cape honey bee continues to thrive,	もしケープミツバチが繁殖し続けると,
it could be a threat	脅威になってしまうのではないかと
to bee populations	ハチの個体数にとって
around the world.	世界中の。

Lesson
09

READING

Lesson 10

問題
Questions

W 単語数 ▶ **492** 語

⏱ 制限時間 ▶ **12** 分

✓ 目標得点 ▶ **30** /40点

DATE

▶次の英文の内容に関して，(1)～(4)の質問に対する最も適切な答え (または文を完成させるのに最も適切なもの) を **1**，**2**，**3**，**4** の中から 1 つ選びなさい。

The Hartz Reforms

In 2002, former German leader Gerhard Schröder launched a program known as the Hartz Reforms to increase economic growth and improve his country's social welfare system and labor market. By 2012, the unemployment rate had fallen from 13.4 percent to 5.5 percent, and economic growth had become steady. However, the Hartz reforms had various negative consequences for the German people. For example, currently, in order to receive unemployment insurance money, workers are forced to sign a contract with a government job agency in which both the individual and agency agree to make efforts to ensure that the person finds employment as soon as possible. If the job agency finds that the worker is not making sufficient effort to find employment, the agency has the power to cut their payments significantly. Such rules, combined with general cuts to benefits and limitations on how long they can be received, have created widespread and lasting opposition to the Hartz Reforms.

However, many German politicians have credited the Hartz Reforms with bringing about the surge in prosperity that Germany has experienced in recent years. According to them, the Hartz Reforms have been highly beneficial to the nation's business climate. For example, they claim that the threat of diminished support from the government for the unemployed has helped limit the bargaining power of unions and workers in wage negotiations, making Germany more attractive and profitable for companies. They also claim the reforms were effective because they

reduced the incentive to retire early and take advantage of the country's
unemployment benefits.

Critics, on the other hand, disagree with these claims. They admit that
the reforms have had a small effect in lowering the unemployment rate.
However, they also say that the numbers have only gone down because
the government puts so much pressure on the jobless that they are forced
to settle for unpleasant jobs with wages so inadequate that they still need
welfare to survive. Even worse, critics say, despite all the suffering that the
Hartz Reforms have caused, the economic improvements that have
occurred are actually the result of factors like new management systems,
outsourcing, and a general trend toward prosperity in most European
nations. These had been ongoing trends that were just taking shape as the
Hartz Reforms began, and they merely helped create the illusion that the
reforms were boosting the economy.

While supporters and critics strongly disagree about what effect the
Hartz Reforms have had on the unemployed, the impact on poverty is
unmistakable. Poverty rates in Germany have increased from 4.8 percent in
2004 to 7.5 percent in 2006, and the increase in poverty has been far
higher among the unemployed. Furthermore, this has been occurring at a
time when the incomes of wealthier people in society have been
increasing. As a result, there are increasing calls for the Hartz Reforms to
be replaced with a new system that utilizes incentives instead of penalties
to motivate the unemployed to return to the workforce.

Lesson
10

Questions ☞

(1) One effect of the Hartz Reforms has been that

    1 while the economy expanded, the unemployment rate did not go down nearly as quickly as people expected it would.

    2 although people are able to get more unemployment benefits, it takes much longer to find job agencies that can help them find work.

    3 people feel they do not receive sufficient support from the German government in finding new jobs when they are unemployed.

    4 there is much more pressure from the German government on people to find work quickly if they lose their jobs.

(2) What do many German politicians say about the Hartz reforms?

    1 By reducing the amount of money that the government has to pay to workers, they have strengthened the economy.

    2 Germany could have much greater prosperity if the Hartz Reforms had done more to reduce Germany's unemployment levels.

    3 They have solved a serious problem that once faced unemployed workers who were nearing retirement age.

    4 Unions and workers are more to blame than they are for the problems that have occurred since the reforms took effect.

(**3**)　What do critics say about the Hartz Reforms?

1　It is unfair that Germany has made the Hartz Reforms because they have created serious problems for many European countries.

2　Although the Hartz reforms have been effective in bringing prosperity to Germany, they have created problems for managers and outsourcing companies.

3　It is just a coincidence that the period of economic prosperity began in Germany after the Hartz Reforms occurred.

4　Although many people have gotten better jobs because of the Hartz Reforms, it is unlikely that the changes will be permanent.

(**4**)　What do statistics show about the Hartz Reforms?

1　They appear to have contributed to the problem of income inequality, particularly for people who are unemployed.

2　They are likely to be responsible for the fact that although there is more poverty, there is also more chance for people to escape from it.

3　They have benefited the wealthy to some extent, but not as much as they have helped people who live in poverty.

4　They are such an important part of the German welfare system that it would be very dangerous to replace them with another type of system.

Lesson
10

ANSWER		
(**1**)　① ② ③ ④	(**2**)　① ② ③ ④	
(**3**)　① ② ③ ④	(**4**)　① ② ③ ④	

Answers & Explanations ☞

Lesson 10
解答・解説
Answers & Explanations

□（**1**）　ハルツ改革による結果の 1 つは……

1　経済が発展する中，失業率は人々が期待するほど急速には下がらなかった。

2　人々はより多くの失業手当をもらえるが，仕事を探すのを手伝ってくれる労働機関を見つけるのにずっと時間がかかる。

3　人々は失業中に新しい仕事を探すうえでドイツ政府から十分な支援を受けていないと感じている。

④　仕事を失った場合，早く仕事を見つけるようにというドイツ政府からのさらに多くの圧力がある。

解説▶第 1 段落の最後の 3 文より，失業者は政府労働機関と契約を結び，できる限り早く新しい仕事を見つけることを約束し，**努力が十分でないと判断された場合には失業手当が削減される**ことなどがわかる。したがって，**4** が正解。第 1 段落の最後の文より失業手当が削減されたことに人々が反感を抱いたことはわかるが，仕事を探すうえでの政府の支援については触れられていないので，**3** は誤り。

□（**2**）　多くのドイツの政治家たちはハルツ改革について何と言っているか。

①　労働者に対して政府が支払わなければならない金額を減らすことで，経済を強化した。

2　もしハルツ改革がドイツの失業水準を下げるためにもっと多くのことをしていたらドイツはより繁栄することができたかもしれない。

3　定年に近づいている失業者が一度直面した深刻な問題を解決することができた。

4　改革が効果を現して以来起きた問題に対して，改革よりも労働組合と労働者の方に責任がある。

解説▶第 2 段落の最初の文にある「**多くのドイツの政治家たちは，ハルツ改革がここ数年でドイツが経験した急激な繁栄をもたらしたと評価した**」より，政治家たちはハルツ改革がドイツの経済に良い影響をもたらしたと考えていることがわかる。そして第 2 段落の最後の 2 文より，その影響はハルツ改革によって労働者の賃金交渉における交渉力が制限されたり，労働者が国からの失業手当を利用する動機が減ったりしたことによるものだと政治家が主張したことがわかるので，**1** が正解。

重要語句　□ strengthen（働）～を強化する，強固にする）

□（**3**）　批判者はハルツ改革について何と言っているか。

1　ハルツ改革は多くのヨーロッパ諸国に深刻な問題をもたらしたため，ドイツがこれをつくったことは不当である。

2　ハルツ改革はドイツに繁栄をもたらしたという意味では効果的であったが，経営者や外部委託企業に問題を引き起こした。

（**3**）ハルツ改革が起きたあとに経済繁栄期がドイツで始まったのは偶然の一致にすぎない。

4　ハルツ改革のおかげで多くの人がより良い仕事につけたが，その変化が永続する可能性は低い。

解説▶第3段落第4文より，批判者はドイツの経済が繁栄した実際の理由について，新たな経営システムや外部委託，ほとんどのヨーロッパ諸国における繁栄の一般的な傾向が生じたためだと考えているとわかる。続く第3段落の最後の文より，これらの傾向が見え始めた時期とハルツ改革の開始時期が重なっていたことで，**ドイツの繁栄はハルツ改革によるものだという錯覚が生まれた**ことが読み取れる。したがって，**3** が正解。

□（**4**）　ハルツ改革についての統計は何を示しているか。

（**1**）特に失業者にとって所得不平等に関する問題の一因となったように思われる。

2　さらなる貧困はあるものの，貧困から抜け出す可能性もより多くあるという事実の要因であるようだ。

3　裕福な人にもある程度の利益はあったが，貧困生活を送っている人に対するものほどの助けにはならなかった。

4　ドイツの福祉制度の大変重要な部分であるため，別の制度と置き換えることは非常に危険である。

解説▶第4段落第2〜3文より，「**ドイツの貧困率は 2004 年の 4.8% から 2006 年の 7.5% に増加し，貧困は失業者の間ではるかに増加している**」こと，そしてこの変化が「**社会のより裕福な人々の所得が増加しているときに起きている**」という統計結果が得られたことがわかる。ここから所得はさらに不平等になっていることがわかるので，**1** が正解。

重要語句　□ contribute（働（良い結果または悪い結果を生じる）一因となる）

ANSWER		SCORE	CHECK YOUR LEVEL
（**1**）① ② ③ **④**　（**2**）**①** ② ③ ④		／**40**点　（4問×各10点）	0〜20点 ➡ *Work harder!*　21〜30点 ➡ *OK!*　31〜40点 ➡ *Way to go!*
（**3**）① ② **③** ④　（**4**）**①** ② ③ ④			

【和訳】

ハルツ改革

❶ 元ドイツ首相のゲアハルト・シュレーダーは，経済成長を高め，自分の国の社会福祉制度と労働市場を改善するため，2002年にハルツ改革として知られる計画を開始した。2012年までには失業率は13.4%から5.5%まで下がり，経済成長は安定してきた。しかしハルツ改革は，ドイツ人にとって様々な悪い結果をもたらした。例えば，現在では，失業保険金を受け取るために，労働者は個人と政府労働機関の両者が，その人自身ができる限り早く確実に仕事を見つけられるよう努力することに同意する契約書に署名するよう強いられる。もし労働者が仕事を見つけるために十分な努力をしていないと労働機関が発見すれば，その機関は支払いを大幅に削減する権限をもっている。これらのルールは，手当の全体的な削減や受け取れる期間についての制限と相まって，ハルツ改革に対して広く，持続的な反対を生んだ。

❷ しかし多くのドイツの政治家たちは，ハルツ改革がここ数年でドイツが経験した急激な繁栄をもたらしたと評価した。彼らによると，ハルツ改革は国家の景況に非常に役立っている。例えば，失業者に対する政府からの支援が少なくなるというおそれは，賃金交渉における労働組合と労働者の交渉力を制限する後押しをし，それによってドイツを企業にとってより魅力的であり利益になるようにしたと，政治家たちは主張する。また改革は，早期退職して国からの失業手当を利用するという動機を減らしたため，効果的であったとも主張する。

❸ 一方で批判者は，これらの主張に同意しない。彼らはこの改革が失業率の減少に多少の影響を与えたと認める。しかし，数字が下がったのは，政府が失業者に対して圧力をかけすぎ，彼らが生きていくのにまだ福祉を必要とするくらい不十分な賃金しか支払われない不快な仕事で我慢することを余儀なくされているだけだとも言う。さらに悪いことに，ハルツ改革が引き起こしたすべての苦難にかかわらず，起こった経済進歩は実際のところ，新たな経営システムや外部委託，ほとんどのヨーロッパ諸国における繁栄の一般的な傾向のような要因による結果であると批判者は言う。これらはハルツ改革が始まったときに具体的に見え始めたばかりの進行していた傾向であり，それらは改革が経済を押し上げているという錯覚を生み出す後押しをしたにすぎない。

❹ 支持者と批判者はハルツ改革が失業者に対してどのような影響を与えたかについて強く対立しているが，貧困への影響は明白である。ドイツの貧困率は，2004年の4.8%から2006年の7.5%に増加し，そして貧困は失業者の間ではるかに増加している。さらに，これは社会のより裕福な人々の所得が増加しているときに起きている。結果として，失業者が労働人口に戻るように促すために，ハルツ改革は，罰を与えるのではなくやる気を利用する新しい制度と置き換えられるべきとの要求が増えている。

重要語句リスト

❶

☐ social welfare system	
	名 社会福祉制度
☐ labor	名 労働, 労働者
☐ unemployment	名 失業 (状態)
☐ consequence	名 結果
☐ contract	名 契約書, 協定
☐ make effort	熟 努力する

❷

☐ credit ~ with...	熟 ~に…の功績があると思う
☐ surge	名 (物価, 利益などの) 急上昇,
	急増
☐ prosperity	名 繁栄, 隆盛
☐ diminished	形 減少した
☐ bargaining	名 交渉, 取引
☐ union	名 労働組合
☐ negotiation	名 交渉
☐ incentive	名 動機

❸

☐ critic	名 批判する人, 批評家, 評論家
☐ the jobless	名 失業者たち
☐ settle for ~	熟 ~で我慢する
☐ ongoing	形 進行中の, 継続している
☐ illusion	名 錯覚, 幻想

❹

☐ poverty	名 貧困, 貧乏
☐ utilize	動 ~を利用する
☐ workforce	名 労働人口

Lesson
10

Lesson 10
要点整理
Paragraph Summary

▶音声を聞きながら, ①〜⑥の空欄を埋め, 段落ごとの要旨を確認しましょう(解答は下部にあります)。

The Hartz Reforms

❶ ◇ the Hartz Reforms：

to increase [① e_____ g_____] and improve the social welfare system and labor market by 2012

positive consequences	negative consequences
• the unemployment rate had fallen • economic growth had become steady	• workers are forced to sign a contract with a government job agency • if the worker is not making sufficient effort to find employment → the agency has the power to cut their payments

→ created widespread and lasting [② o_____]

❷ ◇ **many German politicians : the Hartz Reforms = highly beneficial**

→ (1) helped limit the bargaining power of unions and workers in wage negotiations

(2) reduced the [③ i_____] to retire early and take advantage of the country's unemployment benefits

❸ ◇ **critics : disagree with these claims**[※1]

※1 these claims : the Hartz Reforms = highly beneficial

→ (1) the numbers of the unemployed have only gone down because the government puts so much pressure on the jobless that they are forced to settle for [④ u_____] jobs

(2) the economic improvements are actually the result of factors like new management systems, outsourcing, and a general trend toward prosperity in most European nations

【解答】 ① economic growth ② opposition ③ incentive ④ unpleasant

```
【和訳】                    ハルツ改革
```

❶　◇ ハルツ改革：

　　経済成長を高め，社会福祉制度と労働市場を改善するため

　　2012 年までに

良い結果	悪い結果
• 失業率が下がった • 経済成長が安定してきた	• 労働者は政府労働機関との契約書に署名するよう強いられる • もし労働者が仕事を見つけるために十分な努力をしていないと→ その機関は支払いを削減する権限をもっている

　　→ 広く，持続的な反対を生んだ

❷　◇ 多くのドイツの政治家たち：ハルツ改革 ＝ 非常に役立っている

　　　→ (1) 賃金交渉における労働組合と労働者の交渉力を制限する後押しをした

　　　　 (2) 早期退職して国からの失業手当を利用するという動機を減らした

❸　◇ 批判者：これらの主張[※1]に同意しない

　　　※1 これらの主張：ハルツ改革 ＝ 非常に役立っている

　　　→ (1) 失業者の数が減ったのは，政府が失業者に対して圧力をかけすぎ，

　　　　　　 彼らが不快な仕事で我慢することを余儀なくされているだけだ

　　　　 (2) 経済進歩は実際のところ，新たな経営システムや外部委託，ほとん

　　　　　　 どのヨーロッパ諸国における繁栄の一般的な傾向のような要因に

　　　　　　 よる結果である

❹ ◇ the impact on poverty is unmistakable

(1) poverty rates in Germany have increased from 4.8 percent in 2004 to 7.5 percent in 2006

(2) the increase in poverty has been far higher among the unemployed

→ this has been occurring at a time when the incomes of wealthier people in society have been [5] i_____]

→ increasing calls for the Hartz Reforms to [6] b_ r_____ w___] a new system

❹ ◇ **貧困への影響は明白である**

(1) ドイツの貧困率が 2004 年の 4.8% から 2006 年の 7.5% に増加した

(2) 貧困は失業者の間ではるかに増加している

→ これは社会のより裕福な人々の所得が増加しているときに起きている

→ ハルツ改革は新しい制度と置き換えられるべきとの増えている要求

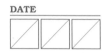

◀)) 英文音声 ▶ **L&R_LV5_10-ST**

英語	和訳
The Hartz Reforms	ハルツ改革
❶ In 2002,	2002 年に,
former German leader Gerhard Schröder launched	元ドイツ首相のゲアハルト・シュレーダーは, 開始した
a program	計画を
known as the Hartz Reforms	ハルツ改革として知られる
to increase economic growth	経済成長を高めるために
and improve his country's social welfare system and labor market.	また自分の国の社会福祉制度と労働市場を改善するために。
By 2012,	2012 年までには,
the unemployment rate had fallen	失業率は下がり
from 13.4 percent to 5.5 percent,	13.4% から 5.5% まで,
and economic growth had become steady.	経済成長は安定してきた。
However,	しかし,
the Hartz reforms	ハルツ改革は
had various negative consequences	様々な悪い結果をもたらした
for the German people.	ドイツ人にとって。
For example,	例えば,
currently,	現在では,
in order to receive unemployment insurance money,	失業保険金を受け取るために,
workers are forced to sign a contract	労働者は契約書に署名するよう強いられる
with a government job agency	政府労働機関と
in which both the individual and agency agree	個人と機関の両者が同意する
to make efforts	努力することを
to ensure	確実にするよう
that the person finds employment	その人が仕事を見つけることを
as soon as possible.	できる限り早く。
If the job agency finds	もし労働機関が発見すれば
that the worker is not making sufficient effort	労働者が十分な努力をしていないと

to find employment,	仕事を見つけるために，
the agency has the power	その機関は権限をもっている
to cut their payments significantly.	支払いを大幅に削減する。
Such rules,	これらのルールは，
combined with general cuts to benefits and limitations	手当の全体的な削減や制限と相まって
on how long they can be received,	受け取れる期間についての，
have created widespread and lasting opposition	広く，持続的な反対を生んだ
to the Hartz Reforms.	ハルツ改革に対して。
❷ However,	しかし，
many German politicians	多くのドイツの政治家たちは，
have credited	評価した
the Hartz Reforms	ハルツ改革を
with bringing about the surge in prosperity	急激な繁栄をもたらしたと
that Germany has experienced	ドイツが経験した
in recent years.	ここ数年で。
According to them,	彼らによると，
the Hartz Reforms have been highly beneficial	ハルツ改革は非常に役立っている
to the nation's business climate.	国家の景況に。
For example,	例えば，
they claim	彼らは主張する
that the threat	おそれは
of diminished support from the government	政府からのサポートが少なくなるという
for the unemployed	失業者に対する
has helped limit	制限する後押しをし
the bargaining power	交渉力を
of unions and workers	労働組合と労働者の
in wage negotiations,	賃金交渉における，
making Germany more attractive and profitable	ドイツがより魅力的であり利益になるようにした
for companies.	企業にとって。
They also claim	彼らはまた主張する

Lesson **10**

the reforms were effective	改革は効果的であったと
because they reduced the incentive	それらは動機を減らしたため
to retire early	早期退職して
and take advantage of the country's unemployment benefits.	国からの失業手当を利用するという。
❸ Critics,	批判者は、
on the other hand,	一方で、
disagree with these claims.	これらの主張に同意しない。
They admit	彼らは認める
that the reforms have had a small effect	この改革は多少の影響を与えたと
in lowering the unemployment rate.	失業率の減少に。
However,	しかし、
they also say	彼らはまた言う
that the numbers have only gone down	数字は下がっているだけだと
because the government puts so much pressure	政府が圧力をかけすぎているので、
on the jobless	失業者に対して
that they are forced	彼らが余儀なくされており
to settle for unpleasant jobs	不快な仕事で我慢することを
with wages so inadequate	不十分な賃金の
that they still need welfare to survive.	彼らが生きていくのにまだ福祉を必要とするくらいの。
Even worse,	さらに悪いことに、
critics say,	批判者は言う、
despite all the suffering	すべての苦難にかかわらず
that the Hartz Reforms have caused,	ハルツ改革が引き起こした、
the economic improvements	経済進歩は
that have occurred	起こった
are actually the result of factors	実際のところ要因の結果であると
like new management systems,	新たな経営システムのような、
outsourcing,	外部委託、
and a general trend toward prosperity	そして繁栄の一般的な傾向の
in most European nations.	ほとんどのヨーロッパ諸国における。
These had been ongoing trends	これらは進行形の傾向であった
that were just taking shape	具体化し始めたばかりの
as the Hartz Reforms began,	ハルツ改革が始まったときに、

and they merely helped create the illusion	そしてそれらは錯覚を生み出す後押しをしたにすぎない
that the reforms were boosting the economy.	改革が経済を押し上げていたという。
❹ While supporters and critics strongly disagree	支持者と批判者は強く対立しているが
about what effect the Hartz Reforms have had	ハルツ改革がどのような影響を与えたかについて
on the unemployed,	失業者に対して,
the impact on poverty is unmistakable.	貧困への影響は明白である。
Poverty rates in Germany have increased	ドイツの貧困率は増加し
from 4.8 percent in 2004	2004 年の 4.8% から
to 7.5 percent in 2006,	2006 年の 7.5% に,
and the increase in poverty has been far higher	そして貧困ははるかに増加している
among the unemployed.	失業者の間で。
Furthermore,	さらに,
this has been occurring	これは起きている
at a time	ときに
when the incomes of wealthier people in society	社会のより裕福な人々の所得が
have been increasing.	増加している。
As a result,	結果として,
there are increasing calls	要求が増えている
for the Hartz Reforms	ハルツ改革は
to be replaced	置き換えられるべきという
with a new system	新しい制度と
that utilizes incentives	やる気を利用する
instead of penalties	罰の代わりに
to motivate the unemployed	失業者を促すために
to return to the workforce.	労働人口に戻るように。

Lesson

10

END 131

Q 4技能試験（英語資格・検定試験）について それぞれの特徴を教えてください！

A 一口に4技能試験といっても様々な種類の試験があり，それぞれ目的や用途が異なっています。そして，種々の4技能試験を用途別に分けるうえで非常に重要なのが，「TLU（Target Language Use）：目標使用言語領域」という指標です。これは，それぞれの4技能試験にどのような種類の英語が使われているかを示すものであり，どの試験でもこのTLUが最初に設定されたうえで問題がつくられています。

　例えば，英検のような試験の場合，一般的な英語の習熟度をはかることを目的としています。そのため出題されるトピックや内容は，日常生活全般のこととなり，多岐にわたります。一方で，TEAPやTOEFL iBT，IELTS（アカデミック・モジュール）といった試験は，アカデミックと呼ばれる領域をTLUとしています。これらの試験は，大学の講義や論文の閲読など，学問をするうえで必要な英語が身についているかどうかをはかる内容となっています。そして，もう1つの代表的なTLUが，ビジネスです。この領域のテストでは，仕事をする際に必要な英語の運用能力をはかることができます。TOEICがその代表例ですね。

　このように，同じ4技能試験の中でも用途はかなり異なっています。自分が大学に入ってやりたいことや，将来どのような領域の英語を使いたいのかということから逆算し，また，試験の難易度を考慮して，自分が受験する試験を選ぶとよいでしょう。例えば，海外大学への進学を目指す人には，世界で広く認められているIELTSやTOEFL iBTの受験をおすすめしたいですね。

Part 3
Lesson 11–15
Reading

内容一致問題
Reading Comprehension

London School of Economics and Political Science

READING

Lesson 11
問題
Questions

W 単語数 ▶ **556** 語
🕐 制限時間 ▶ **15** 分
☑ 目標得点 ▶ **30** /40点

DATE

▶次の英文の内容に関して，(1)～(4)の質問に対する最も適切な答え（または文を完成させるのに最も適切なもの）を **1**，**2**，**3**，**4** の中から1つ選びなさい。

Overpopulation

Thomas Malthus's book *An Essay on the Principle of Population* has been influential ever since it came out in 1798. Malthus pointed out that, although it is relatively easy for humans to have more children, it is relatively difficult for humans to increase their food supply. Malthus therefore believed that population growth naturally increases at a much faster rate than growth in the food supply does. He wanted to understand the methods by which society acted against this phenomenon. He argued that things like social customs, which encourage people to marry later in life, as well as political entities like the government not helping poor people, were some of the ways that society kept population growth in check.

Since its publication, politicians and scholars have attempted to apply the ideas from Malthus's book to real life. For example, a 1601 law passed by Queen Elizabeth I had provided financial assistance to people living in poverty. However, when criticisms grew that such assistance was encouraging them to have more children, politicians influenced by Malthus's ideas changed the law in 1834. People feared that a population explosion could be a disaster for society, leading to widespread starvation. The politicians therefore attempted to discourage people living in poverty from having children by forcing them into "workhouses" where they were made to perform hard labor and were given so little food that they sometimes starved to death. Biologist and author Matt Ridley sums up this type of misguided thinking as the belief that "we must be cruel to be kind."

In the 1960s, a famous biologist named Paul Ehrlich predicted that mass starvation was coming due to population growth in countries such as India and China. Ehrlich called for taxes on children and other measures to limit population growth. In countries like India, governments even forced people to have operations that made them unable to reproduce. Although the world's population at the time was still less than four billion, it seemed unimaginable that it could continue to increase without bringing a worldwide disaster. However, Ehrlich failed to anticipate the Green Revolution in which things like the genetic alteration of crops increased harvests so greatly that it allowed the population to rise to its current total of more than seven billion. Critics argue that this failure to anticipate technological advances in agriculture production is the problem with trying to limit population growth.

Although the "population bomb" never exploded, overpopulation does remain a problem in some countries. However, rather than imposing restrictions that make it difficult for people to have children, many experts now argue that there is a much better way to reduce population. Studies show that the more financially secure people become, the fewer children they have. People living in poverty know that there is a significant chance that their children will fall victim to diseases or starvation, so they tend to have larger families to ensure that some members will survive. When people expect that their children are likely to survive to adulthood, they typically want to support their growth with high-quality education and healthcare, among other services. However, such benefits come at a price, and people realize that they can provide them only to a limited number of children. Therefore, many charities are now focusing on providing medical care and basic necessities as a way to reduce populations.

Questions ☞

(**1**) What question did Thomas Malthus look at in *An Essay on the Principle of Population*?

1 When the increase in population growth is likely to overtake the growth in the food supply.

2 Why certain social customs had so far been ineffective in preventing population growth from overtaking growth in the food supply.

3 How humans are able to prevent population growth from increasing more quickly than the food supply.

4 How it was possible that the human population had stopped increasing even though the food supply was increasing.

(**2**) Which of the following statements best describes the idea that "we must be cruel to be kind"?

1 The extremely strict laws of 1601 were replaced with the kinder laws of 1834, and these later laws had a better effect on poor people.

2 Although the workhouses seemed strict at first, in the long term, they had a beneficial effect on the people who lived in them.

3 When poor people began starving due to a population explosion, it was necessary to make stricter laws that prevented poor people from having children.

4 Some people thought that the only way to prevent terrible food shortages was to make the lives of the poor miserable.

(**3**) What do some critics say is the main problem in the arguments of people who are trying to limit population growth?

    1 They do not realize that technology and other factors are able to compensate for the increase in population.

    2 The methods that people like Paul Ehrlich called for are so unpopular that people will not accept them.

    3 Countries such as India and China will always have large populations even if the governments take measures to limit them.

    4 The fact that the population has more than doubled since the 1960s shows that there will always be room for more people in the world.

(**4**) Some people claim the best way to deal with the problem of overpopulation is

    1 educating poor people about the dangers of overpopulation to convince them to accept restrictions on how many children they can have.

    2 placing restrictions that require people to be wealthy enough to provide education and healthcare for children.

    3 doing studies designed to show poor people the benefits of having fewer children.

    4 providing aid to people to give them confidence that their children will survive into adulthood so they will have fewer children.

ANSWER		
(1) ① ② ③ ④	**(2)**	① ② ③ ④
(3) ① ② ③ ④	**(4)**	① ② ③ ④

Answers & Explanations ☞

Lesson 11
解答・解説
Answers & Explanations

□**(1)** トマス・マルサスは，「人口論」の中でどんな疑問に目を向けたか。

　1 人口増加の増加量がいつ食糧供給の増加を上回りそうか。

　2 人口増加が食糧供給の増加を追い越すのを防ぐのに，なぜある種の社会的慣習が今までのところ効果的ではなかったのか。

　③ 人口増加が食糧供給よりも速く進行するのを人間がどのように防げるか。

　4 食糧供給は増加しているのに人口の増加が止まってしまったという事態が，どうしてありえたのか。

解説▶第1段落の第4文に，He wanted to understand the methods by which society acted against this phenomenon とある。この文の this phenomenon は，前の文中の「人口増加の方が必然的に食糧供給の増加よりもはるかに速いペースになる」という内容を指す。したがって **3** が正解。**1** の「いつ」，**2** の「効果的ではなかった」という内容は本文中に記述されていない。本文の内容からマルサスは人口増加に危機感を抱いていたことがわかるので **4** は誤り。

重要語句　□ overtake（働 ～に追いつく，～を追いこす）

□**(2)** 「私たちは親切であるために残酷であらねばならない」という思想を最も的確に表すのは次のうちどれか。

　1 1601 年の非常に厳しい法律が 1834 年のより寛大な法律に変わり，これらの後者の法律が貧しい人々により良い影響を与えた。

　2 救貧院は最初のうちは厳しいように思われたが，長い目で見るとそこで暮らす人々に有益な影響を与えた。

　3 人口の爆発的増加のせいで貧しい人々が餓え始めたとき，貧しい人々が子どもをもつのを防ぐより厳しい法律をつくる必要があった。

　④ ひどい食糧不足を防ぐための唯一の方法は，貧しい人々の生活を不幸なものにすることだ，と一部の人々は考えた。

解説▶第2段落に書かれている救貧院の目的は，人口の爆発的増加によって多くの餓死者を出さないよう，貧しい人々が子どもをつくる気にならないようにすることである。具体的には貧しい人々に重労働を強いたり，食事を減らしたりしていた。その内容に合う **4** が正解。to be kind は「国民全体（あるいは貧しい人々以外）に親切であるために」と解釈すればよい。

重要語句　□ miserable（働 不幸な）

□（**3**）　一部の批評家は，人口増加を制限しようとしている人々の論拠の主な問題は何
　　　　だと言っているか。

　　　①　科学技術とその他の要因が人口増加の埋め合わせをできることに，彼らは気
　　　　　づいていない。

　　　2　パウル・エールリヒのような人々が呼びかけた方法は非常に不人気なので，
　　　　　人々はそれらを受け入れないだろう。

　　　3　インドや中国などの国では，たとえ政府が制限する方策を取っても，人口が
　　　　　常に多いだろう。

　　　4　人口が 1960 年代から 2 倍以上になったという事実は，世界には常に人口
　　　　　が増加する余地があることを示している。

解説▶第 3 段落の最後の文の内容から考えて，**1** が正解。本文では「世界規模の大災害
を引き起こすことなく，人口が増加し続けることは考えられないように思えた。しかし，
実際には，（エールリヒが予想できなかった）『緑の革命』などによる農業生産の技術的進
歩によって，人口が増加した」と説明されている。**2, 3** のような内容は本文中に記述さ
れておらず，**4** は常識的に考えても不自然なので誤り。

□（**4**）　一部の人々の主張によると，過剰人口の問題に対処する最善の策は……

　　　1　もてる子どもの数についての制限を受け入れるよう説得するために，過剰人
　　　　　口の危険性を貧しい人々に教えることだ。

　　　2　子どもに教育や医療を提供できるほど十分に裕福になるよう求める制限を
　　　　　人々に課すことだ。

　　　3　より少ない子どもをもつことの利点を貧しい人々に示すよう計画された研究
　　　　　を行うことだ。

　　　④　自分の子どもが成人になるまで生き延びるという確信を与えるために人々に
　　　　　援助を提供し，人々が子どもを減らすようにすることだ。

解説▶第 4 段落の後半の内容に合う **4** が正解。この段落の説明によると，貧しい人々
は，自分の子どもが死ぬ可能性を考えて，多くの子どもをもつ。対して経済的に安定し
た人々は，自分の子どもが成人になるまで生き残れそうだと期待するので，子どもに質
の高い教育や医療を提供し，大事に育てる。それにはお金がかかるので，限られた数の
子どもをもつようになり，人口の減少につながる。

ANSWER		SCORE	CHECK YOUR LEVEL
（**1**）　① ② ③ ④	（**2**）　① ② ③ ④	／40点 （4問×各10点）	0〜20点 ➡ *Work harder!* 21〜30点 ➡ *OK!* 31〜40点 ➡ *Way to go!*
（**3**）　① ② ③ ④	（**4**）　① ② ③ ④		

過剰人口

❶ トマス・マルサスの著書『人口論』は，1798年に出版されて以来影響力を保ち続けている。マルサスは，人間がより多くの子どもをもつことは比較的簡単だが，人間が食糧供給を増やすのは比較的難しいと指摘した。したがって，マルサスは，人口増加の方が必然的に食糧供給の増加よりもはるかに速いペースになると考えた。彼は，社会がこの現象に逆らう方法を理解したかった。彼は，人々に晩婚を推奨する社会的慣習のようなことや，政府のような政治的実体が貧しい人々を援助しないといったことが，社会が人口増加を抑制するための方法の一部であると主張した。

❷ それが出版されて以降，政治家たちや学者たちはマルサスの本の思想を実生活に適用しようと試みた。例えば，エリザベス1世によって可決された1601年の法律は，貧しい暮らしを送る人々に金銭的援助を与えていた。しかし，そのような援助は彼らがより多くの子どもをもつことを推奨しているという批判が高まると，マルサスの思想に影響を受けた政治家たちは，1834年にその法律を改正した。人口の爆発的増加は社会にとって大きな災いとなり，多くの人の餓死につながりうると人々はおそれた。そこで政治家たちは，貧しい暮らしを送る人々が子どもをもつ気にならないよう試み，彼らを「救貧院」に強制収容した。彼らはそこで重労働をするよう強いられ，与えられる食事が少なすぎて餓死することもあった。生物学者かつ作家のマット・リドリーは，この種の見当違いの思考を「私たちは親切であるために残酷であらねばならない」という信念だと要約している。

❸ 1960年代に，パウル・エールリヒという有名な生物学者が，インドや中国などの国では人口増加によって大規模な飢餓が起こると予測した。エールリヒは，人口増加を制限するために子どもに課す税などの方策を呼びかけた。インドなどの国では，政府が人々に不妊手術まで強制した。当時の世界の人口はまだ40億に満たなかったが，世界規模の大災害を引き起こすことなく増加し続けることは考えられないように思えた。しかし，エールリヒは「緑の革命」を予測できなかった。その革命を通じて作物の遺伝子変化などが収穫を大幅に増加させた結果，総人口は現在の70億を超えるまでに増えた。この農業生産における技術的進歩を予想できなかったことが，人口増加を制限しようとする試みの課題だ，と批評家たちは主張している。

❹ 「人口爆弾」は一度も爆発しなかったが，過剰人口は一部の国々では依然として問題である。しかし，人々が子どもをもちにくくなるような制限を課すよりも，人口を減らすためのずっと優れた方法があると今日，多くの専門家たちは主張する。いくつかの研究によれば，経済的に安定すればするほど，人々がもつ子どもの数は少なくなる。貧しい暮らしを送る人々は，自分の子どもが病気や飢餓の犠牲になる見込みがかなりあるとわかっているので，何人かが確実に生き残れるよう大家族をもつ傾向がある。自分の子どもが成人になるまで生き残れそうだと期待する場合，人々は普通，ほかのサービスもあるが，質の高い教育や医療によって彼らの成長を支援したいと考える。しかし，そのような援助は高くつき，限られた数の子どもにしか与えられないことに人々は気づく。したがって，今では多くの慈善団体が，人口を減らすための1つの方法として医療と基本的な生活必需品の提供を重視している。

重要語句リスト

❶

☐ overpopulation	⑧ 過剰人口
☐ influential	⑱ 影響力の大きい
☐ come out	⑲ 出版される
☐ relatively	⑳ 相対的に，比較的
☐ keep ～ in check	⑲ ～を抑制する，食い止める

❷

☐ publication	⑧ 出版，発表
☐ population explosion	
	⑧ 人口の爆発的増加
☐ disaster	⑧ 大災害
☐ starvation	⑧ 餓え，餓死
☐ workhouse	⑧ 救貧院
☐ hard labor	⑧ 重労働
☐ starve to death	⑲ 餓死する
☐ sum up ～	⑲ ～を要約する
☐ misguided	⑱ 間違った
☐ cruel	⑱ 残酷な

❸

☐ call for ～	⑲ ～を呼びかける，要求する
☐ reproduce	⑩ 生殖する，子どもをつくる
☐ unimaginable	⑱ 考えられない
☐ anticipate	⑩ ～を予測する
☐ genetic alteration	⑧ 遺伝子の変化
☐ crop	⑧ 作物
☐ harvest	⑧ 収穫

❹

☐ explode	⑩ 爆発する
☐ impose	⑩ ～を課す
☐ fall victim to ～	⑲ ～の犠牲になる
☐ healthcare	⑧ 医療
☐ benefit	⑧ 援助，手助け
☐ come at a price	⑲ 高くつく
☐ medical care	⑧ 医療
☐ necessities	⑧ 生活必需品

Lesson

11

Lesson 11
要点整理
Paragraph Summary

Overpopulation

❶ ◇ **Thomas Malthus's book = influential**

- Malthus pointed out

difficult	to increase food supply
easy	to have more children

  → population growth > growth in the food supply

- the methods by which society acted against this phenomenon

  (1) encouraging people to [① m____ l____] in life

  (2) political entities like the government not helping poor people

❷ ◇ **politicians and scholars : applied the ideas from Malthus's book**

(1)

> a 1601 law : provide financial assistance to people living in poverty
>
> ↑
>
> criticism : such assistance was encouraging them to have more children

↓

politicians   changed the 1601 law

(2)

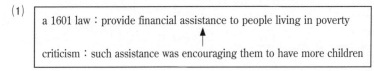

people

feared a [② p_____ e_____]
could be a disaster for society

↓

politicians

forced people living in poverty into
"workhouses" in order to discourage
them from having children

【解答】 ① marry later ② population explosion

【和訳】

過剰人口

❶ ◇ **トマス・マルサスの著書 ＝ 影響力がある**

• マルサスは指摘した

難しい	食糧供給を増やすこと
簡単	より多くの子どもをもつこと

→ 人口増加 **>** 食糧供給の増加

• 社会がこの現象に逆らう方法

(1) 人々に晩婚を推奨する

(2) 政府のような政治的実体が貧しい人々を援助しない

❷ ◇ **政治家や学者：マルサスの本の思想を適用した**

(1)

> 1601年の法律：貧しい暮らしを送る人々に金銭的援助を与える
>
> ↑
>
> 批判：そのような援助は彼らがより多くの子どもをもつことを推奨している

↓

政治家たち　　　1601年の法律を改正した

(2)

人々

人口の爆発的増加は社会にとって大きな
災いとなりかねないとおそれた

↓

政治家たち

貧しい暮らしを送る人々が子どもをもつ
気にならないよう，彼らを「救貧院」に強
制収容した

❸ ◇ **Paul Ehrlich**：**predicted that mass starvation was coming due to population growth**

→ called for $\boxed{3}$ t____ on children and other measures to limit population growth

→ in countries like India：governments forced people to have operations that made them unable to reproduce

◇ **Green Revolution**：**things like the genetic alteration of crops**

• Ehrlich failed to anticipate the Green Revolution

• Green Revolution increased harvests so greatly

→ allowed the population to $\boxed{4}$ r___

❹ ◇ **overpopulation remains a problem**

• a much better way to reduce population

= more $\boxed{5}$ f_____ secure → have fewer children

people living in poverty

their children may fall victim to diseases or starvation → have larger families

financially secure people

their children are likely to survive to adulthood → have fewer children

→ many charities are now focusing on providing medical care and basic necessities as a way to reduce populations

❸   ◇ **パウル・エールリヒ：人口増加によって大規模な飢餓が起こると予測した**

　　　→人口増加を制限するために子どもに課す税などの方策を呼びかけた

　　　→インドなどの国：政府が人々に不妊手術を強制した

　　◇ **緑の革命：作物の遺伝子変化など**

　　　• エールリヒは「緑の革命」を予測できなかった

　　　• 「緑の革命」は収穫を大幅に増加させた

　　　　→人口は増えた

❹   ◇ **過剰人口は依然として問題である**

　　　• 人口を減らすためのずっと優れた方法

　　　　= より経済的に安定する→より少ない子どもをもつ

貧しい暮らしを送る人々

子どもが病気や飢餓の犠牲になるかもしれない
→ 大家族をもつ

経済的に安定した人々

子どもが成人になるまで生き残れそう
→ より少ない子どもをもつ

　　　→今では多くの慈善団体が，人口を減らすための１つの方法として医
　　　　療と基本的な生活必需品の提供を重視している

Lesson 11
速読練習
Sight Translation

 ◀)) 英文音声 ▶**L&R_LV5_11-ST**

英語	和訳
Overpopulation	過剰人口
❶ Thomas Malthus's book *An Essay on the Principle of Population*	トマス・マルサスの著書『人口論』は
has been influential	影響力を保ち続けている
ever since it came out in 1798.	1798年に出版されて以来。
Malthus pointed out that,	マルサスは指摘した,
although it is relatively easy	比較的簡単だが
for humans	人間にとって
to have more children,	より多くの子どもをもつことは,
it is relatively difficult	比較的難しい
for humans	人間にとって
to increase their food supply.	食糧供給を増やすことは。
Malthus therefore believed	したがってマルサスは考えた
that population growth naturally increases	人口増加は必然的に大きくなると
at a much faster rate	はるかに速いペースで
than growth in the food supply does.	食糧供給の増加よりも。
He wanted to understand the methods	彼は方法を理解したかった
by which society acted against this phenomenon.	社会がこの現象に逆らう。
He argued that	彼は主張した
things like social customs,	社会的慣習のようなことが,
which encourage people to marry	人々に結婚することを推奨する
later in life,	人生の後半で,
as well as political entities like the government	政府のような政治的実体だけでなく
not helping poor people,	貧しい人々を援助しない,
were some of the ways	方法の一部であると
that society kept population growth in check.	社会が人口増加を抑制するための。
❷ Since its publication,	それが出版されて以降,
politicians and scholars have attempted	政治家たちや学者たちは試みた
to apply the ideas	思想を適用することを
from Malthus's book	マルサスの本の

to real life.	実生活に。
For example,	例えば,
a 1601 law passed	可決された 1601 年の法律は
by Queen Elizabeth I	エリザベス 1 世によって
had provided financial assistance	金銭的援助を与えていた
to people living in poverty.	貧しい暮らしを送る人々に。
However,	しかし,
when criticisms grew	批判が高まると
that such assistance was encouraging them	そのような援助は彼らに推奨しているという
to have more children,	より多くの子どもをもつことを,
politicians influenced by Malthus's ideas	マルサスの思想に影響を受けた政治家たちは
changed the law	その法律を改正した
in 1834.	1834 年に。
People feared	人々はおそれた
that a population explosion	人口の爆発的増加は
could be a disaster for society,	社会にとって大きな災いとなりうり,
leading to widespread starvation.	多くの人の餓死につながると。
The politicians therefore attempted	そこで政治家たちは試みた
to discourage people living in poverty	貧しい暮らしを送る人々が〜する気にならないよう
from having children	子どもをもつ
by forcing them into "workhouses"	彼らを「救貧院」に強制収容することで
where they were made	彼らはそこで強いられた
to perform hard labor	重労働をするように
and were given so little food	そしてほんの少ししか食事を与えられなかったので
that they sometimes starved to death.	餓死することもあった。
Biologist and author Matt Ridley	生物学者かつ作家のマット・リドリーは
sums up	要約する
this type of misguided thinking	この種の見当違いの思考を
as the belief	信念だと
that "we must be cruel to be kind."	「私たちは親切であるために残酷であらねばならない」という。
❸ In the 1960s,	1960 年代に,

a famous biologist named Paul Ehrlich predicted	パウル・エールリヒという有名な生物学者は予測した
that mass starvation was coming	大規模な飢餓が起こると
due to population growth	人口増加によって
in countries	国では
such as India and China.	インドや中国などの。
Ehrlich called for	エールリヒは呼びかけた
taxes on children	子どもに課す税を
and other measures	またそのほかの方策を
to limit population growth.	人口増加を制限するために。
In countries like India,	インドなどの国では,
governments even forced people	政府が人々を強制さえした
to have operations	手術をすること
that made them unable to reproduce.	子どもをつくれないようにする。
Although the world's population at the time	当時の世界の人口は〜だけれども
was still less than four billion,	まだ40億に満たなかった,
it seemed unimaginable	考えられないように思えた
that it could continue to increase	増加し続けることが
without bringing a worldwide disaster.	世界規模の大災害を引き起こすことなく。
However,	しかし,
Ehrlich failed	エールリヒはできなかった
to anticipate the Green Revolution	「緑の革命」を予測することを
in which things like the genetic alteration of crops	その革命を通じて作物の遺伝子変化などが
increased harvests so greatly	収穫を大幅に増加させたので
that it allowed the population to rise	人口を増加させた
to its current total of more than seven billion.	現在の総人口が70億を超えるまで。
Critics argue	批評家たちは主張している
that this failure	この失敗は
to anticipate technological advances in agriculture production	農業生産における技術的進歩を予想することとの
is the problem	課題である
with trying to limit population growth.	人口増加を制限しようとする試みの。
❹ Although the "population bomb" never exploded,	「人口爆弾」は一度も爆発しなかったが,

overpopulation does remain a problem	過剰人口は依然として問題である
in some countries.	一部の国々では。
However,	しかし,
rather than imposing restrictions	制限を課すよりも
that make it difficult for people	人々がしにくくなる
to have children,	子どもをもつことを,
many experts now argue	今日, 多くの専門家たちは主張する
that there is a much better way	ずっと優れた方法がある
to reduce population.	人口を減らすための。
Studies show	研究によれば
that the more financially secure people become,	経済的に安定すればするほど,
the fewer children they have.	人々がもつ子どもの数が少なくなる。
People living in poverty know	貧しい暮らしを送る人々はわかっている
that there is a significant chance	見込みがかなりあると
that their children will fall victim	自分の子どもが犠牲になる
to diseases or starvation,	病気や飢餓の,
so they tend to have larger families	だから大家族をもつ傾向がある
to ensure	確実にするために
that some members will survive.	何人かが生き残ることを。
When people expect	人々が期待する場合
that their children are likely to survive	自分の子どもが生き残れそうだという
to adulthood,	成人まで,
they typically want to support their growth	人々は普通, 彼らの成長を支援したいと考える
with high-quality education and healthcare, among other services.	質の高い教育や医療, ほかのサービスの中で。
However,	しかし,
such benefits come at a price,	そのような援助は高くつき,
and people realize	そして人々は気づく
that they can provide them	それらを与えられることに
only to a limited number of children.	限られた数の子どもにのみ。
Therefore,	したがって,
many charities are now focusing	今では多くの慈善団体が重視している
on providing medical care and basic necessities	医療と基本的な生活必需品の提供を
as a way to reduce populations.	人口を減らすための1つの方法として。

END 149

READING

Lesson 12
問題
Questions

W 単 語 数 ▶ **522** 語
🕐 制限時間 ▶ **15** 分
☑ 目標得点 ▶ **30** /40点

DATE

▶ 次の英文の内容に関して，（ 1 ）～（ 4 ）の質問に対する最も適切な答え（または文を完成させるのに最も適切なもの）を **1**，**2**，**3**，**4** の中から 1 つ選びなさい。

Aging, Emotion, and Memory

According to psychologist Laura Carstensen, as people age, they begin to realize that their time on Earth is limited. Therefore, while younger people tend to focus on seeking out new information and exploring their world, aging brings a shift in priorities. The aging brain begins to focus on emotion-related goals and social life. In an experiment, Carstensen showed both positive images, such as an adult hugging children, and negative images, such as a duck stuck in an oil spill, to people of various ages. She discovered that, while older subjects remembered fewer of the images overall, they had a tendency to recall a higher proportion of the positive ones than the younger subjects did. While it is commonly believed that most individuals experience a decline in overall happiness as they age, Carstensen's research indicates that the opposite may be true.

Some researchers suggested that perhaps positive thoughts are easier to remember because they are less complex. They said that since people were losing their ability to process information, they could be focusing on the information that would be the easiest to comprehend. Since older people tend to experience declining memory performance, this theory could explain why they tended to remember more of the positive images. Carstensen, however, conducted more research comparing older individuals whose mental abilities remained strong with older people whose minds showed signs of decline. She found that the sharper an older person's mind was, the more likely the person was to remember positive

23 images.

24   For young people, a tendency to focus on and remember negative things
25 could be extremely valuable. When one is young, there are many harsh
26 lessons to be learned, and someone who forgets them may be less likely to
27 survive into old age. Carstensen believes that there may be an evolutionary
28 reason for older people tending to remember things that make them
29 happy, which is related to a theory known as the "grandmother
30 hypothesis." Long ago, older people often took on leadership roles, and
31 those with strong negative emotions could bring conflict to the group. In
32 contrast, being calm and staying positive could contribute significantly to
33 the group's unity. Having a grandmother who cared about others and
34 cultivated deep relationships within the group could contribute to its
35 chances of survival.

36   Carstensen has found, however, that a tendency to focus on good things
37 is not always beneficial. In an experiment in which people were asked to
38 play a video game where they could win or lose money, the brains of both
39 older and younger people tended to become active when they thought
40 about winning. However, when it came to losing, age differences became
41 apparent. The brains of older subjects still seemed to be seeking rewards,
42 whereas those of younger subjects did not. This concerned Carstensen
43 because it indicated that older people may have more trouble detecting
44 things like fraud. Similarly, when reading a complicated contract, they may
45 tend to ignore or forget negative aspects that could cause trouble for them
46 in the future. Carstensen believes those who work with seniors must be
47 aware of such tendencies so that they can warn older people who may do
48 something risky.

Questions ☞

(1) According to Laura Carstensen, as people get older,

    1 the decline in their ability to remember things well causes a decline in their overall happiness.

    2 the realization that they will not live forever causes them to focus more on positive things in life.

    3 they stop trying to take in as much new information because they know they are unlikely to remember it all.

    4 they become better at remembering images, but their ability to remember things decreases overall.

(2) Carstensen's experiment comparing older people with varying mental abilities suggested that

    1 it was unlikely that a decline in memory is the reason for the change in the type of images older people tend to remember.

    2 since people's memories get worse as they age, they tend to focus more on simple things.

    3 there is little or no relationship between a person's memory and their other mental abilities.

    4 people who had the greatest degree of mental decline tended to be the most positive overall.

(**3**)　How does the grandmother hypothesis relate to Carstensen's theory about older people's memories?

 1 The conflicts between older and younger members of groups may have required people in the past to have better memories than people do now.

 2 Older people who lost their tendency to focus on negative things were less likely to be effective leaders for the groups they belonged to.

 3 Only older people who were in leadership roles needed to have better memories than other people.

 4 The stronger relationships built by older leaders who had a positive outlook may have helped their groups to survive.

(**4**)　What is one thing that concerns Carstensen about older people's memories?

 1 They could make older people less likely to read through complicated contracts because they know they will forget what they learned.

 2 They could cause older people to be afraid of trying new things that could bring them rewards.

 3 They could cause older people to lose money or make poor decisions because they tend not to think about negative things as much.

 4 They could make older people lose confidence in their ability to compete with younger people.

Lesson
12

ANSWER		
(**1**) ① ② ③ ④	(**2**)	① ② ③ ④
(**3**) ① ② ③ ④	(**4**)	① ② ③ ④

Answers & Explanations ☞

Lesson 12
解答・解説
Answers & Explanations

□**（1）** ローラ・カーステンセンによると，人々は年を取るにつれて，……

1 物事をよく思い出す能力の低下が全体的な幸福度の低下を引き起こす。

② 自分が永遠に生きられないという認識によって，生活のポジティブな面により目を向けるようになる。

3 自分が全部を記憶していそうにないことを知っているので，以前と同じ量の新しい情報を取りこもうとするのを止める。

4 画像を思い出すのはより上手になるが，物を覚えている能力は全体的に減退する。

解説▶第1段落第1文に「人々は年を取るにつれて，この世での自分の時間が限られていることに気づき始める」とある。またカーステンセンの実験によれば，高齢者は若者よりも高い割合でポジティブな画像を思い出す傾向があった。したがって **2** が正解。**1**，**3**，**4** のような内容は本文中に記述されていないので誤り。

重要語句 □ realization（图 認識）

□**（2）** 様々な知能をもつ高齢者を比較したカーステンセンの実験は，……ということを示唆した。

① 記憶力の低下によって高齢者が思い出しがちな画像の種類が変化する可能性は低い

2 人々の記憶力は年を取るにつれて衰えるので，単純なことにより目を向ける傾向がある

3 人の記憶力とほかの知能との間には，ほとんどあるいは全く関係がない

4 知能の低下の程度が最も高い人は，全体的に最も前向きな傾向があった

解説▶第2段落の高い知能を維持している高齢者と判断に衰えの兆候がある高齢者とを比較するカーステンセンのさらなる調査によれば，高い知能を維持している高齢者ほどポジティブな画像を思い出す傾向が強かった。したがって，それが示唆することとして適当な **1** が正解。

重要語句 □ varying（图 様々な）

□**（3）** おばあさん仮説は，高齢者の記憶に関するカーステンセンの理論とどのような関係があるか。

1 集団の高齢者と若者との対立は，昔の人々に現代の人々よりも良い記憶力を
もつことを求めたかもしれない。

2 ネガティブなことを重視する傾向を失った高齢者が，自分の所属する集団の
印象的な指導者である可能性は低い。

3 指導的役割にある高齢者だけが，ほかの人よりも優れた記憶力をもつ必要が
あった。

(4) 前向きな物の見方をする高齢の指導者によって築かれたより強固な関係は，
その集団が生き残るのに役立ったかもしれない。

解説 ▶ 第3段落によれば，カーステンセンは高齢者の記憶の傾向を生物的進化と結びつ
けて考えた。それによると，昔は高齢者が指導者であることが多く，指導者がプラスの
感情をもつことが，集団の生き残る可能性の向上に貢献したのかもしれない。その説明
の内容に合う **4** が正解。**2** はその内容に反するので誤り。昔の人と現代人との記憶力の
比較や，指導者とそのほかの者との記憶力の比較は本文中に記述されていない。した
がって **1**，**3** は誤り。

重要語句 □ outlook (⑧ 物の見方)

□ **(4)** 高齢者の記憶についてカーステンセンを不安にさせる1つのことは何か。

1 高齢者は自分が覚えたことを忘れるとわかっているので，複雑な契約書に目
を通す可能性が低くなるかもしれない。

2 高齢者は自分に報いをもたらしうる新しいことをやってみるのを怖がるよう
になるかもしれない。

(3) 高齢者はネガティブなことを若者ほど考えない傾向があるので，お金を失っ
たり下手な決定をしたりしかねない。

4 高齢者は若者と競争する能力に対する自信を失うかもしれない。

解説 ▶ 第4段落第5文に「高齢者は詐欺のようなものを見抜くのに苦労するかもしれな
い」とあり，カーステンセンは，高齢者がポジティブなものだけに目を向けてネガティブ
なことを無視したり忘れたりする結果，様々なトラブルに巻き込まれることを懸念して
いるので，**3** が正解。また，第6文の内容より，**1** は誤り。**2**，**4** のような内容は本文
に記述されていないので誤り。

ANSWER		SCORE	CHECK YOUR LEVEL
(1) ① ② ③ ④　**(2)** ① ② ③ ④		╱40点 (4問×各10点)	0〜20点 ➡ *Work harder!* 21〜30点 ➡ *OK!* 31〜40点 ➡ *Way to go!*
(3) ① ② ③ ④　**(4)** ① ② ③ ④			

老化と感情と記憶

❶ 心理学者ローラ・カーステンセンによると，人々は年を取るにつれて，この世での自分の時間が限られていることに気づき始める。そのため，若者は新しい情報の探求や自分の世界の探検を重視しがちだが，老化は優先事項に変化をもたらす。老化する脳は，感情に関連した目標や社会生活を重視し始める。ある実験でカーステンセンは，子どもを抱いている大人などのポジティブな画像と，流出した石油の中で身動きの取れないアヒルなどネガティブな画像の両方を，様々な年齢の人に見せた。彼女の発見によれば，高齢の被験者の方が全体的に少ない画像を記憶していたが，若年の被験者よりも高い割合でポジティブな画像を思い出す傾向があった。ほとんどの人は年を取るにつれて全体的な幸福の減退を経験すると一般には考えられているが，カーステンセンの調査はその逆が正しいのかもしれないことを示している。

❷ ポジティブな思考の方がより複雑でないので，それだけ思い出しやすいのかもしれないと示唆した研究者もいた。人々は情報を処理する能力を失っているので，最も理解しやすいであろう情報を重視しているのかもしれないと彼らは言った。高齢者は記憶力の低下を経験しがちなので，この説は彼らがポジティブな画像をより多く思い出す傾向があった理由を説明しうる。しかしカーステンセンは，高い知能を維持している高齢者と判断に衰えの兆候がある高齢者とを比較するさらなる調査を行った。その結果，高齢者の判断力が鋭いほどポジティブな画像を思い出す傾向があることがわかった。

❸ 若者にとっては，ネガティブなことを重視したり思い出したりする傾向が極めて価値をもちうる。若い頃は学ぶべき厳しい教訓が多く，それらを忘れる人は老齢期まで生き残る可能性が低くなるかもしれない。高齢者が自分たちを幸せにするものを思い出す傾向があることには，進化論上の理由があるかもしれないとカーステンセンは考えており，それは「おばあさん仮説」として知られる理論と関係がある。遠い昔，高齢者は指導的役割を担うことが多く，強いマイナス感情がある高齢者は集団に対立をもたらす可能性があった。一方，穏やかで前向きであり続けることは，集団の結束に大いに役立つこともあった。他人を気にかけて集団内で深い関係を育むおばあさんがいることは，その集団が生き残る可能性に貢献したのかもしれない。

❹ しかしカーステンセンは，良いことを重視する傾向が常に有益とは限らないことを発見した。お金を勝ち取るか失うかというテレビゲームをするよう求められた人々の実験では，高齢者の脳と若者の脳の両方が，勝つことを考えたとき活性化する傾向があった。しかし負けることに関しては，年齢の違いが明白になった。高齢の被験者の脳は依然として報いを求めているように思われたが，若者の被験者の脳はそうではなかった。これはカーステンセンを不安にさせた。なぜなら，高齢者は詐欺のようなものを見抜くのにより苦労するかもしれないということを示唆したからである。同様に高齢者は，複雑な契約書を読むとき，将来自分にとって問題を引き起こすかもしれないネガティブな面を無視したり忘れたりする傾向があるかもしれない。高齢者と一緒に働く人は，危険なことをするかもしれない高齢者に警告できるように，このような傾向を意識しておく必要があるとカーステンセンは考えている。

重要語句リスト

❶

☐ aging	❷	老化
☐ age	❸	年を取る
☐ seek out 〜	❹	〜を追求する
☐ shift	❷	変化
☐ priority	❷	優先事項
☐ emotion-related	❺	感情に関連した
☐ hug	❸	〜を抱きしめる
☐ stuck in 〜	❹	〜の中で身動きが取れない
☐ spill	❷	流出
☐ subject	❷	被験者
☐ overall	❻	全体的に
	❺	全体的な
☐ recall	❸	〜を思い出す

❷

☐ process	❸	〜を処理する

❸

☐ harsh	❺	厳しい
☐ evolutionary	❺	進化論的な
☐ hypothesis	❷	仮説
☐ conflict	❷	対立
☐ unity	❷	結束
☐ care about 〜	❹	〜を気にかける，大切にする
☐ cultivate	❸	〜を育てる

❹

☐ concern	❸	〜を不安にさせる
☐ detect	❸	〜を見抜く
☐ fraud	❷	詐欺

Lesson
12

要点整理
Paragraph Summary

▶音声を聞きながら，①～⑥の空欄を埋めるもしくは適語を選び，
段落ごとの要旨を確認しましょう（解答は下部にあります）。

Aging, Emotion, and Memory

❶ ◇ **psychologist Laura Carstensen**

younger people	focus on seeking out new information and exploring their world
the aging brain	focus on emotion-related goals and social life

- an experiment：showed both positive images and negative images
  to people of various ages

→ older subjects：(1) remember fewer of the images

　　　　　　　　(2) recall a higher proportion of the [① p_____]

　　　　　ones

→ × common belief that most individuals experience a decline in
　overall happiness as they age

❷ ◇ **researchers and Laura Carstensen**

some researchers

- positive thoughts are less complex
  → easier to remember
- older people tend to experience declining
  memory performance
  → remember more of the positive images

Laura Carstensen

- older people with [② s_____] minds
  → more likely to remember positive
  images

【解答】　① positive　② sharper

158

【和訳】

老化と感情と記憶

❶ ◇ 心理学者ローラ・カーステンセン

若者	新しい情報の探求や自分の世界の探検を重視する
老化する脳	感情に関連した目標や社会生活を重視する

- 実験：ポジティブな画像とネガティブな画像の両方を様々な年齢の人に見せた

→高齢の被験者：(1) より少ない画像を記憶している

(2) 高い割合でポジティブな画像を思い出す

→ × ほとんどの人は年を取るにつれて全体的な幸福度の減退を経験するという一般的な考え方

❷ ◇ 研究者とローラ・カーステンセン

研究者

- ポジティブな思考はより複雑でない
  →思い出しやすい
- 高齢者は記憶力の低下を経験しがちである
  →ポジティブな画像をより多く思い出す

- -

ローラ・カーステンセン

- より鋭い判断力をもつ高齢者
  → ポジティブな画像を思い出す傾向がある

❸ ◇ **young people** : **many harsh lessons to be learned**

→ focus on and remember [③ n_____] things = valuable

◇ **older people** : **"grandmother hypothesis"**[※1]

→ tend to remember things that make them happy

※1 "grandmother hypothesis" :

older people with strong negative emotions → bring conflict to the group

↔ being calm and staying positive → contribute to the group's [④ u____]

❹ ◇ **a tendency to focus on good things** : **not always beneficial**

• an experiment : asked people to play a video game where they
could win or lose money

	when people thought about **winning**	when people thought about **losing**
the brains of [⑤ older / younger] subjects	active	seeking rewards
the brains of [⑥ older / younger] subjects	active	not seeking rewards

→ older people : (1) may have more trouble detecting things like fraud

(2) ignore or forget negative aspects that cause trouble

【解答】 ③ negative ④ unity ⑤ older ⑥ younger

160

❸ ◇ **若者：多くの学ぶべき厳しい教訓**

　　→ ネガティブなことを重視したり思い出したりする ＝ 価値がある

　◇ **高齢者：おばあさん仮説**[※1]

　　→ 自分たちを幸せにするものを思い出す傾向がある

　※1 おばあさん仮説：

　　強いマイナス感情がある高齢者→ 集団に対立をもたらす

　　↔ 穏やかで前向きでいること→ 集団の結束に役立つ

❹ ◇ **良いことを重視する傾向：常に有益とは限らない**

　　• 実験：お金を勝ち取るか失うかというテレビゲームをするよう人々に求めた

	勝つことを考えたとき	負けることを考えたとき
高齢の被験者の脳	活性化する	報いを求める
若者の被験者の脳	活性化する	報いを求めない

　　→ 高齢者：(1)詐欺のようなものを見抜くのにより苦労するかもしれない

　　　　　　　(2)問題を引き起こすネガティブな面を無視したり忘れたりする

英文音声 ▶ **L&R_LV5_12-ST**

DATE

英語	和訳
Aging, Emotion, and Memory	老化と感情と記憶
❶ According to psychologist Laura Carstensen,	心理学者ローラ・カーステンセンによると,
as people age,	人々は年を取るにつれて,
they begin to realize	気づき始める
that their time on Earth is limited.	この世での自分の時間が限られていることに。
Therefore,	そのため,
while younger people tend to focus	若者は重視しがちだが
on seeking out new information	新しい情報を探求することを
and exploring their world,	また自分の世界を探検することを,
aging brings a shift in priorities.	老化は優先事項に変化をもたらす。
The aging brain begins to focus	老化する脳は重視し始める
on emotion-related goals	感情に関連した目標を
and social life.	そして社会生活を。
In an experiment,	ある実験で,
Carstensen showed both	カーステンセンは両方を見せた
positive images,	ポジティブな画像と,
such as an adult hugging children,	子どもを抱いている大人などの,
and negative images,	そしてネガティブな画像を,
such as a duck stuck in an oil spill,	流出した石油の中で身動きの取れないアヒルなどの,
to people of various ages.	様々な年齢の人に。
She discovered that,	彼女は発見した,
while older subjects remembered	高齢の被験者は記憶していたが
fewer of the images overall,	全体的により少ない画像を,
they had a tendency	彼らには傾向があった
to recall a higher proportion of the positive ones	より高い割合でポジティブな画像を思い出すという
than the younger subjects did.	若年の被験者よりも。
While it is commonly believed	一般には考えられているが
that most individuals experience	ほとんどの人は経験すると
a decline in overall happiness	全体的な幸福の減退を

as they age,	年を取るにつれて,
Carstensen's research indicates	カーステンセンの調査は示している
that the opposite may be true.	その逆が正しいのかもしれないと。
❷ Some researchers suggested	示唆した研究者もいた
that perhaps positive thoughts are easier	おそらくポジティブな思考の方が〜しやすい
to remember	思い出すことを
because they are less complex.	より複雑でないので。
They said	彼らは言った
that since people were losing	人々は失っているので
their ability	能力を
to process information,	情報を処理する,
they could be focusing	彼らは重視しているのかもしれない
on the information	情報を
that would be the easiest to comprehend.	最も理解しやすいであろう。
Since older people tend to experience	高齢者は経験しがちなので
declining memory performance,	記憶力の低下を,
this theory could explain	この説は説明しうる
why they tended to remember more	彼らがより多く思い出す傾向があった理由を
of the positive images.	ポジティブな画像を。
Carstensen, however, conducted	しかし, カーステンセンは行った
more research	さらなる調査を
comparing older individuals	高齢者を比較して
whose mental abilities remained strong	高い知能を維持している
with older people	高齢者と
whose minds showed signs of decline.	判断に衰えの兆候がある。
She found	彼女はわかった
that the sharper an older person's mind was,	高齢者の判断力が鋭いほど,
the more likely the person was	人は傾向がある
to remember positive images.	ポジティブな画像を思い出す。
❸ For young people,	若者にとっては,
a tendency	傾向が
to focus on and remember	重視したり思い出したりする

Lesson 12

negative things	ネガティブなことを
could be extremely valuable.	極めて価値をもちうる。
When one is young,	若い頃は,
there are many harsh lessons	厳しい教訓が多い
to be learned,	学ぶべき,
and someone who forgets them	そしてそれらを忘れる人は
may be less likely to survive into old age.	老齢期まで生き残る可能性が低くなるかもしれない。
Carstensen believes	カーステンセンは考えている
that there may be an evolutionary reason	進化論上の理由があるかもしれないと
for older people	高齢者が
tending to remember	思い出す傾向があることに
things that make them happy,	自分たちを幸せにするものを,
which is related to a theory	それは理論と関係がある
known as the "grandmother hypothesis."	「おばあさん仮説」として知られる。
Long ago,	遠い昔,
older people often took on	高齢者は担うことが多かった
leadership roles,	指導的役割を,
and those with strong negative emotions	そして強いマイナス感情がある高齢者は
could bring conflict to the group.	集団に対立をもたらす可能性があった。
In contrast,	一方,
being calm and staying positive	穏やかで前向きであり続けることは
could contribute significantly	大いに役立つこともあった
to the group's unity.	集団の結束に。
Having a grandmother	おばあさんがいることは
who cared about others	他人を気にかける
and cultivated deep relationships	そして深い関係を育む
within the group	集団内で
could contribute	貢献したかもしれない
to its chances of survival.	その集団が生き残る可能性に。
❹ Carstensen has found,	カーステンセンは発見した,
however,	しかし,
that a tendency	傾向が
to focus on good things	良いことを重視する

is not always beneficial.	常に有益とは限らない。
In an experiment	実験では
in which people were asked	人々が求められた
to play a video game	テレビゲームをするように
where they could win or lose money,	お金を勝ち取るか失うかという，
the brains of both older and younger people	高齢者の脳と若者の脳の両方が
tended to become active	活性化する傾向があった
when they thought	彼らが考えたとき
about winning.	勝つことを。
However,	しかし，
when it came to losing,	負けることに関しては，
age differences became apparent.	年齢の違いが明白になった。
The brains of older subjects	高齢者の被験者の脳は
still seemed to be seeking rewards,	依然として報いを求めているように思われた，
whereas those of younger subjects did not.	その一方で若者の被験者の脳はそうではなかった。
This concerned Carstensen	これはカーステンセンを不安にさせた
because it indicated	示唆したので
that older people may have more trouble	高齢者はより苦労するかもしれないということを
detecting things like fraud.	詐欺のようなものを見抜くのに。
Similarly,	同様に，
when reading a complicated contract,	複雑な契約書を読むとき，
they may tend to ignore or forget	彼らは無視したり忘れたりする傾向があるかもしれない
negative aspects	ネガティブな面を
that could cause trouble for them in the future.	将来自分にとって問題を引き起こすかもしれない。
Carstensen believes	カーステンセンは考えている
those who work with seniors	高齢者と一緒に働く人は
must be aware of such tendencies	このような傾向を意識しておく必要がある
so that they can warn older people	高齢者に警告できるように
who may do something risky.	危険なことをするかもしれない。

Lesson
12

END　165

Lesson 13
問題
Questions

READING

W 単語数 ▶ **547** 語

制限時間 ▶ **15** 分

目標得点 ▶ **30** /40点

DATE

▶次の英文の内容に関して，(1)～(4)の質問に対する最も適切な答え（または文を完成させるのに最も適切なもの）を 1，2，3，4 の中から 1 つ選びなさい。

The Vinland Map

In 1957, book dealer Larry Witten discovered an unusual map that showed Europe, Africa, and Asia, but it also contained an image of "Vinland," the Viking name for North America. Although the Vinland Map appeared to have been produced around the year 1440, writing on it indicated that the image of Vinland was based on a journey there made by Vikings around the year 1000. If the map were authentic, then Norwegian Vikings had visited North America hundreds of years before Christopher Columbus "discovered" it in 1492. Witten, an experienced book dealer, found no obvious signs that the map might not be genuine. It was made from animal skin dated to the 1400s and was drawn with writing instruments appropriate to the period. Furthermore, since Witten had purchased the map for a reasonable price, he did not think the map was a fake produced merely for the sake of profit. Therefore, he decided that the map was likely authentic.

At first, Witten was reluctant to make his discovery public because he was still not completely sure of the map's authenticity. Unknown to him, however, another book dealer had shown the map to two leading experts at the British Museum. Having the British Museum's seal of approval would have been a big help in convincing the world that the Vinland Map was real. Indeed, both experts believed the map to be genuine, but they also knew that admitting as much would be controversial. Were the map ultimately discovered to be fake, the experts' careers could be ruined. Witten felt much the same, so he kept his map secret for many years.

Witten had found the Vinland Map inside a book called the *Hystoria Tartarorum*. Curiously, the Vinland Map had small holes made by insects that did not match the shape of the holes in the other maps in the book. Sometime later, a friend named Tom Marston, who worked at Yale University, showed Witten maps from the same time period with similar words on them. When he borrowed one, Witten found that the holes in the Vinland Map matched up perfectly with the ones in the Yale map. This indicated that the Vinland Map had originally been in a book together with the maps owned by Yale. This convinced him that the map was real, and he decided to make his discovery public.

Over the years, historians and book experts have argued about the Vinland Map. In 1974, it was found that up to 50 percent of the ink contained a titanium pigment that had not been invented until the 1920s. However, an analysis conducted in 1985 revealed that not only was there little titanium, but also there were many other inks that were used in medieval times but not today. Furthermore, titanium pigment has been found in the Gutenberg Bible, which dates back to the 1400s. Another solid piece of evidence supporting the map's authenticity is the discovery by archaeologists that Vikings did indeed settle in North America in the tenth century and inhabited the area continuously for nearly 500 years. Taking into account the archaeological discoveries and various analyses of the map itself, it seems likely to be genuine. It must be remembered, however, that for centuries people were certain that Columbus discovered North America, too.

Lesson
13

Questions ☞

(1) What was Larry Witten's reaction when he found the Vinland Map?

    1 He was suspicious because of the writing instruments that it appeared to have been made with.

    2 He was unable to come up with any convincing reason to doubt that the map was actually produced during the 1400s.

    3 He was unsure of what to do with it because his expertise was in the field of books rather than maps.

    4 He found it difficult to believe that Norwegian Vikings could have visited the Americas before Christopher Columbus.

(2) The two experts who examined the Vinland Map at the British Museum

    1 warned Witten that he would be making a serious mistake if he tried to convince people that the map was real.

    2 were afraid of the damage it would cause to their reputations if they went public with their real opinions about the Vinland Map.

    3 argued with workers at the British Museum about whether the Vinland Map was based on reality.

    4 refused to admit that the Vinland Map was real because they felt foolish for missing the chance to make such a major discovery.

(**3**) The holes in the Vinland Map

    1 suggested that it was not originally a part of the map collection that Larry Witten had bought it with.

    2 made Tom Marston think that it was certain that the Vinland Map had once been part of the *Hystoria Tartarorum.*

    3 were shown to have been made by a type of insect that did not exist in Europe when the Vinland Map was said to have been drawn.

    4 made Marston believe that his maps, rather than the Vinland Map, had originally come from the *Hystoria Tartarorum.*

(**4**) The author of the passage suggests that the question of whether the Vinland Map is real

    1 was finally decided by the 1985 analysis that showed the titanium found in the map was commonly used by Vikings.

    2 is likely to be solved when more archaeological discoveries are made regarding when the Vikings left their North American colonies.

Lesson
13

    3 will never be answered with complete certainty but that multiple sources of evidence make a convincing argument that it is real.

    4 demonstrates the danger of relying only on documents and ignoring important archaeological discoveries.

ANSWER		
(**1**) ① ② ③ ④	(**2**) ① ② ③ ④	
(**3**) ① ② ③ ④	(**4**) ① ② ③ ④	

Answers & Explanations ☞

□（**1**）　ラリー・ウィッテンは，ビンランド・マップを発見したときどう反応したか。

1　それをつくるのに使われたらしい筆記具のせいで，疑いをもっていた。

②　地図が実際に 1400 年代につくられたことを疑う説得力のある理由を全く思いつくことができなかった。

3　自分の専門分野は地図よりむしろ本だったので，その地図をどうすればよいのかよくわからなかった。

4　ノルウェーのバイキングがクリストファー・コロンブスより前にアメリカを訪れたかもしれないと信じるのは難しかった。

解説▶第 1 段落第 4 文に「**経験豊富な書籍販売者であるウィッテンは，その地図が本物ではないかもしれないという明白な証拠を発見しなかった**」とあり，地図が 1400 年代の動物の皮でできていることやその時代にふさわしい筆記具で描かれていること，手頃な価格で購入できたことなどから，ウィッテンはその地図が本物の可能性があると判断したことがわかる。したがって **2** が正解。

重要語句　□ suspicious（⑮ 疑っている）　□ convincing（⑯ 説得力のある）

□（**2**）　大英博物館でビンランド・マップを調べた 2 人の専門家は，……

1　もし地図は本物だと人々に信じさせようとすれば，重大な間違いを犯すだろうとウィッテンに警告した。

②　ビンランド・マップに関する本当の考えを公表した場合に，それが自分たちの評判に及ぼしそうな害をおそれた。

3　ビンランド・マップが事実に基づくかどうかについて，大英博物館の職員と議論した。

4　それほどの大発見をする好機を逃したのはばかげたことだと思ったので，ビンランド・マップは本物だと認めようとしなかった。

解説▶第 2 段落によれば，ウィッテンとは別の書籍販売者が大英博物館にビンランド・マップを持ち込み，2 人の専門家はそれが本物らしいと考えた。しかし万が一間違っていれば自分たちの経歴が損なわれるかもしれないので，公に本物だと認めようとしなかったことが読み取れる。したがって **2** が正解。

重要語句　□ reputation（⑧ 評判）　□ go public with ～（⑯ ～を公開する）

□（**3**）　ビンランド・マップの穴は，……

① それがもともとラリー・ウィッテンが一緒に買った地図収集物の一部ではないことを示唆していた。

2 ビンランド・マップはかつて「ヒストリア・タータロラム」の一部だったにちがいないとトム・マーストンに思わせた。

3 ビンランド・マップが描かれたと言われる当時はヨーロッパに存在しなかった種類の虫によってつくられたとわかった。

4 ビンランド・マップよりむしろ自分の地図が，もともと「ヒストリア・タータロラム」の中にあったのだとマーストンに信じさせた。

解説▶第3段落の内容から考えて **1** が正解。ウィッテンは「ヒストリア・タータロラム」という本の中でビンランド・マップを見つけたが，同じ本に含まれていたほかの地図とビンランド・マップでは，虫食いの穴の形が異なることに気づいた。その後，友人のマーストンから借りたイェール大学所蔵の地図の穴の形がビンランド・マップと一致した。このことは，ビンランド・マップがもともと，「ヒストリア・タータロラム」ではない別の本の中に入っていたことを意味する。確信したのはウィッテンだから，**2**，**4** は誤り。**3** の内容は本文中に記述されていないので誤り。

□**(4)** 本文の著者が示唆するところでは，ビンランド・マップが本物かどうかという疑問は，……

1 地図の中で発見されたチタンがバイキングによって一般に使われていたことを示す 1985 年の分析によって最終的に判断された。

2 いつバイキングが北アメリカの居留地を去ったのかに関するより多くの考古学的発見がなされれば解決される可能性がある。

③ 完全な確信をもって答えることは決してできないだろうが，多数の証拠資料はそれが本物だという説得力のある主張をする。

4 文書だけに頼り重要な考古学的発見を無視することの危険性を実証している。

解説▶第4段落の最後から2番目の文に「**考古学的発見と地図自体の様々な分析を考慮すれば，それは本物らしく思われる**」とあるので，**3** が正解。チタンの証拠としての信憑性には諸説あることがわかるので **1** は誤り。**2**，**4** のような内容は本文中に記述されていないので誤り。

ANSWER		SCORE	CHECK YOUR LEVEL
(1) ① ② ③ ④　**(2)** ① ② ③ ④		／40点	0〜20点 ➡ *Work harder!* 21〜30点 ➡ *OK!*
(3) ① ② ③ ④　**(4)** ① ② ③ ④		(4問×各10点)	31〜40点 ➡ *Way to go!*

ビンランド・マップ

❶ 1957 年にラリー・ウィッテンという書籍販売者が珍しい地図を発見した。それはヨーロッパ，アフリカ，アジアを示すだけでなく北アメリカでのバイキングの呼び名である「ビンランド」の絵も含んでいた。ビンランド・マップは 1440 年頃に作られたようだったが，地図の記述によればビンランドの絵は 1000 年頃にバイキングが行った旅に基づいていた。もしその地図が本物なら，1492 年にクリストファー・コロンブスが北アメリカを「発見」する数百年前に，ノルウェーのバイキングが北アメリカを訪れていたことになる。経験豊富な書籍販売者であるウィッテンは，その地図が本物ではないかもしれないという明白な証拠を発見しなかった。それは 1400 年代の動物の皮でできており，その時代にふさわしい筆記具で描かれていた。そのうえ，ウィッテンは地図を手頃な値で購入したので，彼は地図が単に利益のためにつくられた偽物だとは思わなかった。それゆえに彼は，地図は本物の可能性があると判断した。

❷ 最初のうちはその地図の真正性をまだ完全に確信していなかったので，ウィッテンはその発見を公にするのをためらった。しかし彼は知らなかったが，ほかの書籍販売者が大英博物館で 2 人の一流の専門家にその地図を見せていた。大英博物館の承認印があれば，ビンランド・マップが本物だと世界中の人々を納得させるのに大いに役立っただろう。実のところ，2 人の専門家はどちらもその地図が本物だと信じていたが，そう認めれば物議を醸すだろうということも彼らは知っていた。もし地図が結局偽物だったとわかれば，専門家の経歴が損なわれるかもしれない。ウィッテンもほぼ同じように感じていたので，彼は長年の間その地図を秘密にしたままだった。

❸ ウィッテンは「ヒストリア・タータロラム」という本の中でビンランド・マップを見つけていた。不思議なことに，ビンランド・マップには虫がつくったいくつかの小さな穴があり，それらの穴は本にあるほかの地図の穴の形と一致しなかった。それからしばらくして，イェール大学に勤めていたトム・マーストンという友人が，似た言葉の載っている同時期の地図をウィッテンに見せた。1 つの地図を借りたとき，ウィッテンはビンランド・マップの穴がイェール大学の地図の穴と完全に一致することを発見した。これは，ビンランド・マップがもともとイェール大学の所有する地図と一緒に 1 冊の本の中に入っていたことを意味した。これによって地図が本物だと彼は確信し，自分の発見を公表する決心をした。

❹ 長年にわたり，歴史家や本の専門家はビンランド・マップについて議論し続けてきた。1974 年に，（地図を描くのに使われた）インクのうち最大で 50％が，1920 年代まで発明されていなかったチタン顔料を含むことがわかった。しかし，1985 年に行われた分析は，チタンがほとんど存在しなかっただけでなく，現代では使われていない，中世に使われたほかの多くのインクも存在したことを明らかにした。しかも，チタン顔料は 1400 年代に遡るグーテンベルク聖書で発見されている。その地図の真正性を裏付けるもう 1 つの確かな証拠は，10 世紀にバイキングは北アメリカに確かに定住しており，500 年近くの間その地域に住み続けていたという考古学者たちの発見である。その考古学的発見と地図自体の様々な分析を考慮すれば，それは本物らしく思われる。しかし，人々はコロンブスが北アメリカを発見したと何世紀にもわたって確信していたことも覚えておかねばならない。

重要語句リスト

❶

☐ Viking	②	バイキング
☐ authentic	⑯	本物の
☐ genuine	⑯	本物の
☐ writing instrument		
	②	筆記具
☐ appropriate to 〜	⑩	〜にふさわしい

❷

☐ be reluctant to *do*		
	⑩	〜したがらない
☐ make 〜 public	⑩	〜を公にする
☐ authenticity	②	真正性, 信頼性
☐ seal of approval	②	承認印
☐ as much	⑩	ちょうどそれだけ, 等しく
☐ controversial	⑯	物議を醸す
☐ ruin	⑩	〜を損なう, 台無しにする

❸

☐ curiously	⑩	不思議なことに
☐ convince	⑩	〜に確信させる

❹

☐ titanium	②	チタン
☐ pigment	②	顔料
☐ medieval times	②	中世
☐ Gutenberg Bible	②	グーテンベルク聖書
☐ date back to 〜	⑩	〜に遡る
☐ archaeologist	②	考古学者
☐ inhabit	⑩	〜に住む
☐ continuously	⑩	絶え間なく

Lesson

13

READING

Lesson 13
要点整理
Paragraph Summary

◀)) 音声 ▶ **L&R_LV5_13-Q**

▶ 音声を聞きながら, ①〜⑥の空欄を埋め, 段落ごとの
要旨を確認しましょう (解答は下部にあります)。

The Vinland Map

❶ ◇ **Larry Witten : discovered an unusual map that contained an image of "Vinland"**

- if the Vinland Map were authentic
  → Norwegian Vikings visited North America before 1492
- the Vinland Map :
  (1) made from animal skin dated to the 1400s
  (2) drawn with writing instruments appropriate to the period
  (3) did not seem to be a fake produced for the sake of profit
  → likely [① a_ _ _ _ _ _ _ _]

❷ ◇ **Witten : reluctant to make his discovery public**

◇ **another book dealer : showed it to two leading experts**

  → both experts believed the map to be [② g_ _ _ _ _ _]

  ↔ admitting as much would be controversial

   + Were the map ultimately discovered to be fake, the experts' careers could be ruined

    → the Vinland Map was kept [③ s_ _ _ _ _] for many years

❸ ◇ **Witten had found the Vinland Map inside a book**

  → the small holes made by insects did not match the shape of the holes in the other maps in the book

◇ **Tom Marston who worked at Yale university showed Witten maps from the same time period**

  → the holes in the Vinland Map [④ m_ _ _ _ _ _ u_] perfectly with the ones in the Yale map

【解答】 ① authentic ② genuine ③ secret ④ matched up

【和訳】

ビンランド・マップ

❶ ◇ ラリー・ウィッテン：「ビンランド」の絵を含む珍しい地図を発見した

- もしビンランド・マップが本物だったら

  → ノルウェーのバイキングが 1492 年より前に北アメリカを訪れた

- ビンランド・マップ：

  (1) 1400 年代の動物の皮でできていた

  (2) その時代にふさわしい筆記具で描かれていた

  (3) 利益目的でつくられた偽物のようには思われなかった

  → 本物の可能性がある

❷ ◇ **ウィッテン：彼の発見を公にするのをためらう**

◇ **ほかの書籍販売者：2 人の一流の専門家にそれを見せた**

  → 2 人の専門家はどちらもその地図が本物であると信じていた

  ↔ そう認めれば物議を醸すだろう

  ＋ もし地図が結局偽物だったとわかれば，専門家の経歴が損なわれる
    かもしれない

  → ビンランド・マップは長年の間秘密にされたままだった

❸ ◇ **ウィッテンはある本の中でビンランド・マップを見つけていた**

  → 虫がつくった小さな穴は，本にあるほかの地図の穴の形と一致しなかった

◇ **イェール大学に勤めていたトム・マーストンが同時期の地図をウィッテン
に見せた**

  → ビンランド・マップの穴がイェール大学の地図の穴と完全に一致した

→ the Vinland Map was in a book together with the maps owned by Yale

→ Witten decided to make his discovery [5] p_ _ _ _ _]

❹ ◇ **historians and book experts : have argued about the Vinland Map**

in 1974	in 1985
• up to 50 percent of the ink : a titanium pigment • titanium pigment was not invented until the 1920s	• the ink : little titanium • titanium pigment has been found in the Gutenberg Bible, which dates back to the 1400s

• another evidence supporting the map's authenticity

  → Vikings : settled in North America in the tenth century

      + [6] i_ _ _ _ _ _ _ _] the area continuously for nearly

    500 years

→ the Vinland Map seems likely to be genuine

→ ビンランド・マップはイェール大学の所有する地図と一緒に1冊の本
　の中に入っていた

→ ウィッテンは自分の発見を公にする決心をした

❹　◇ 歴史家や本の専門家：ビンランド・マップについて議論し続けてきた

1974 年	1985 年
• インクの最大 50%：チタン顔料 • チタン顔料は 1920 年代まで発明されていなかった	• インク：わずかなチタン • チタン顔料は 1400 年代に遡るグーテンベルク聖書で発見されている

• その地図の真正性を裏付けるもう1つの証拠

　→ バイキング：10 世紀に北アメリカに定住した

　　　　　＋500 年近くの間，その地域に住み続けていた

→ ビンランド・マップは本物らしく思われる

速読練習
Sight Translation

 ◀)) 英文音声 ▶L&R_LV5_13-ST

DATE

英語	和訳
The Vinland Map	ビンランド・マップ
❶ In 1957,	1957 年に,
book dealer Larry Witten discovered	ラリー・ウィッテンという書籍販売者が発見した
an unusual map	珍しい地図を
that showed Europe, Africa, and Asia,	ヨーロッパ，アフリカ，アジアを示した,
but it also contained an image of "Vinland,"	しかしそれは「ビンランド」の絵も含んでいた,
the Viking name for North America.	北アメリカでのバイキングの呼び名である。
Although the Vinland Map appeared to have been produced	ビンランド・マップはつくられたようだったが
around the year 1440,	1440 年頃に,
writing on it indicated	それの記述は示した
that the image of Vinland was based	ビンランドの絵は基づいていたと
on a journey there	そこでの旅に
made by Vikings	バイキングによって行われた
around the year 1000.	1000 年頃に。
If the map were authentic,	もしその地図が本物なら,
then Norwegian Vikings had visited	ノルウェーのバイキングが訪れていた
North America	北アメリカを
hundreds of years before	数百年前に
Christopher Columbus "discovered" it	クリストファー・コロンブスが「発見」する
in 1492.	1492 年に。
Witten, an experienced book dealer,	経験豊富な書籍販売者であるウィッテンは,
found no obvious signs	明白な証拠を発見しなかった
that the map might not be genuine.	その地図が本物ではないかもしれないという。
It was made from animal skin	それは動物の皮でできていた
dated to the 1400s	1400 年代の
and was drawn with writing instruments	そして筆記具で描かれていた
appropriate to the period.	その時代にふさわしい。
Furthermore,	そのうえ,
since Witten had purchased the map	ウィッテンは地図を購入したので

for a reasonable price,	手頃な値で,
he did not think	彼は思わなかった
the map was a fake	地図が偽物だと
produced merely for the sake of profit.	単に利益のためにつくられた。
Therefore,	それゆえに,
he decided	彼は判断した
that the map was likely authentic.	地図は本物の可能性があると。
❷ At first,	最初のうちは,
Witten was reluctant	ウィッテンはためらった
to make his discovery public	彼の発見を公にすることを
because he was still not completely sure	彼はまだ完全には確信していなかったので
of the map's authenticity.	その地図の真正性を。
Unknown to him,	彼に知られずに,
however,	しかし,
another book dealer had shown the map	ほかの書籍販売者がその地図を見せていた
to two leading experts	2人の一流の専門家に
at the British Museum.	大英博物館で。
Having the British Museum's seal of approval	大英博物館の承認印があれば
would have been a big help	大いに役立っただろう
in convincing the world	世界中の人々を納得させるのに
that the Vinland Map was real.	ビンランド・マップが本物だと。
Indeed,	実のところ,
both experts believed the map	2人の専門家はどちらもその地図を信じていた
to be genuine,	本物だと,
but they also knew	しかし彼らはまた知っていた
that admitting as much would be controversial.	等しく認めれば物議を醸すだろうと。
Were the map ultimately discovered	もし地図が結局わかれば
to be fake,	偽物だと,
the experts' careers could be ruined.	専門家の経歴が損なわれるかもしれない。
Witten felt much the same,	ウィッテンもほぼ同じように感じていた,
so he kept his map secret	だから彼はその地図を秘密にしたままだった

Lesson
13

for many years.	長年の間。
❸ Witten had found the Vinland Map	ウィッテンはビンランド・マップを見つけていた
inside a book	本の中で
called the *Hystoria Tartarorum*.	「ヒストリア・タータロラム」という。
Curiously,	不思議なことに,
the Vinland Map had	ビンランド・マップにはあった
small holes	小さな穴が
made by insects	虫がつくった
that did not match the shape of the holes	それはその穴の形と一致しなかった
in the other maps in the book.	本にあるほかの地図の。
Sometime later,	それからしばらくして,
a friend named Tom Marston,	トム・マーストンという友人が,
who worked at Yale University,	イェール大学に勤めていた,
showed Witten maps	ウィッテンに地図を見せた
from the same time period	同時期の
with similar words on them.	それらに似た言葉の載っている。
When he borrowed one,	1つの地図を借りたとき,
Witten found	ウィッテンは発見した
that the holes in the Vinland Map	ビンランド・マップの穴が
matched up perfectly	完全に一致すると
with the ones in the Yale map.	イェール大学の地図の穴と。
This indicated	これは意味した
that the Vinland Map had originally been	ビンランド・マップがもともとあったことを
in a book together	一緒に1冊の本の中に
with the maps	その地図と
owned by Yale.	イェール大学に所有される。
This convinced him	これによって彼は確信した
that the map was real,	その地図が本物だと,
and he decided	そして彼は決心した
to make his discovery public.	彼の発見を公表することを。
❹ Over the years,	長年にわたり,
historians and book experts	歴史家や本の専門家は
have argued	議論し続けてきた

about the Vinland Map.	ビンランド・マップについて。
In 1974,	1974 年に,
it was found	わかった
that up to 50 percent of the ink contained	インクのうち最大で 50%が含んでいると
a titanium pigment	チタン顔料を
that had not been invented	発明されていなかった
until the 1920s.	1920 年代まで。
However,	しかし,
an analysis conducted in 1985 revealed	1985 年に行われた分析は明らかにした
that not only was there little titanium,	チタンがほとんど存在しなかっただけでなく,
but also there were many other inks	ほかの多くのインクが存在したこともまた
that were used in medieval times	中世に使われた
but not today.	けれども現在では使われていない。
Furthermore,	しかも,
titanium pigment has been found	チタン顔料は発見されている
in the Gutenberg Bible,	グーテンベルク聖書で,
which dates back to the 1400s.	1400 年代に遡る。
Another solid piece of evidence	もう 1 つの確かな証拠は
supporting the map's authenticity	その地図の真正性を裏付ける
is the discovery	発見である
by archaeologists	考古学者たちの
that Vikings did indeed settle	バイキングは確かに定住していたという
in North America in the tenth century	10 世紀に北アメリカに
and inhabited the area continuously	そしてその地域に住み続けていたという
for nearly 500 years.	500 年近くの間。
Taking into account	考慮すると
the archaeological discoveries	その考古学的発見を
and various analyses of the map itself,	そして地図自体の様々な分析を,
it seems likely to be genuine.	それは本物らしく思われる。
It must be remembered,	覚えておかねばならない,
however,	しかし,
that for centuries people were certain	人々は何世紀にもわたって確信していたことを
that Columbus discovered North America, too.	コロンブスが北アメリカを発見したとも。

Lesson

13

Lesson 14
問題
Questions

W 単 語 数 ▶ 504 語
制限時間 ▶ 15 分
✔ 目標得点 ▶ 30 /40点

DATE

▶次の英文の内容に関して，(1)～(4)の質問に対する最も適切な答え（または文を完成させるのに最も適切なもの）を 1，2，3，4 の中から 1 つ選びなさい。

The Cambridge-Somerville Youth Study

Richard Clarke Cabot was a professor of medicine at Harvard University who wanted to help troubled youth. He became interested in the idea that the environment people grew up in could have an influence on whether they became criminals. In the 1930s, a study conducted on young people who had committed crimes revealed that 88.2 percent were arrested again within the next five years. This depressing statistic motivated Cabot to perform a study of his own to look into the effects of having honest, well-educated people spend time with at-risk youth in order to influence their behavior. It was called the Cambridge-Somerville Youth Study.

Cabot wanted to ensure that his study was performed scientifically. He found 506 boys from poor backgrounds, half of whom were considered "difficult" children and half of whom were considered "average" children. Each of the boys was matched with another boy of a similar age and background. The pairs were then randomly divided into two groups. Social workers were assigned to one of the groups, providing them with aid such as counseling, tutoring, and medical treatment. This group was also sent to summer camps and community programs. The other group received no aid whatsoever. Cabot hoped that by studying the differences between the results of the two groups, he could determine the degree to which the treatment had influenced them.

The study lasted from 1939 until 1945, but the results were extremely disappointing. When they were first analyzed, it was found that the boys who received treatment were no more or less likely to commit crimes than the boys who did not. However, in the 1970s, a sociologist named Joan McCord had the idea that, since the boys were now in their 40s, there was a possibility that positive effects from the study might have been delayed. She contacted as many of the boys as she could find, interviewed them, and analyzed all of the data again, this time using computers and new analysis techniques. This time, in each of the seven categories that she studied, such as alcoholism, mental health, and criminal records, she found that the boys who received aid were, in fact, worse off than the boys who had received no special treatment.

Some critics of social programs say that the Cambridge-Somerville Youth Study is evidence that social programs that try to influence youth do not work. However, there are several theories about why the program backfired. For example, in group counseling sessions and summer camps, boys often told stories about how they had stolen things or drunk alcohol. These actions may have appeared glamorous to the other boys and increased the likelihood that they would engage in the same behaviors. Therefore, perhaps it was not receiving counseling, but rather the type of counseling, that caused problems. Instead of eliminating programs that try to influence young people, defenders of social programs believe that we should conduct new studies that examine whether there are effective techniques that can be used to improve the outcomes for troubled youth.

Lesson

14

Questions ☞

(1) Why did Richard Clarke Cabot first start the Cambridge-Somerville Youth Study?

   1 He wanted to know about the effects of schooling on whether or not people became criminals.

   2 There were not enough statistics about how many young people were being arrested every year.

   3 Evidence showed that youths who had committed crimes were extremely likely to commit them again.

   4 He wanted to know why young people who seemed honest and well-educated were being arrested.

(2) Why were some of the boys not given treatment?

   1 Some of the boys were found not to have any risk of becoming criminals, so they did not need treatment.

   2 Cabot wanted to compare their results with those of the boys who were given treatment.

   3 There were not enough social workers to provide treatment to all of the boys in the study.

   4 It was found that there were few differences between the groups, so treatment for both was not necessary.

(**3**)　What was the difference between the first and second analyses of the Cambridge-Somerville Youth Study?

   1　Although the first study found that the treatment prevented people from committing crimes, the second one found that it had other good effects, too.

   2　The first study failed to include the boys' criminal records, and when they were examined, it showed that there had been a positive effect.

   3　The second study included interviews that revealed that there had been problems in how the first analysis had been carried out.

   4　While the first one indicated that the treatment had not had an effect, the second one indicated the effect had been harmful.

(**4**)　What do defenders of programs that try to influence young people say in response to critics of the Cambridge-Somerville Youth Study?

   1　It may be that it was the methods used to treat the boys that caused the unexpected results of the study.

   2　Although it may not be able to stop young people from drinking or committing crimes, the treatment may have had other less obvious effects.

   3　Because the situation has changed so much since the 1930s, the results of the study are not relevant to the effective techniques used today.

   4　No one knows what really caused the boys' negative behavior, so it was a mistake to stop the study.

Lesson 14

ANSWER		
(**1**) ① ② ③ ④	(**2**)	① ② ③ ④
(**3**) ① ② ③ ④	(**4**)	① ② ③ ④

Answers & Explanations ☞

Lesson 14
解答・解説
Answers & Explanations

□**(1)**　リチャード・クラーク・キャボットが最初にケンブリッジ・サマービル青少年調査を始めたのはなぜか。

1　人々が犯罪者になるかどうかに対する学校教育の効果について知りたかった。

2　毎年どのくらい多くの若者が逮捕されているかについての十分な統計がなかった。

③　証拠は，罪を犯した青少年は再び罪を犯す可能性が極めて高いと示した。

4　誠実で十分な教育を受けたように思える若者がなぜ逮捕されているのかを知りたかった。

解説▶第1段落第4文に This depressing statistic motivated Cabot to perform ... とあるので，前の文に出てくる統計がキャボットの研究の動機だったことがわかる。その統計は若者の再犯率が9割に近いという内容だから，**3**が正解。学校教育や逮捕者の人数などには触れられていないから**1**，**2**は誤り。**4**は第1段落の内容と全く異なるので誤り。

重要語句　□schooling（⑧ 学校教育）

□**(2)**　一部の少年たちに治療が与えられなかったのはなぜか。

1　一部の少年たちは犯罪者になる危険が全くないことがわかったので，治療は必要なかった。

②　キャボットは彼らの結果を，治療を受けた少年たちの結果と比較したかった。

3　研究対象の少年全員に治療を提供できるほど十分な数のソーシャルワーカーがいなかった。

4　グループ間の違いがほとんどないとわかったので，両方に治療をする必要はなかった。

解説▶第2段落の最初の文に「キャボットは自分の研究が科学的に行われていることを保証したかった」とある。その方法として彼は，治療を行うグループと行わないグループとに分けることで治療の成果を客観的に検証しようとした。したがって**2**が正解。分ける必要があったから分けたのであり，**1**，**4**は誤り。**3**の内容は本文中に記述されていないので誤り。

□**(3)**　最初のケンブリッジ・サマービル青少年調査の分析と２番目の分析との間には，どんな違いがあったか。

1　最初の研究から治療は人々が罪を犯すのを防ぐことがわかったが，２番目の研究からほかの良い効果もあることがわかった。

2　最初の研究は少年たちの犯罪歴を含まず，それが詳細に調べられたときプラスの効果があったことがわかった。

3　２番目の研究はインタビューを含んでおり，そのインタビューで最初の分析の実施方法に問題があったことが明らかになった。

④　最初の分析は治療に効果がなかったことを示していたが，２番目の分析で影響が有害だったことがわかった。

解説▶第３段落の第２文と最後の文の内容に合う**4**が正解。最初の研究では２つのグループの間に有意な差は見られなかったことがわかるので，**1**は誤り。２番目の研究からは治療がマイナスの影響を与えたことがわかったので，**2**は誤り。**3**の内容は本文中に記述されていないので誤り。

□**(4)**　若者に影響を与えようとするプログラムを擁護する人々は，ケンブリッジ・サマービル青少年調査の批判者に応えて何と言っているか。

①　研究の予期せぬ結果を引き起こしたのは，少年を治療するために利用された方法だったかもしれない。

2　若者の飲酒や犯罪を止めることはできないかもしれないが，治療にはそれに比べて目立たない別の効果があったかもしれない。

3　状況は1930年代から大きく変化しているので，その研究の結果は現在利用されている効果的な技術とは関係がない。

4　少年たちの好ましくない行動の本当の原因を誰も知らないので，研究をやめたことは誤りだった。

解説▶第４段落第５文に「**問題を引き起こしたのは，カウンセリングを受けることではなくむしろカウンセリングの種類だったのかもしれない**」とあるので，**1**が正解。この文はit was not A but B that ...（…なのはAではなくBだ）という形の強調構文である。ほかの選択肢の内容は本文中に記述されていないので誤り。

Lesson **14**

ANSWER		SCORE	CHECK YOUR LEVEL
(1) ① ② ❸ ④　**(2)** ① ❷ ③ ④		╱40点 (4問×各10点)	0〜20点 ➡ *Work harder!* 21〜30点 ➡ *OK!* 31〜40点 ➡ *Way to go!*
(3) ① ② ③ ❹　**(4)** ❶ ② ③ ④			

[和訳]
ケンブリッジ・サマービル青少年調査

❶ リチャード・クラーク・キャボットは問題を抱えた青少年を助けたいと思ったハーバード大学医学部の教授であった。彼は人々が育った環境が犯罪者になるかどうかに影響を与える可能性があるという考えに興味をもった。1930年代に罪を犯した若者を対象にして行われた研究によって，その後の5年以内に88.2%が再び逮捕されたことが明らかになった。この憂うつな統計はキャボットを触発し，キャボットは若者の行動に影響を与えるため，誠実で十分な教育を受けた人々に，危険にさらされている［非行化のおそれがある］青少年とともに時を過ごしてもらうことの効果を調査する自らの研究を行った。それは「ケンブリッジ・サマービル青少年調査」と呼ばれた。

❷ キャボットは，自分の研究が科学的に行われていることを保証したかった。彼は，貧しい生い立ちの506人の少年を見つけ，その半分は「あつかいにくい」子どもたちとみなされ，あとの半分は「平均的な」子どもたちとみなされた。それぞれの少年は年齢や生い立ちが同じ，ほかの1人の少年と組まされた。次にそのペアは無作為に2つのグループに分けられた。ソーシャルワーカーはグループの1つに割り当てられ，彼らにカウンセリング，個別指導，医療といった援助を提供した。このグループはまた夏季キャンプやコミュニティープログラムへ派遣された。もう一方のグループは一切の援助を受けなかった。キャボットは，2つのグループの結果の違いを研究することによって，治療が彼らに与えた影響の度合いを判断できると期待した。

❸ 研究は1939年から1945年まで続いたが，その結果は全くの期待外れだった。それらが最初に分析されたとき，治療を受けた少年たちは，治療を受けなかった少年たちに比べて，罪を犯す可能性が高くも低くもないことがわかった。しかし1970年代に，ジョーン・マッコードという社会学者が，少年たちは今では40代になっているので，研究による好影響が遅れて（出て）いる可能性があるという考えをもった。彼女は発見できたうち，できる限り多くの少年に連絡を取り，彼らにインタビューを行い，このときはコンピューターと新しい分析技術を使ってすべてのデータを再び分析した。今度は，アルコール依存症，精神的健康，犯罪歴など，彼女が研究した7つの分野のそれぞれにおいて，実際のところ，援助を受けた少年たちは，特別な治療を一切受けなかった少年たちよりも悪いことがわかった。

❹ 社会プログラムの批判者の中には，ケンブリッジ・サマービル青少年調査は，青少年に影響を与えようとする社会プログラムに効果がないということの証拠だと言う人もいる。しかし，そのプログラムが裏目に出た理由についてはいくつかの理論がある。例えば集団カウンセリング会や夏季キャンプでは，少年たちは自分がどのようにしてものを盗んだり酒を飲んだりしたかについての話をよくした。このような行動がほかの少年たちにとっては魅力的に見え，彼らが同じ行動を取る可能性を高めたのかもしれない。したがって，もしかしたら問題を引き起こしたのは，カウンセリングを受けることではなくむしろカウンセリングの種類だったのかもしれない。若者に影響を与えようとするプログラムを撤廃する代わりに，問題を抱えた青少年にとっての結果を改善するのに利用できる効果的な技術があるかどうかを調べる新しい研究を行うべきだと，そうした社会プログラムを擁護する人々は信じている。

重要語句リスト

❶

☐ commit a crime	勵 罪を犯す
☐ reveal	動 ～を明らかにする
☐ arrest	動 ～を逮捕する
☐ depressing	形 憂うつな，気のめいるような
☐ motivate O to *do*	勵 O を～する気にさせる
☐ at-risk	形 危険にさらされている

❷

☐ ensure	動 ～を保証する，確実にする
☐ randomly	副 無作為に
☐ social worker	名 ソーシャルワーカー，社会福祉指導員
☐ be assigned to ～	勵 ～に割り当てられる
☐ tutoring	名 個別指導
☐ no ～ whatsoever	勵 全く～ない

❸

☐ sociologist	名 社会学者
☐ alcoholism	名 アルコール依存症
☐ criminal record	名 犯罪歴

❹

☐ backfire	動 裏目に出る
☐ glamorous	形 魅力的な
☐ eliminate	動 ～を取り除く，撤廃する

READING

Lesson 14

要点整理

Paragraph Summary

◀)) 音声 ▶ **L&R_LV5_14-Q**

▶音声を聞きながら、①～⑧の空欄を埋め、段落ごとの
要旨を確認しましょう（解答は下部にあります）。

The Cambridge-Somerville Youth Study

❶ ◇ **Richard Clarke Cabot became interested in the idea that**

• the [① e_____] people grew up in

→ could have an influence on whether they became criminals

◇ **in the 1930s**

• a study : many young people who had committed crimes were

[② a_____] again

→ Cabot performed a study about the effects of having honest, well-

educated people spend time with at-risk youth

= the Cambridge-Somerville Youth Study

❷ ◇ **Cabot wanted to ensure that his study was performed scientifically**

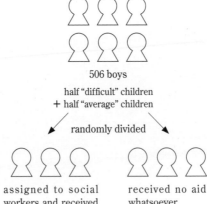

506 boys

half "difficult" children
+ half "average" children

randomly divided

assigned to social
workers and received
aid

received no aid
whatsoever

【解答】　① environment　② arrested

190

【和訳】

ケンブリッジ・サマービル青少年調査

❶　◇ リチャード・クラーク・キャボットは考えに興味をもった

- 人々が育った環境

→ 犯罪者になるかどうかに影響を与える可能性がある

◇ 1930 年代

- 研究：罪を犯した多くの若者は再び逮捕された

→ キャボットは誠実で十分な教育を受けた人々に，非行化のおそれがある
青少年とともに時を過ごしてもらうことの効果について研究を行った

= ケンブリッジ・サマービル青少年調査

❷　◇ キャボットは自分の研究が科学的に行われていることを保証したかった

506 人の少年

半分の「あつかいにくい」子どもたち
+ 半分の「平均的な」子どもたち

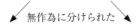無作為に分けられた

ソーシャルワーカーに割り
当てられ，援助を受けた

一切の援助を受けな
かった

→ Cabot hoped：studying the [③ d_____] between the two groups

        → could determine the degree to which the treatment had influenced them

❸ ◇ **the study from 1939 until 1945**

  → the results = disappointing

   • the boys who received treatment were no more or less likely to [④ c_____ c_____] than the boys who did not

◇ **in the 1970s**

   • Joan McCord had an idea：
positive effects from the study might have been [⑤ d_____]

    → interviewed the boys

    → the boys who received aid were [⑥ w____ o__] than the boys who had received no special treatment

❹ ◇ **some critics say**

   • the Cambridge-Somerville Youth Study
= evidence that social programs do not work

  ↔ several theories about why the program backfired

   • boys in group counseling sessions and summer camps told stories about how they had stolen things or drunk alcohol

    → increased the likelihood of the same behavior

  → receiving counseling < the [⑦ t___] of counseling = problems

  → we should conduct new studies about [⑧ e_____] techniques to improve the outcomes for troubled youth

---

【解答】　③ differences　④ commit crimes　⑤ delayed　⑥ worse off　⑦ type　⑧ effective

→キャボットは期待した：2つのグループの違いを研究すること

→治療が彼らに与えた影響の度合いを判断できる

❸　◇ **1939 年から 1945 年までの研究**

→結果 ＝ 期待外れ

- 治療を受けた少年たちは，治療を受けなかった少年たちに比べて，罪を犯す可能性が高くも低くもなかった

◇ **1970 年代**

- ジョーン・マッコードには考えがあった：

研究による好影響が遅れて（出て）いるかもしれない

→少年たちにインタビューを行った

→援助を受けた少年たちは，特別な治療を一切受けなかった少年たちよりも（結果が）悪かった

❹　◇ **批判者たちは言う**

- ケンブリッジ・サマービル青少年調査

＝ 社会プログラムには効果がないということの証拠

↔プログラムが裏目に出た理由についてのいくつかの理論

- 集団カウンセリング会や夏季キャンプでの少年たちは，自分がどのようにしてものを盗んだり酒を飲んだりしたかについての話をした

→同じ行動を取る可能性を高めた

→カウンセリングを受けること ＜ カウンセリングの種類 ＝ 問題

→問題を抱えた青少年にとっての結果を改善する効果的な技術についての新しい研究を行うべき

Lesson
14

193

英語	和訳
The Cambridge-Somerville Youth Study	ケンブリッジ・サマービル青少年調査
❶ Richard Clarke Cabot was a professor of medicine at Harvard University	リチャード・クラーク・キャボットはハーバード大学医学部の教授だった
who wanted to help	助けたいと思った
troubled youth.	問題を抱えた青少年を。
He became interested in the idea	彼は考えに興味をもった
that the environment	環境が
people grew up in	人々が育った
could have an influence	影響を与える可能性があるという
on whether they became criminals.	犯罪者になるかどうかに。
In the 1930s,	1930年代に,
a study	研究は
conducted on young people	若者を対象にして行われた
who had committed crimes	罪を犯した
revealed	明らかにした
that 88.2 percent were arrested again	88.2%が再び逮捕されたことを
within the next five years.	その後の5年以内に。
This depressing statistic motivated Cabot	この憂うつな統計はキャボットを触発し
to perform a study of his own	自らの研究を行うよう
to look into the effects	効果を調査する
of having honest, well-educated people	誠実で, 十分な教育を受けた人々に
spend time	時を過ごしてもらうことの
with at-risk youth	危険にさらされている [非行化のおそれがある] 青少年とともに
in order to influence their behavior.	彼らの行動に影響を与えるために。
It was called	それは〜と呼ばれた
the Cambridge-Somerville Youth Study.	「ケンブリッジ・サマービル青少年調査」と。
❷ Cabot wanted to ensure	キャボットは保証したかった
that his study was performed scientifically.	自分の研究が科学的に行われていることを。
He found 506 boys	彼は, 506人の少年を見つけた

from poor backgrounds,	貧しい生い立ちの,
half of whom were considered "difficult" children	その半分は「あつかいにくい」子どもたちとみなされ
and half of whom were considered "average" children.	あとの半分は「平均的な」子どもたちとみなされた。
Each of the boys was matched	それぞれの少年は組まされた
with another boy	ほかの1人の少年と
of a similar age and background.	年齢や生い立ちが同じ。
The pairs were then randomly divided into two groups.	そのペアは次に無作為に分けられた2つのグループに。
Social workers were assigned	ソーシャルワーカーは割り当てられ
to one of the groups,	グループの1つに,
providing them with aid	彼らに援助を提供した
such as counseling, tutoring, and medical treatment.	カウンセリング, 個別指導, 医療のような。
This group was also sent	このグループはまた派遣された
to summer camps and community programs.	夏季キャンプやコミュニティープログラムへ。
The other group received no aid whatsoever.	もう一方のグループは一切の援助を受けなかった。
Cabot hoped	キャボットは期待した
that by studying the differences	違いを研究することによって
between the results of the two groups,	2つのグループの結果の,
he could determine the degree	度合いを判断できると
to which the treatment	治療が
had influenced them.	彼らに与えた影響の。
❸ The study lasted	研究は続いた
from 1939 until 1945,	1939年から1945年まで,
but the results were extremely disappointing.	しかしその結果は全くの期待外れだった。
When they were first analyzed,	それらが最初に分析されたとき,
it was found	わかった
that the boys who received treatment	治療を受けた少年たちは
were no more or less likely to commit crimes	罪を犯す可能性が高くも低くもないと
than the boys who did not.	治療を受けなかった少年たちに比べて。

Lesson **14**

195

However,	しかし,
in the 1970s,	1970年代に,
a sociologist	社会学者が
named Joan McCord	ジョーン・マッコードという
had the idea that,	考えをもった,
since the boys were now	少年たちは今ではなっているので
in their 40s,	40代に,
there was a possibility	可能性があるという
that positive effects from the study	研究による好影響が
might have been delayed.	遅れて(出て)いるかもしれない。
She contacted as many of the boys	彼女はできる限り多くの少年に連絡を取り
as she could find,	彼女が発見できた,
interviewed them,	彼らにインタビューを行い,
and analyzed all of the data again,	すべてのデータを再び分析した,
this time	このときは
using computers and new analysis techniques.	コンピューターと新しい分析技術を使って。
This time,	今度は,
in each of the seven categories	7つの分野のそれぞれにおいて
that she studied,	彼女が研究した,
such as alcoholism,	アルコール依存症,
mental health,	精神的健康,
and criminal records,	犯罪歴など,
she found	彼女はわかった
that the boys who received aid were,	援助を受けた少年たちは,
in fact,	実際のところ,
worse off than the boys	少年たちよりも悪いと
who had received no special treatment.	特別な治療を一切受けなかった。
❹ Some critics of social programs say	社会プログラムの批判者の中には～と言う人もいる
that the Cambridge-Somerville Youth Study	ケンブリッジ・サマービル青少年調査は
is evidence	証拠だと,
that social programs	社会プログラムには
that try to influence youth	青少年に影響を与えようとする
do not work.	効果がないという。

However,	しかし,
there are several theories	いくつかの理論がある
about why the program backfired.	そのプログラムが裏目に出た理由については。
For example,	例えば,
in group counseling sessions	集団カウンセリング会や
and summer camps,	夏季キャンプでは,
boys often told stories	少年たちは話をよくした
about how they had stolen things	彼らがどのようにしてものを盗んだかについて
or drunk alcohol.	もしくは酒を飲んだりしたかについて。
These actions may have appeared	このような行動が魅力的に見えたのかもし
glamorous	れない
to the other boys	ほかの少年たちにとっては
and increased the likelihood	そして可能性を高めたのかもしれない
that they would engage	彼らが携わる
in the same behaviors.	同じ行動に。
Therefore,	したがって,
perhaps it was not receiving counseling,	もしかしたらカウンセリングを受けることではなく,
but rather the type of counseling,	むしろカウンセリングの種類だったのかもしれない,
that caused problems.	問題を引き起こしたのは。
Instead of eliminating programs	プログラムを撤廃する代わりに
that try to influence young people,	若者に影響を与えようとする,
defenders of social programs believe	社会プログラムを擁護する人々は信じている
that we should conduct new studies	私たちが新しい研究を行うべきだと
that examine	調べる
whether there are effective techniques	効果的な技術があるかどうかを
that can be used	利用できる
to improve the outcomes	結果を改善するのに
for troubled youth.	問題を抱えた青少年にとって。

Lesson
14

READING

Lesson 15
問題
Questions

W 単 語 数 ▶ 512 語
🕐 制限時間 ▶ 15 分
✅ 目標得点 ▶ 30 /40点

DATE

▶次の英文の内容に関して, (1)～(4)の質問に対する最も適切な答え (または文を完成させるのに最も適切なもの) を 1, 2, 3, 4 の中から 1 つ選びなさい。

SWAT Teams

On August 1, 1966, a mentally ill man named Charles Whitman climbed to the top of the clock tower at the University of Texas and began shooting innocent people with a high-powered rifle, killing 14 and wounding 32 more. Not only was the incident both shocking and tragic, but it also caused outrage because local police had been unable to handle the situation. Lacking the weapons and training of soldiers, they could not carry out their duty of protecting local citizens from Whitman. This, combined with other notable incidents such as riots in which thousands of people became violent, started fires, and destroyed public property, led to the creation of what are known as Special Weapons and Tactics (SWAT) teams in major American cities.

Armed with automatic weapons and sniper rifles, SWAT teams were originally deployed to rescue kidnapping victims, stop terrorists, and handle violent confrontations with criminals, among other high-risk missions. SWAT teams were often regarded as heroes. During the 1980s, however, President Ronald Reagan called for a "War on Drugs," making strict laws that significantly increased penalties for selling and using illegal drugs. Ordinary police, fearing for their lives when they tried to arrest drug dealers, increasingly called for the use of SWAT teams when entering buildings where people were thought to be selling drugs. Soon, the media began reporting about SWAT teams accidentally entering the houses of innocent people and frightening the children in neighboring houses when they were on such missions. As they became more heavily armed and used more aggressive methods, many people came to believe that the actions of SWAT teams were getting out of hand.

In 1980, SWAT teams were deployed about 3,000 times. Now they are used about 50,000 times a year. In some high-crime areas, SWAT teams even patrol the area every day. However, whether local police are able to obtain the trust and cooperation of local citizens may be one of the main factors in determining whether crimes get solved or not. If SWAT teams become a source of fear in the local community, it can completely alter the relationship between a police force and the people it strives to protect. The result is that when crimes are committed, citizens may not be as willing to cooperate.

Ever since the 2001 attacks on the United States by the terrorist organization known as Al-Qaeda, the government has been trying to upgrade the abilities of its police to deal with terrorist threats. Not only has it been increasing funding for SWAT teams, but it has also been encouraging the military to give them weapons and equipment. However, critics point out that the military's role is to cause maximum damage to enemy forces. In contrast, the duty of police in a democratic society is to protect and serve the community using the minimum of force necessary. Critics fear that, while protecting citizens from terrorism is an admirable goal, the current trend may be dangerous if it leads to police abandoning the principles they have operated under in the past to become more like the military.

Lesson
15

Questions ☞

(**1**) Why were many people angry about the incident involving Charles Whitman?

    1 There was a long delay before soldiers were sent in to stop Whitman from killing people.

    2 The SWAT team that was sent in to stop Whitman killed some innocent people by accident.

    3 The local police were unable to deal with the heavily armed Whitman in an effective way.

    4 There were rules that prevented the SWAT team from entering the university and arresting Whitman.

(**2**) How did people's attitudes about SWAT teams change in the 1980s?

    1 People became thankful that SWAT teams were protecting innocent children from the threat of drugs.

    2 People started to worry that SWAT teams were causing problems by doing things beyond the scope of their original purpose.

    3 People thought that SWAT teams were not equipped with the necessary equipment to carry out their duties effectively.

    4 People became angry that SWAT team members had been caught selling the same types of drugs they were arresting people for using.

(**3**) What effect do experts think SWAT teams could have on their communities?

1 Because SWAT teams are being used more but have become less successful in stopping crimes, people have come to see them as less useful.

2 By spending time in high-crime areas, SWAT teams are able to frighten criminals and prevent crimes.

3 Because SWAT teams make people realize there are serious crimes happening around them, they could increase cooperation by individuals.

4 By changing the public's attitude to the police in their communities, SWAT teams could make it more difficult for the police to stop crimes.

(**4**) Some critics fear that since the 2001 Al-Qaeda terrorist attacks,

1 police have begun to be encouraged to take on a role that is not suitable in a democratic society.

2 although they have improved their weapons and training, police are still not ready to deal with the terrorist threat.

3 police have put so much effort into stopping terrorism that they have ignored crimes that are occurring in their communities.

4 the physical damage that has been done to communities during police missions has increased.

Lesson **15**

ANSWER		
(**1**) ① ② ③ ④	(**2**) ① ② ③ ④	
(**3**) ① ② ③ ④	(**4**) ① ② ③ ④	

Answers & Explanations ☞

Lesson 15
解答・解説
Answers & Explanations

青文字＝設問・選択肢の和訳　赤文字＝正解

□（**1**）　なぜ多くの人々はチャールズ・ホイットマンが関与した事件について怒ったのか。

    1　ホイットマンの殺人を止めるために兵士が送り込まれるのが大幅に遅れた。

    2　ホイットマンを止めるために送り込まれた SWAT チームが，罪のない人々を誤って殺した。

    ③　地元警察は，重装備したホイットマンに効果的に対処できなかった。

    4　SWAT チームが大学に入ってホイットマンを逮捕することを妨げる規則があった。

解説▶第1段落第2〜3文に，「地元警察が状況に対処できなかったために暴動も引き起こした」「武器と兵士の訓練が足りず，警察はホイットマンから地元住民を守るという義務を遂行することができなかった」とあることから考えて，**3** が正解。**1**，**4** の内容は本文中に記述されていないので誤り。**2** についても事件は SWAT チームが創設される前なので誤り。

重要語句　□ involve（動 〜を関与させる）

□（**2**）　1980 年代に，SWAT チームに関する人々の態度はどのように変化したか。

    1　SWAT チームが薬物の脅威から無実の子どもを守っていることに，人々は感謝するようになった。

    ②　SWAT チームが彼らの元来の目的の範囲を超えたことをして問題を起こしていることを，人々は心配し始めた。

    3　SWAT チームは彼らの職務を効果的に実行するために必要な装備を備えていないと人々は思った。

    4　SWAT チームのメンバーたちが，その使用のために人々を逮捕しているのと同じタイプの薬物を売っていたことに人々は怒った。

解説▶第2段落より，SWAT チームは元来，誘拐された被害者を救助し，テロリストを阻止し，犯罪者との暴力的衝突に対処するために配置された。しかし，違法薬物の売買の捜査にまで行動範囲が広がり，その手法も過激になったことで人々は不安になったとわかる。その内容に合う **2** が正解。ほかの選択肢は第2段落の内容と合わないので誤り。

□（**3**）　SWAT チームは地域社会にどんな影響を与えうると専門家は考えているか。

1 SWAT チームの利用機会は増えているが，犯罪防止の成功率が下がったので，人々は彼らが以前ほど役に立たないとみなすようになっている。

2 SWAT チームは犯罪多発地域で時間を過ごすことで，犯罪者を怖がらせ，犯罪を防ぐことができる。

3 SWAT チームは自分のまわりで深刻な犯罪が起きていることを人々に気づかせるので，個人による協力を増やせそうだ。

④ 地域内で警察に対する大衆の態度を変えることによって，SWAT チームは警察が犯罪を防止するのをより難しくするかもしれない。

解説▶第2段落の最後の文と第3段落の最後の2文では，SWAT チームの重装備化と捜査方法の過激化が進んで市民が彼らを怖がるようになると，市民は警察に協力する気にならないかもしれないという懸念が述べられている。したがって **4** が正解。**3** はその反対の内容なので誤り。**1**，**2** の内容は本文中に記述されていないので誤り。

□ **(4)** 2001 年のアルカイダのテロ攻撃以来，……とおそれる評論家もいる。

① 警察が民主主義社会に適さない役割を引き受けるよう促され始めている

2 警察は武器や訓練を改良しているが，テロリストの脅威に対処する準備がまだできていない

3 警察はテロ行為を止めるために大変な努力をしているので，自分の地域で起こっている犯罪を無視してきた

4 警察の任務中の地域に対する物理的損害が増加している

解説▶第4段落の第3文以降の内容から考えて，**1** が正解。SWAT チームを含む警察が，元来の職務の範囲を超えて軍隊のようになってしまうと，民主主義社会にとって危険な存在になりかねないというのが本文の趣旨である。ほかの選択肢の内容は第4段落の内容に合わないため誤り。

Lesson 15

重要語句 □ take on a role（熟 役割を担う）　□ put effort into ～（熟 ～するよう努力する）

ANSWER		SCORE	CHECK YOUR LEVEL
(1) ① ② ③ ④　**(2)** ① ② ③ ④		／40点	0～20点 ➡ *Work harder!*
			21～30点 ➡ *OK!*
(3) ① ② ③ ④　**(4)** ① ② ③ ④		(4問×各10点)	31～40点 ➡ *Way to go!*

【和訳】

SWATチーム

❶ 1966年8月1日に，チャールズ・ホイットマンという名の精神疾患のある男性がテキサス大学の時計塔の頂上に登り，高性能ライフルで罪のない人々を撃ち始め，14人が死亡し32人以上が負傷した。事件は衝撃的で悲惨だっただけではなく，地元警察が状況に対処できなかったために暴動も引き起こした。武器と兵士の訓練が足りず，警察はホイットマンから地元住民を守るという義務を遂行することができなかった。この事件，および数千人が暴徒と化して火をおこし公共財を破壊した暴動などほかの有名な事件が相まって，アメリカの主要都市での特別機動隊（SWAT）チームとして知られる組織の創設につながった。

❷ 自動小銃や狙撃銃で武装して，SWATチームは元来，ほかの危険性の高い使命の中でも特に，誘拐された被害者を救助し，テロリストを阻止し，犯罪者との暴力的衝突に対処するために配置された。SWATチームはしばしば英雄とみなされた。また一方，1980年代に，ロナルド・レーガン大統領は違法薬物の販売と使用に対する罰を大いに強化する厳しい法律をつくって，「薬物撲滅運動」を呼びかけた。薬物の密売人を逮捕しようとする際の命の危険をおそれた一般警察は，薬物の販売が行われていると思われる建物に入る際には，ますますSWATチームを使うよう求めた。まもなくマスコミは，彼らがそのような任務を負っている際に，無実の人々の家に誤って侵入し，隣家の子どもたちを怖がらせたSWATチームのことを報道し始めた。彼らがより重装備になり，より攻撃的な方法を使うにつれて，多くの人々はSWATチームの行動が制御不能になりつつあると思うようになった。

❸ 1980年に，SWATチームは約3,000回配置された。現在彼らは1年に約50,000回利用される。一部の犯罪多発地域では，SWATチームは毎日その地域を巡回さえしている。しかし地元警察が地元住民の信頼と協力を得られるかどうかは，犯罪が解決されるかどうかを決定づける大きな要因の1つになるかもしれない。もしSWATチームが地域社会で脅威の元凶となれば，警察部隊とそれが守ろうと励む人々との関係を完全に変化させうる。結果として，犯罪が起きた際に市民は，以前ほど進んで協力する気にならないかもしれない。

❹ アルカイダとして知られるテロリスト組織による2001年のアメリカへの攻撃以来，政府はテロリストの脅威に対処するために警察の能力を向上させようとしている。政府はSWATチームへの財政支援を増やすだけでなく，武器や装備を彼らに与えるよう軍に促してもいる。しかし評論家たちは，軍の役割は敵軍に最大の損害を与えることだと指摘している。一方，民主主義社会における警察の義務は，最低限必要な力を使って地域を守り，地域に尽くすことである。テロ行為から市民を守ることは立派な目標だがそれによって警察が過去に守っていた行動原理を捨てて，より軍隊のようになることにつながるなら，現在の傾向は危険かもしれないと評論家たちはおそれている。

重要語句リスト

❶

☐ high-powered rifle
　　　　　　　　　　 ⑧ 高性能ライフル
☐ outrage　　　　　⑧ 暴動
☐ handle　　　　　 ⑩ ～に対処する
☐ combined with ～
　　　　　　　　　　 ⑰ ～と相まって
☐ notable　　　　　⑯ 有名な
☐ riot　　　　　　　⑧ 暴動
☐ public property　⑧ 公共財

❷

☐ armed with ～　⑰ ～で武装して
☐ automatic weapon
　　　　　　　　　　 ⑧ 自動小銃
☐ sniper rifle　　　⑧ 狙撃銃
☐ kidnapping　　　⑧ 誘拐
☐ mission　　　　　⑧ 使命，任務
☐ call for ～　　　 ⑰ ～を呼びかける，求める
☐ illegal drug　　 ⑧ 違法薬物
☐ arrest　　　　　 ⑩ ～を逮捕する
☐ dealer　　　　　⑧ 売人
☐ aggressive　　　⑯ 攻撃的な
☐ get out of hand ⑰ 手に負えなくなる

❸

☐ high-crime area ⑧ 犯罪多発地域
☐ police force　　 ⑧ 警察部隊

❹

☐ upgrade　　　　⑩ ～を向上する
☐ funding　　　　 ⑧ 財政的支援，資金提供
☐ admirable　　　⑯ 立派な
☐ abandon　　　　⑩ ～を捨てる

Lesson
15

SWAT Teams

❶ ◇ **on August 1, 1966**

- a mentally ill man named Charles Whitman：
  killed 14 and wounded 32 more
  → local police could not handle the situation
- lacking the weapons and training of soldiers
  → local police could not carry out their duty of [① p_____]
    local citizens
  → the [② c_____] of SWAT teams

❷ ◇ **SWAT teams were originally** [③ d_____]

(1) to rescue kidnapping victims

(2) to stop terrorists

(3) to handle violent confrontations with criminals

◇ **during the 1980s**

- President Ronald Reagan called for a "War on Drugs," making strict laws for selling and using illegal drugs
  → ordinary police called for the use of SWAT teams when entering buildings where people were thought to be selling drugs
  → SWAT teams：entering the houses of innocent people + frightening children
- SWAT teams：became more heavily armed and used more aggressive methods
  → people came to believe：
    the actions of SWAT teams = getting [④ o__ o_ h___]

【解答】 ① protecting ② creation ③ deployed ④ out of hand

206

【和訳】

SWAT チーム

❶ ◇ **1966 年 8 月 1 日**

- チャールズ・ホイットマンという名の精神疾患のある男性：

  14 人を死亡させ 32 人以上を負傷させた

  → 地元警察はその状況に対処できなかった

- 武器と兵士の訓練の不足

  → 地元警察は地元住民を守るという義務を遂行することができな

  かった

  → 特別機動隊（SWAT）チームの創設

❷ ◇ **SWAT チームが配置されたのは元来**

(1) 誘拐された被害者を救助するため

(2) テロリストを阻止するため

(3) 犯罪者との暴力的衝突に対処するため

◇ **1980 年代**

- ロナルド・レーガン大統領は，違法薬物の販売と使用に対する厳しい

  法律をつくって「薬物撲滅運動」を呼びかけた

  → 一般警察は，薬物の販売が行われていると思われる建物に入る際に

  は，SWAT チームを使うよう求めた

  → SWAT チーム：無実の人々の家に侵入する ＋ 子どもたちを怖がら

  せる

- SWAT チーム：より重装備になり，より攻撃的な方法を使った

  → 人々は思うようになった：

  SWAT チームの行動 ＝ 制御不能になりつつある

Lesson

15

❸ ◇ **SWAT teams were deployed**

- in 1980 : about 3,000 times a year
- now : about 50,000 times a year
  → in some high-crime areas : patrol every day

◇ **cooperation of local citizens = one of the main factors in solving crimes**

- if SWAT teams become a source of [5 f___]
  → citizens may not be as willing to cooperate

❹ ◇ **the United States government**

(1) increasing funding for SWAT teams

(2) encouraging the military to give SWAT teams weapons and [6 e_____]

→ trying to upgrade the abilities of its police to deal with terrorist threats

◇ **critics**

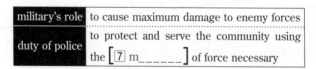

military's role	to cause maximum damage to enemy forces
duty of police	to protect and serve the community using the [7 m_____] of force necessary

- the current trend = dangerous
  ← police abandon the principles + become more like the military

❸　◇ **SWAT チームは配置された**

　　• 1980 年：1 年に約 3,000 回

　　• 現在：1 年に約 50,000 回

　　　→ 一部の犯罪多発地域：毎日巡回している

　◇ **地元住民の協力 ＝ 犯罪を解決する大きな要因の 1 つ**

　　• もし SWAT チームが脅威の元凶となれば

　　　→ 市民は以前ほど進んで協力する気にならないかもしれない

❹　◇ **アメリカ政府**

　　⑴ SWAT チームへの財政支援を増やす

　　⑵ 武器や装備を SWAT チームに与えるよう軍に促す

　　→ テロリストの脅威に対処するために警察の能力を向上させようとしている

　◇ **評論家たち**

軍の役割	敵軍に最大の損害を与えること
警察の義務	最低限必要な力を使って地域を守り，地域に尽くすこと

　　• 現在の傾向 ＝ 危険

　　　← 警察が行動原理を捨てる ＋ より軍隊のようになる

Lesson
15

Lesson 15
速読練習
Sight Translation

◀)) 英文音声 ▶**L&R_LV5_15-ST**

英語	和訳
SWAT Teams	**SWAT チーム**
❶ On August 1, 1966,	1966 年 8 月 1 日に，
a mentally ill man	精神疾患のある男性が
named Charles Whitman	チャールズ・ホイットマンという名の
climbed	登り
to the top of the clock tower	時計塔の頂上に
at the University of Texas	テキサス大学の
and began shooting	そして撃ち始め
innocent people	罪のない人々を
with a high-powered rifle,	高性能ライフルで，
killing 14 and wounding 32 more.	14 人を死亡させ 32 人以上を負傷させた。
Not only was the incident both shocking and tragic,	事件は衝撃的で悲惨だっただけではなく，
but it also caused outrage	暴動も引き起こした
because local police had been unable to handle	地元警察が対処できなかったために
the situation.	その状況に。
Lacking the weapons and training of soldiers,	武器と兵士の訓練が足りず，
they could not carry out	彼らは遂行できなかった
their duty	彼らの義務を
of protecting local citizens	地元住民を守るという
from Whitman.	ホイットマンから。
This,	これは，
combined with other notable incidents	ほかの有名な事件と相まって
such as riots	暴動などの
in which thousands of people became violent,	数千人が暴徒と化して，
started fires,	火をおこし，
and destroyed public property,	そして公共財を破壊した，
led to the creation	創設につながった
of what are known as Special Weapons and Tactics (SWAT) teams	特別機動隊 (SWAT) チームとして知られる

in major American cities.	アメリカの主要都市での。
❷ Armed with automatic weapons and sniper rifles,	自動小銃や狙撃銃で武装して，
SWAT teams were originally deployed	SWAT チームは元来，配置された
to rescue kidnapping victims,	誘拐された被害者を救助し，
stop terrorists,	テロリストを阻止し，
and handle violent confrontations with criminals,	犯罪者との暴力的衝突に対処するために，
among other high-risk missions.	ほかの危険性の高い使命の中でも特に。
SWAT teams were often regarded	SWAT チームはしばしばみなされた
as heroes.	英雄と。
During the 1980s,	1980 年代に，
however,	しかし，
President Ronald Reagan called for	ロナルド・レーガン大統領は呼びかけた
a "War on Drugs,"	「薬物撲滅運動」を，
making strict laws	厳しい法律をつくって
that significantly increased penalties	罰を大いに強化する
for selling and using illegal drugs.	違法薬物の販売と使用に対する。
Ordinary police,	一般警察は，
fearing for their lives	命の危険をおそれた
when they tried to arrest	逮捕しようとする際の
drug dealers,	薬物の密売人を，
increasingly called for the use of SWAT teams	ますます SWAT チームを使うよう求めた
when entering buildings	建物に入る際には
where people were thought	人々が思われる
to be selling drugs.	薬物の販売が行われていると。
Soon,	まもなく，
the media began reporting	マスコミは報道し始めた
about SWAT teams	SWAT チームについて
accidentally entering the houses	家に誤って侵入し
of innocent people	無実の人々の
and frightening the children	そして子どもたちを怖がらせた
in neighboring houses	隣家の
when they were on such missions.	彼らがそのような任務を負っている際に。
As they became more heavily armed	彼らがより重装備になり

Lesson **15**

and used more aggressive methods,	より攻撃的な方法を使うようになるにつれて,
many people came to believe	多くの人々が思うようになった
that the actions of SWAT teams	SWAT チームの行動は
were getting out of hand.	制御不能になりつつあると。
❸ In 1980,	1980 年に,
SWAT teams were deployed	SWAT チームは配置された
about 3,000 times.	約 3,000 回。
Now	現在
they are used	彼らは利用される
about 50,000 times	約 50,000 回
a year.	1 年に。
In some high-crime areas,	一部の犯罪多発地域では,
SWAT teams even patrol	SWAT チームは巡回さえしている
the area	その地域を
every day.	毎日。
However,	しかし,
whether local police are able to obtain	地元警察が得られるかどうかは
the trust and cooperation	信頼と協力を
of local citizens	地元住民の
may be one of the main factors	大きな要因の 1 つになるかもしれない
in determining	決定づける
whether crimes get solved or not.	犯罪が解決されるかどうかを。
If SWAT teams become	もし SWAT チームがなれば
a source of fear	脅威の元凶と
in the local community,	地域社会で,
it can completely alter	それは完全に変化させうる
the relationship	関係を
between a police force	警察部隊と
and the people	人々との
it strives to protect.	それが守ろうと励む。
The result is	結果は
that when crimes are committed,	犯罪が起きた際に,
citizens may not be as willing to	市民は以前ほど進んで協力する気にならな
cooperate.	いかもしれないということだ。
❹ Ever since the 2001 attacks	2001 年の攻撃以来

on the United States	アメリカへの
by the terrorist organization	テロリスト組織による
known as Al-Qaeda,	アルカイダとして知られる，
the government has been trying to upgrade	政府は向上させようとしている
the abilities of its police	警察の能力を
to deal with terrorist threats.	テロリストの脅威に対処するために。
Not only has it been increasing	政府は増やすだけでなく
funding	財政支援を
for SWAT teams,	SWAT チームへの，
but it has also been encouraging the military	それは軍に促してもいる
to give them weapons and equipment.	武器や装備を彼らに与えるよう。
However,	しかし，
critics point out	評論家たちは指摘している
that the military's role is	軍の役割は
to cause maximum damage	最大の損害を与えることだと
to enemy forces.	敵軍に。
In contrast,	一方，
the duty of police	警察の義務は
in a democratic society	民主主義社会における
is to protect	守ることであり
and serve the community	そして地域に尽くすことである
using the minimum of force necessary.	最低限必要な力を使って。
Critics fear that,	評論家たちはおそれている，
while protecting citizens from terrorism	テロ行為から市民を守ることは
is an admirable goal,	立派な目標だが，
the current trend may be dangerous	現在の傾向は危険かもしれないと
if it leads to police abandoning	警察が捨てることにつながるなら
the principles	行動原理を
they have operated under	彼らが守っていた
in the past	過去に
to become more like the military.	そしてより軍隊のようになるのなら。

Lesson **15**

Q 英語力を上げるには，留学が一番なのでしょうか？

A 多く頂く質問ですが，この質問に対して私は，「留学はした方がよい」という答えを返したいと思います。

一口に留学といっても様々なパターンがありますね。何年間もかけて長期的に留学することもあれば，1年間の交換留学に行く場合もあります。期間が夏休み，1週間，3日間などに限られる，短期の留学プログラムも存在しています。まずは自分に合った留学のパターンを探し，そのうえでぜひ留学に挑戦してほしいです。

ただし，留学の目的を単なる英語学習のみに定めないようにしてください。留学の最終的な目標は，「英語を覚えること」ではありません。本来の留学の目的とは，**世界の人々と出会い，コミュニケーションを取り，人間関係を構築すること。**そして，**日本にいたときとは異なる視点から物事を学び，自分の視野を広げること**です。あくまでも，英語学習は留学のたくさんある目的の1つにすぎません。

そもそも，「留学をしなければ英語が使えるようにならない」などということは決してありません。人間としての成長を目指すうえでぜひ留学をしてほしいと思う一方，英語を話せるようになりたいだけなのであれば，留学は必須ではないと思います。なぜかというと，日本にいながらでもオンラインで世界中の人と話すことができるからです。インターネットを通して世界の大学の講義を受講したり，世界中の知識や情報を動画から入手したりすることもできます。また，日本に住む外国人の数は年々増加しており，コミュニケーションを取る機会を自らつくることもできるでしょう。日本にいては英語に触れられない，英語を学べないなどということは全くありません。

つまり，留学の目的を単なる英語学習としないことが大切です。私がおすすめするのは，英語の勉強自体は日本でたくさんしておいて，いざ留学に行ったら，その国の文化に触れる中で自分を成長させつつ，日本で学んできた英語もさらにレベルアップさせることです。

Part 4
Lesson 16-20
Listening
会話文・ナレーション問題
Conversation & Narration

Duke University

Lesson 16
問題
Questions

▶対話を聞き，その最後にある質問に対して最も適切なものを **1**，**2**，**3**，**4** の中から１つ選びなさい。

(**1**) **1** Where to find the most recent information.

　　　 2 What she can do to improve her Spanish.

　　　 3 Whether she can change her essay topic.

　　　 4 Why Peru is having economic problems.　①②③④

(**2**) **1** Convince Greg to participate in the fun run.

　　　 2 Organize the fun run.

　　　 3 Tell him about the fun run.

　　　 4 Change her plan for the fun run.　①②③④

(**3**) **1** It did not contain enough information.

　　　 2 It focused too much on computer software.

　　　 3 It was too technical.

　　　 4 It was too long.　①②③④

(**4**) **1** Ask Rachel to write more songs.

　　　 2 Tell Rachel she should change instruments.

　　　 3 Convince Rachel to stay in the band.

　　　 4 Remind Rachel about the next practice.　①②③④

(**5**) **1** He has a drone pilot's license.

　　　 2 He uses his drone for his business.

　　　 3 He takes pictures with his drone.

　　　 4 He wants a drone that can stay in the air longer.　①②③④

(6) **1** The quality of their factory's products.

  2 Hiring more people for the maintenance department.

  3 Complaints from an important customer.

  4 Ways to meet a difficult deadline.　　　①②③④

(7) **1** He got a promotion at work recently.

  2 He feels less successful than his brother.

  3 He has a plan for earning more money.

  4 He is reluctant to help his brother.　　　①②③④

(8) **1** Get a new smartphone.

  2 Try another shop.

  3 Leave the screen as it is.

  4 Pay extra for a quick repair.　　　①②③④

(9) **1** Getting a different credit card.

  2 Reducing the number of their cars.

  3 Going on an overnight trip with Barbara.

  4 Borrowing money from a friend.　　　①②③④

(10) **1** Getting new security cameras.

  2 Talking more to customers.

  3 Hiring a security guard.

  4 Moving frequently stolen items.　　　①②③④

Lesson
16

Answers & Explanations ☞

LISTENING

Lesson 16
解答・解説
Answers & Explanations

青文字＝放送される英文（スクリプト）　赤文字＝正解・語義
■＝男性　■＝女性

□（1）　スクリプト / 和訳

英文	和訳
Professor Abrams, I'm doing research for my essay on the economy of Peru, but I'm having trouble finding up-to-date sources. Most of the books in the library are at least 10 years old.	エイブラムス教授，私はペルーの経済に関する自分の小論のために調査していますが，最新の情報源を見つけるのに苦労しています。図書館のほとんどの本は，少なくとも10年前のものです。
Hmm. Have you tried looking for articles? I think there are some economics journals that cover South American countries in the library. You can read Spanish, right?	ふむ。記事を探してみたかい？　図書館には南米の国をあつかった経済誌が何冊かあると思う。君はスペイン語が読めるね？
Well, my Spanish isn't perfect, but maybe I can make some sense of them.	そうですね，私のスペイン語は完璧ではありませんが，たぶん何とか理解できます。
It's a tough topic that you've chosen, but I think there should be enough material if you really look.	君が選んだのは難しいテーマだが，真剣に探せば十分な資料があるはずだよ。

What is the woman asking her professor about?

① Where to find the most recent information.
2 What she can do to improve her Spanish.
3 Whether she can change her essay topic.
4 Why Peru is having economic problems.

女性は教授に何について尋ねているか。

1 どこで最新の情報を見つけるべきか。
2 スペイン語を上達させるために自分に何ができるか。
3 自分の小論のテーマを変えることができるかどうか。
4 ペルーが経済的な問題を抱えているのはなぜか。

解説▶学生［女性］がエイブラムス教授［男性］に，小論についての相談をしている場面。女性が最初の発言で「**最新の情報源を見つけるのに苦労しています。**図書館のほとんどの本は，少なくとも10年前のものです」と言い，エイブラムス教授がそれに対して経済誌の記事を読んでみるよう提案している。したがって **1** が正解。ほかの選択肢の内容は会話中に出てこないので誤り。

重要語句　□ essay（⑧ 小論，評論，エッセイ）　□ up-to-date（⑯ 最新の）
□ cover（⑭ ～をあつかう，掲載している）

218

□（**2**） スクリプト / 和訳

Carol, as you know, Greg Anderson usually organizes the charity, fun run, every year for our NPO.	キャロル，君も知っているように，普段はグレッグ・アンダーソンが私たちのNPOのために毎年，ファン・ランという慈善事業を計画してくれている。
He always does a great job, doesn't he?	彼はいつもすばらしい仕事をしてくれますよね？
Yes, but this year his wife has been having health problems, so he's not available. We were wondering if you could be in charge of it.	そうだね，しかし今年は奥さんの体の具合が悪くて，手があいていないんだ。私たちは，君がそれを担当できればと思っているのだが。
I don't know. I've never done anything like that before.	どうでしょうか。私は以前にそのようなことをした経験が一度もありません。
Well, we've noticed you're good at planning things and motivating people, so we think you'd be perfect.	いや，私たちは君が物事を計画して人々をやる気にさせるのが上手だとわかっているから，君なら申し分ないと思っているよ。
Hmm. Well, I guess I can give it a try.	うーん。そうですね，やってみようかと思います。

What does the man ask the woman to do?

1 Convince Greg to participate in the fun run.
②　Organize the fun run.
3 Tell him about the fun run.
4 Change her plan for the fun run.

男性は女性に何をするよう頼んでいるか。

1 グレッグを説得してファン・ランに参加させる。
2 ファン・ランの計画をする。
3 ファン・ランについて彼に話す。
4 彼女のファン・ランの計画を変更する。

解説 ▶男性がキャロル［女性］に，毎年行われる慈善事業について話している場面。男性の2回目の発言に「**君がそれを担当できればと思っているのだが**」とあり，「それ」は男性の最初の発言より，ファン・ランという慈善事業を計画することを指す。したがって**2**が正解。

重要語句 □ organize（動（催し物など）を計画する）　□ available（形 手があいている，応対できる）
　　　□ in charge of ～（熟 ～を担当して）　□ motivate（動 ～をやる気にさせる）
　　　□ convince O to *do*（熟 O を説得して～させる）

219

Lesson 16
解答・解説
Answers & Explanations

☐（**3**）　スクリプト / 和訳

What did you think of the presentation, Gail?	プレゼンテーションについてどう思った？　ゲイル。
Well, they seem to have a lot of experience in designing computer software. They might be a good company to hire for our project.	そうね，先方はコンピューター・ソフトの設計において豊富な経験があるようだわ。私たちの企画を依頼するのによい会社かもしれない。
One thing that concerns me was the lack of detail in their presentation, though.	でも，僕が1つ懸念していることは，彼らのプレゼンテーションに詳しい内容が足りなかったことだよ。
I noticed that, too. Maybe we should make a list of technical questions and send it to them.	私もそれに気づいたわ。専門的な質問のリストをつくってそれを彼らに送るのが良さそうね。
That sounds like a good idea. Let's do that.	それは良い考えだね。早速それをやろう。

What did the man think about the presentation?

男性はプレゼンテーションについてどう思ったか。

① It did not contain enough information.
2 It focused too much on computer software.
3 It was too technical.
4 It was too long.

1 十分な情報を含んでいなかった。
2 コンピューター・ソフトに重点を置きすぎていた。
3 専門的すぎた。
4 長すぎた。

解説▶男性がゲイル［女性］に，プレゼンテーションの感想について尋ねている場面。男性は2回目の発言で「**彼らのプレゼンテーションに詳しい内容が足りなかった**」と言っているので，**1**が正解。ほかの選択肢の内容は会話中に出てこないので誤り。

重要語句 ☐ design（動 ～を設計する）　☐ hire（動 （賃金を払って人）を雇う）
☐ concern（動 ～を不安にさせる）　☐ focus on ～（熟 ～に重点を置く）

□ (4) スクリプト / 和訳

Steve, what are we going to do about Rachel?	スティーブ，私たちはレイチェルについてどうしたらいいと思う？
I don't know. If she quits, there'll be no one to write our songs. And she's the best bass player we've ever had.	さあね。もし彼女がやめたら，僕らの歌をつくる人が1人もいなくなってしまう。それに彼女は今までにうちにいた中で最高のベース奏者だ。
Yes, I was wondering if you could talk to her and try to persuade her to stay with us.	ええ，あなたが彼女と話して，私たちのもとに残るよう説得することはできないかしら？
I guess I can, but I don't know what to say. She told me she doesn't have enough time to practice with us these days.	できると思うけど，何て言えばいいかわからない。彼女は，最近私たちと一緒に練習する時間が十分にないと僕に言ったんだ。
Well, you're her friend, and she really respects you. I'm sure you can think of something to change her mind.	あのね，あなたは彼女の友人で，彼女はあなたを本当に尊敬しているわ。あなたは彼女の考えを変える何かを思いつけるはずよ。

What does the woman ask the man to do?

女性は男性に何を頼んでいるか。

1 Ask Rachel to write more songs.
2 Tell Rachel she should change instruments.
③ Convince Rachel to stay in the band.
4 Remind Rachel about the next practice.

1 レイチェルにより多くの歌をつくるよう頼む。
2 レイチェルに楽器を変えるべきだと伝える。
3 バンドに留まるようレイチェルを説得する。
4 次の練習のことを忘れないようレイチェルに伝える。

解説 ▶ 女性とスティーブ［男性］が，バンドをやめようとしているレイチェルについて話し合っている場面。女性は2回目の発言で「**彼女 [レイチェル] と話して，私たちのもとに残るよう説得すること**はできないか」と頼んでいる。男性の最初の発言によれば彼女はベース奏者なので，彼らはバンドのメンバーだとわかる。したがって **3** が正解。

重要語句 □ quit（動 ～をやめる，退職する） □ bass（名 ベース） □ instrument（名 楽器）
□ convince O to do（動 O を説得して～させる）

LISTENING

Lesson 16
解答・解説
Answers & Explanations

青文字＝放送される英文（スクリプト）　赤文字＝正解・語義

░░░＝男性　░░░＝女性

□(5)　スクリプト／和訳

What did you do this weekend, Jeremy?	先週末は何をしたの？　ジェレミー。
I was out flying my drone.	外出してドローンを飛ばしていたんだ。
I didn't know you had a drone. Don't you need a license to fly them or something?	あなたがドローンを持っているとは知らなかったわ。飛ばすのに免許証か何かが必要じゃないの？
Well, if you use them for your business, you're required to take a test and get a certificate from the government, but I just use mine for photography. It's so simple to fly them that anyone can learn to do it in half an hour or so.	あのね，もし仕事でドローンを使うなら，試験を受けて政府から免許証をもらう必要があるけれど，僕は自分のドローンを写真撮影のために使っているだけなんだ。飛ばすのはとても簡単だから，誰でも30分ほどで飛ばせるようになるよ。
I bet you can get some really nice shots with it.	あなたはきっとそれを使って本当にすばらしい写真を撮れるわね。
Yes, the world looks totally different from up in the air.	うん，上空からは世界が全く違って見えるんだ。

What is one thing we learn about the man?

1　He has a drone pilot's license.
2　He uses his drone for his business.
③　He takes pictures with his drone.
4　He wants a drone that can stay in the air longer.

男性についてわかることは何か。

1　彼はドローンの操縦士の免許証を持っている。
2　彼は仕事でドローンを使う。
3　彼はドローンを使って写真を撮る。
4　彼はもっと長く上空に留まることのできるドローンが欲しい。

解説▶女性がジェレミー［男性］に，先週末何をして過ごしたかについて尋ねている場面。ジェレミーの2回目の発言に「**僕は自分のドローンを写真撮影のために使っているだけなんだ**」とあるので，**3**が正解。最後の「あなたはきっとそれ［ドローン］を使ってすばらしい写真を撮れるわね」「うん」というやりとりからも，推測できる。ジェレミーの2回目の発言の内容から考えて，ジェレミーは免許を持っていないので，**1**は誤り。

重要語句　□certificate（⑧ 免許証，証明書）　□I bet 〜（⑲ きっと〜だ）　□up in the air（⑲ 上空で）

☐ **(6)**　スクリプト / 和訳

Gloria, did you hear that one of our customers just ordered 28,000 toasters?	グローリア，取引先の１つがたった今２万８千個のトースターを注文したのを聞いたかい？
When do they need them by?	それはいつまでに必要なの？
September first.	９月１日だ。
That's a huge order. Can our factory handle that much production?	大きな注文ね。うちの工場がそんな大量生産をさばけるかしら。
Well, the contract's already been signed. I guess we're going to have to extend our operating hours.	うーん，契約書にはもう署名が済んでいる。僕たちは稼働時間を延ばさなければならないだろう。
We'd better start seeing which employees are willing to work overtime.	どの社員が残業に前向きかの確認を始める方がいいわね。
Yes, and we'll have to talk to the maintenance department. We don't want to have a breakdown that could delay our production.	うん，それにメンテナンス部と話さなければならない。生産を遅らせうる故障があるのは良くないから。

What are the man and the woman discussing?　**男性と女性は何を話しているか。**

1 The quality of their factory's products.　1 彼らの工場の製品の品質。

2 Hiring more people for the maintenance department.　2 メンテナンス部にもっと多くの人を雇うこと。

3 Complaints from an important customer.　3 重要な取引先からの苦情。

④ Ways to meet a difficult deadline.　4 厳しい締め切りに間に合わせる方法。

解説▶男性とグローリア［女性］が取引先からのトースターの大量受注と今後の業務について話し合っている場面。グローリアが２回目の発言で「うちの工場がそんな大量生産をさばけるかしら」と言い，男性が稼働時間を延ばすなどの考えを語っていることから，**4**が正解。ほかの選択肢の内容は話題になっていないので誤り。

重要語句 ☐ handle（動 〜をさばく，あつかう）　☐ that much（形 それほど多くの）
☐ operating hour（名 稼働時間）　☐ maintenance department（名 メンテナンス部［保守部門］）
☐ breakdown（名 故障）☐ complaint（名 苦情）　☐ meet a deadline（熟 締め切りに間に合う）　223

Lesson 16
解答・解説
Answers & Explanations

青文字＝放送される英文（スクリプト）　赤文字＝正解・語義
▨＝男性　▨＝女性

□ (7)　スクリプト / 和訳

| What's the matter, honey? | どうしたの，あなた？ |

I just found out that my brother got another promotion at the bank. He's a senior vice president now.

僕は，兄が銀行でまた昇進したと今ちょうど知ったんだ。彼は今では上級副社長だよ。

Well, you said you might become the assistant manager at the shoe store soon, right? You're moving up, too.

ねえ，あなたはもうすぐ靴屋のアシスタントマネージャーになるかもしれないと言ったわよね？　あなたも出世しているわ。

Yes, but he earns at least four times as much as me, and people are always talking about how great he is. I'm happy for him, but it's starting to make me really frustrated.

うん，でも彼は少なくとも僕の４倍稼いでいて，人々は彼のすばらしさについていつも話している。彼のことは嬉しいけど，そのことで僕は本当に失望した気持ちになりかけている。

Don't let it bother you, honey. Everyone who knows you thinks you're a wonderful person.

気にしないで，あなた。あなたを知っている人は皆，あなたは素敵な人だと考えているわ。

What is one thing that we learn about the man?

男性についてわかることは何か。

1 He got a promotion at work recently.
② He feels less successful than his brother.
3 He has a plan for earning more money.
4 He is reluctant to help his brother.

1 最近彼は仕事で昇進した。
2 彼は兄より成功していないと感じている。
3 彼にはより多くのお金を稼ぐ計画がある。
4 彼は兄を助けるのを嫌がっている。

解説▶男性は「兄が銀行でまた昇進した」「彼は少なくとも僕の４倍稼いでいる」と言い，frustrated（失望した）という言葉を使っているので，**2**が正解。女性の２回目の発言より，男性は実際に昇進したわけではなく，その可能性があるだけなので **1** は誤り。

重要語句　□ get a promotion（熟 昇進する）　□ senior vice president（名 上級［上席］副社長）
□ move up（熟 出世する）　□ frustrated（形 失望した，いら立った）
□ bother（動 ～を悩ませる）　□ be reluctant to do（熟 ～するのを嫌がる）

□（**8**） スクリプト／和訳

Excuse me. I dropped my smartphone and the screen has cracks in it. Can you repair it?	すみません。スマートフォンを落として，画面にひびが入りました。修理してもらえますか。
A full screen replacement will be $180. We should be able to have it ready for you within three to four days.	画面を全部交換するには 180 ドルかかります。3〜4日以内にお渡しする準備ができるはずです。
Hmm. I was afraid it was going to be expensive. I need my phone for work as soon as possible.	うーん。値段が高くなることを心配していました。仕事でスマートフォンができるだけ早く必要なんです。
Well, we have a same-day repair service for an additional $25. We could have it ready for you by this evening.	では，25 ドルの追加料金で即日お渡しの修理サービスがあります。本日の夕方までにご用意できます。
OK, let's do that.	わかりました，それでお願いします。

What does the man decide to do?	男性は何をすることに決めているか。
1 Get a new smartphone.	**1** 新しいスマートフォンを買う。
2 Try another shop.	**2** ほかの店へ行ってみる。
3 Leave the screen as it is.	**3** 画面を（修理しないで）そのままにしておく。
④ Pay extra for a quick repair.	**4** 迅速な修理のために追加料金を払う。

Lesson
16

解説 ▶男性がスマートフォンの修理を依頼している場面。女性［店員］が最後の発言で「25 ドルの追加料金で即日お渡しの修理サービスがあります」と提案し，男性はそのサービスを使うと答えているので，**4** が正解。ほかの選択肢の内容は会話中に出てこないので誤り。

重要語句 □ crack（名 ひび）　□ replacement（名 交換）　□ same-day（形 即日［同日］の）
□ extra（名 追加料金）

225

Lesson 16
解答・解説
Answers & Explanations

青文字＝放送される英文（スクリプト）　赤文字＝正解・語義

■■＝男性　■■＝女性

□ **(9)** スクリプト / 和訳

Honey, have you seen our credit card bill for this month? We really have to cut our expenses.	君，今月のクレジットカードの請求書を見たかい？　僕たちは本当に出費を減らさなくちゃならないよ。
But what can we do?	でも，何ができるかしら？
Well, with the way fuel prices are, I was thinking we could get rid of one of our cars. We could keep one and take turns riding the bus.	そうだな，ガソリン代がこんな調子だから，僕たちの車のうちの1台を処分してはどうかと思っていたんだ。1台は持っておいて，交代でバスに乗ってもいいし。
Hmm. That would save a lot of money.	なるほど。そうすればたくさんのお金の節約になるでしょうね。
Actually, my friend Barbara is looking for a used vehicle. Maybe she'd be interested in buying it.	実は，友人のバーバラが中古車を探しているんだ。たぶん彼女は僕たちの車を買うことに興味をもつだろう。
It sounds like a good idea, but let's think it over for a day or two before we talk to Barbara.	それは良い考えだけど，バーバラと話す前に1日か2日よく考えましょう。

What does the man suggest doing?

1 Getting a different credit card.
(2) Reducing the number of their cars.
3 Going on an overnight trip with Barbara.
4 Borrowing money from a friend.

男性は何を提案しているか。

1 異なるクレジットカードを手に入れること。
2 彼らの車の数を減らすこと。
3 バーバラと一泊旅行へ行くこと。
4 友人からお金を借りること。

解説▶男性と女性が出費を減らす方法について話し合っている場面。男性が2回目の発言で「（ガソリン代がかさむので）僕たちの車のうちの1台を処分してはどうかと思っていたんだ」と言っているので，**2**が正解。ほかの選択肢の内容は会話中に出てこないので誤り。

重要語句 □ bill（❷ 請求書）　□ get rid of ～（❸ ～を処分する）　□ take turns *doing*（❸ 交代で～する）
□ used vehicle（❷ 中古車）　□ go on an overnight trip（❸ 一泊旅行に行く）

□（**10**）スクリプト / 和訳

Ms. Fender, I've noticed that teenagers seem to be stealing things from our store.	フェンダーさん，十代の若者たちが店から商品を盗んでいるようだと気づきました。
Yes, our security cameras haven't been very effective.	ええ，私たちの防犯カメラはあまり効果がありません。
I've heard that people are often very nervous before they steal something, so if store employees greet customers and ask them if they need help with anything, it can frighten off people who were planning on shoplifting. Do you think we could try something like that?	人が何かを盗む前には，たいていとても緊張すると聞いたので，もし店員が客に挨拶をして「何かお探しですか」と尋ねたら，万引きを計画している人を驚かせることができます。私たちはそのようなことをやってみることができると思いますか？
That might be a good idea. And it could help our sales, too.	それは良い考えかもしれません。そうすれば売り上げにも役立ちそうですね。

What does the man suggest doing?	男性は何を提案しているか。
1 Getting new security cameras.	**1** 新しい防犯カメラを買うこと。
②Talking more to customers.	**2** 客ともっと話すこと。
3 Hiring a security guard.	**3** 警備員を雇うこと。
4 Moving frequently stolen items.	**4** よく盗まれる商品を移動すること。

Lesson
16

解説▶男性とフェンダー［女性］が店の盗難を防止する方法について考えている場面。男性が最後に "Do you think we could try something like that?" と提案しており，**that** は前文の store employees greet ... anything を指している。つまり，**客に挨拶をして話しかけ，万引きを計画している人を驚かせること**を提案しているので，**2** が正解。

重要語句 □ security camera（⊗ 防犯カメラ） □ frighten off ～（働 ～を驚かせる）
□ plan on *do*ing（働 ～する計画を立てる） □ security guard（⊗ 警備員）

SCORE	CHECK YOUR LEVEL
/50点 (10問×各5点)	0～30点 ➡ *Work harder!* 31～40点 ➡ *OK!* 41～50点 ➡ *Way to go!*

227

Lesson 17
問題
Questions

🕐 所要時間 ▶ **9** 分

☑ 目標得点 ▶ **40** /50点

DATE

▶対話を聞き，その最後にある質問に対して最も適切なものを **1**，**2**，**3**，**4** の中から 1 つ選びなさい。

(1) **1** Air pressure might hurt the baby's ears.
    2 Other passengers might upset the baby.
    3 The baby might disturb other passengers.
    4 The baby will need several changes of clothes.   ① ② ③ ④

(2) **1** Go to college.
    2 Dress up for Halloween.
    3 Meet up in the fall.
    4 Remodel their guest room.   ① ② ③ ④

(3) **1** Play video games.
    2 Pay for her first two years of school.
    3 Work on a scholarship application.
    4 Read her friend's essays.   ① ② ③ ④

(4) **1** Put her belongings in a rented storage unit.
    2 Give her furniture to a friend.
    3 Take her belongings across the country in a truck.
    4 Sell all of her furniture online.   ① ② ③ ④

(5) **1** Take the elevator.
    2 Go back home.
    3 Get some coffee.
    4 Buy a new suit.   ① ② ③ ④

(**6**) **1**　To renew his passport.

2　To see a doctor.

3　To stay home and rest.

4　To wear a mask.　　　　　　　①②③④

(**7**) **1**　The woman will need to pick up her dress.

2　The woman wants to have time to eat.

3　The man prefers to get there by train.

4　There is construction on the highway.　①②③④

(**8**) **1**　It is being recalled for polluting the environment.

2　It is currently heading into town for work.

3　It is broken down on the side of the road.

4　It is being equipped with a new hybrid engine.　①②③④

(**9**) **1**　To brush her teeth three times a day.

2　To floss after every meal.

3　To get a special prescription.

4　To consult with her dentist.　　　　①②③④

Lesson
17

(**10**) **1**　Cook pasta.

2　Go to an all-you-can-eat restaurant.

3　Chop up a fruit salad.

4　Eat leftover Chinese food.　　　　①②③④

Answers & Explanations ☞

Lesson 17
解答・解説
Answers & Explanations

□ **(1)**　スクリプト / 和訳

I'm a little worried about taking my newborn on a long-haul international flight.	生まれたばかりの赤ちゃんを長距離の国際便に乗せるのは少し心配だわ。
Because he might cry a lot?	たくさん泣くかもしれないからかい？
No, I'm afraid the air pressure might hurt his ears.	いいえ、気圧が耳を痛めるかもしれないから。
I heard that nursing or using a pacifier helps babies adjust. I'd be more concerned about the people sitting around you.	授乳をしたりおしゃぶりを使ったりすれば、赤ちゃんは慣れるそうだよ。僕は君のまわりに座る人々の方がもっと心配だ。
What do you mean?	どういう意味？
A long flight next to a fussy baby can really wear someone out. But who knows, maybe the engine noise will soothe him to sleep.	騒がしい赤ちゃんが隣にいる長距離飛行は、本当に疲れるかもしれない。でも、ことによったらエンジンの音で赤ちゃんはおとなしく眠るかもしれないね。

What is the man concerned about?

1　Air pressure might hurt the baby's ears.
2　Other passengers might upset the baby.
③　The baby might disturb other passengers.
4　The baby will need several changes of clothes.

男性は何について心配しているか。

1　気圧が赤ちゃんの耳を痛めるかもしれない。
2　ほかの乗客が赤ちゃんを怒らせるかもしれない。
3　赤ちゃんがほかの乗客に迷惑をかけるかもしれない。
4　赤ちゃんは数回着替える必要があるだろう。

解説▶男性が2回目の発言で「君のまわりに座る人々の方がもっと心配だ」と言っており、女性にその理由を問われて「**騒がしい赤ちゃんが隣にいる長距離飛行は、本当に疲れるかもしれない**」と答えているので、**3**が正解。**1**は男性ではなく女性が心配していることなので、誤り。

重要語句　□ newborn（⑧ 新生児）　□ nurse（⑩ 授乳する）　□ pacifier（⑧ おしゃぶり）
□ adjust（⑩ 慣れる、順応する）　□ fussy（⑲ 騒がしい）
□ wear ～ out（⑱ ～を疲れ果てさせる）　□ soothe（⑩ ～を落ち着かせる）
□ upset（⑩ ～を動揺させる、怒らせる）

□（**2**）　スクリプト / 和訳

I'm so sad that graduation is coming soon. I don't want our college life to end!	もうすぐ卒業するのがとても悲しいわ。大学生活が終わってほしくない！
I know! All our friends will be scattered across the country. I'm going to miss them.	そうだね！　友達はみんな国中に散らばってしまう。彼らがいないと寂しくなるよ。
We will have to travel to see each other often. Promise you'll come to visit me at my parents' house in Oregon? They remodeled their guest room, and it has one of the best views in town.	ちょくちょく旅行してみんなと会わなくちゃ。オレゴン州の私の実家を訪ねて来ると約束してね？　来客用の部屋を改装して、そしてそれは町で最高の景色の１つを備えているのよ。
I will try my hardest to come visit. When is the best time to see you?	何とか行くようにしてみるよ。君に会うのに一番良いのはいつ？
Well, I won't actually move until August, so how about this fall?	そうね、実は８月まで引っ越さないから、今年の秋はどう？
That would work for me — we could celebrate Halloween together by going to a haunted house!	僕にとっても好都合だよ。お化け屋敷に行ってハロウィンを一緒に祝おう！

What are the friends planning to do?

1　Go to college.
2　Dress up for Halloween.
③　Meet up in the fall.
4　Remodel their guest room.

友人たちは何を計画しているか。

1　大学に行く。
2　ハロウィンのために着飾る。
3　秋に会う。
4　来客用の部屋を改装する。

解説▶女性と男性が、大学卒業後の予定について話している場面。女性は２回目の発言で男性に実家を訪ねてくれるように頼み、男性がそれに応じている。女性は３回目の発言で秋に会うことを提案し、男性もそれを受け入れている。したがって**3**が正解。

重要語句　□ scattered（形 散らばった）　□ remodel（動 ～を改装する）
　　　　　□ work for ～（熟（物事が）～にとって好都合だ）　□ haunted house（名 お化け屋敷）
　　　　　□ meet up（熟 会う）

Lesson 17
解答・解説
Answers & Explanations

青文字＝放送される英文（スクリプト）　赤文字＝正解・語義
■＝男性　■＝女性

□（3）　スクリプト／和訳

What are you doing after school tomorrow? Do you want to come over to my house to play video games?	明日の放課後は何をする予定なの？テレビゲームをしに僕の家に訪ねてこないかい？
I wish I could, but I have to work on an application for a scholarship to Harvard University.	そうしたいけど，ハーバード大学の奨学金の申請に取りかからないといけないの。
Don't worry about it! How much is the scholarship worth?	それは心配しないで！　その奨学金はどのくらいの価値があるの？
It would cover all my expenses for the first two years of school. I'll have to write several essays and get letters of recommendation, too.	それは最初の2年間の学費すべてをまかなうでしょうね。いくつか小論を書いて，推薦状をもらう必要もあるわ。
When will you find out if you are awarded the scholarship?	君が奨学金をもらえるかどうかがわかるのはいつ？
Hopefully within a few months. I'm already nervous about my application, and I haven't even started it yet.	数ヵ月以内だといいわね。もう申請のことが気になっているけれど，まだそれに手をつけてすらいないの。

What is the woman going to do after school tomorrow?

1　Play video games.
2　Pay for her first two years of school.
③　Work on a scholarship application.
4　Read her friend's essays.

女性は明日の放課後何をする予定か。

1　テレビゲームをする。
2　最初の2年分の学費を支払う。
3　奨学金の申請に取りかかる。
4　友人の小論を読む。

解説▶男性が女性に明日の放課後の予定について尋ねている場面。女性の最初の発言に「ハーバード大学の奨学金の申請に取りかからないといけないの」とあるので，**3** が正解。男性は明日の放課後にテレビゲームをすることを提案したが，女性は奨学金の申請のためにそれを断っているので，**1** は誤り。

重要語句　□come over to ～（熟）～に訪ねてくる）　□award ～ a scholarship（熟）～に奨学金を支給する）

□（**4**）　スクリプト / 和訳

I'm relocating across the country for a year, but I'm not sure what to do with all my furniture and stuff when I move out of my apartment. You don't need a sofa, do you?	私は 1 年間国中を移動する予定だけれど，アパートから出るとき家具などの荷物を全部どうすればいいかわからないの。あなた，ソファはいらないわよね？
Thanks, but no thanks. Have you considered keeping your belongings in a rented storage locker?	ありがとう，でも遠慮しておくよ。賃貸の収納ロッカーに持ち物を保管しておくことは考えたことがあるかい？
To be honest, I hadn't. Do you know how much it costs?	正直なところ，なかったの。どのくらいの費用がかかるか知っている？
The price varies based on how long you rent the locker, but it's not too bad.	値段はどのくらいの期間ロッカーを借りるかに基づいて変わるけれど，そんなに悪くないよ。
That sounds like the best option for me. Then I won't have to deal with the hassle of selling my stuff online or buying new stuff when I return.	私にとってそれが最も良い選択肢のようね。それにオンラインで物を売ることや，戻るときに新しい物を買うという煩わしいことに対処する必要がなさそうね。
Makes sense to me. If you want, I can help you get your belongings there with my truck.	もっともだ。もし良ければ，僕のトラックで君の持ち物をそこへ運ぶのを手伝うよ。

Lesson
17

What is the woman going to do?

① Put her belongings in a rented storage unit.
2 Give her furniture to a friend.
3 Take her belongings across the country in a truck.
4 Sell all of her furniture online.

女性は何をするつもりか。

1 賃貸の収納庫に自分の持ち物を預ける。
2 自分の家具を友人にあげる。
3 国中にトラックで自分の持ち物を持っていく。
4 自分の家具をすべてインターネットで売る。

[解説]▶男性が最初の発言で賃貸の収納ロッカーの利用を女性に勧め，女性が「**私にとってそれが最も良い選択肢のようね**」とそれに同意しているので **1** が正解。女性は最初の発言で自分のソファを男性に譲ることを提案したが，男性に断られているので，**2** は誤り。

[重要語句]　□ relocate（⑩ 移動する，転勤する）　□ belongings（㉃ 持ち物，家財）

□ rented storage locker（㉃ 賃貸の収納ロッカー）　□ hassle（㉃ 煩わしいこと）

233

Lesson 17
解答・解説
Answers & Explanations

青文字＝放送される英文（スクリプト）　赤文字＝正解・語義
　＝男性　　＝女性

□（5）スクリプト／和訳

Hey, Shirley, what's that banging sound?

なあシャーリー，あのバンバンたたくような音は何だい？

Apparently, the elevator was acting up, so they're doing some maintenance on it today. I didn't think it was supposed to be this noisy, though.

どうもエレベーターが故障していて，今日は整備をしているらしいの。でも，こんなに騒々しくなるとは思っていなかったわ。

If it keeps up, I don't think I can get any work done. But I can't afford to fall behind on my big project.

もしそれが続くなら，仕事が全然進まないよ。でも，大きなプロジェクトを遅らせる余裕はないんだ。

Why don't we take our laptops over to the coffee shop across the street?

通りの向こうの喫茶店にノートパソコンを持っていくのはどう？

Nah, I think I'll just work from home today. My wife has a cold, so I should be there for her anyhow.

いいえ，今日は自宅で仕事をするよ。妻が風邪をひいているから，どうしても彼女のそばにいないと。

Suit yourself.

お好きにどうぞ。

What will the man do?

男性は何をするだろうか。

1 Take the elevator.
②　Go back home.
3 Get some coffee.
4 Buy a new suit.

1 エレベーターに乗る。
2 家に帰る。
3 コーヒーを買う。
4 新しいスーツを買う。

解説▶男性がシャーリー［女性］に，騒音の原因について尋ねている場面。男性が最後の発言で「今日は自宅で仕事をするよ」と言っているので，**2**が正解。ほかの選択肢の内容は会話中に出てこないので誤り。"Suit yourself." は「お好きにどうぞ」「勝手にしなさい」という意味。

重要語句 □ banging（働 激しく打つ）　□ act up（働 故障する，調子が悪い）　□ keep up（働 継続する）
□ get work done（働 仕事を済ませる）　□ fall behind（働 遅れる）
□ nah（働 いいえ）　□ work from home（働 自宅で仕事をする）　□ anyhow（働 何としても）

□（ 6 ） スクリプト / 和訳

Hi, Gary, it's me. I'm so excited to go to Bali tomorrow. Don't forget to bring your passport.	ゲーリー, 私よ。明日バリに行くのがとても楽しみだわ。パスポートを持ってくるのを忘れないでね。
Uh, I have some bad news. I still have a lingering cough from the cold I caught last week.	あのね, 悪い知らせがあるんだ。先週ひいた風邪からまだしつこく咳が残っている。
Oh no, I thought you had gotten over it! Didn't you see a doctor?	まあ, 私はあなたが風邪から回復したんだと思っていたわ！ 医者に診てもらわなかったの？
Yeah, he said it's not too serious, but I need to get some rest. I'm also worried you might get sick, so maybe we should postpone the trip.	行ったよ, 医者は大したことはないと言ったけれど, 僕は少し休む必要がある。君が病気になるかもしれないことも心配だから, たぶん延期する方がよさそうだ。
Hey, there's no better place to relax than on the beach. Just wear a mask — I'm sure I'll be fine.	ねえ, ビーチ以上にくつろげる場所はないわ。マスクをすればいいわ, 私はきっと平気よ。
If you say so.	君がそう言うなら。

What does the woman suggest to the man? 女性は男性に何を提案しているか。

1 To renew his passport. 1 パスポートを更新すること。
2 To see a doctor. 2 医者に診てもらうこと。
3 To stay home and rest. 3 家にいて休息すること。
④ To wear a mask. 4 マスクをすること。

解説▶女性とゲーリー［男性］がバリに行く予定について話している場面。女性が最後の発言で「マスクをすればいいわ」と言っているので, 4 が正解。男性の2回目の発言より, 男性はすでに医者に診てもらっていることがわかるので, 2 は誤り。同じく男性の2回目の発言から, 旅行を延期して休息を取ることを提案しているのは男性なので, 3 も誤り。

重要語句 □ lingering（形 長引く） □ get over ～（熟 ～から回復する）
□ postpone（動 ～を延期する） □ renew（動 ～を更新する）

Lesson 17
解答・解説
Answers & Explanations

青文字＝放送される英文（スクリプト）　赤文字＝正解・語義

■＝男性　■＝女性

□ **(7)** スクリプト / 和訳

I printed out the directions for us to get to the wedding. It looks like there's some construction on the highway.	私たちが結婚式に行く道順を印刷したの。幹線道路で建設工事があるみたいよ。
Is it still open or are we going to have to take a detour?	まだ通れるかな，それとも迂回する必要がありそうかな？
It's closed, but there are some alternate routes we can take.	それは通れないけれど，私たちが通れるいくつかの別のルートがあるわ。
Maybe we should just take the train.	電車に乗る方がいいかもしれないね。
I'd rather not — I don't want to be sandwiched between people during rush hour when I'm in a formal dress.	それはしたくないわ。フォーマルなドレスを着ているときにラッシュアワーで人にはさまれたくないの。
In that case, let's get in the car and leave the hotel half an hour early.	それなら，車に乗って30分早くホテルを出発しよう。

Why will the couple need more time to get to the wedding?	2人が結婚式に行くのにより多くの時間を必要とするのはなぜか。
1 The woman will need to pick up her dress.	**1** 女性はドレスを受け取る必要があるだろう。
2 The woman wants to have time to eat.	**2** 女性は食べる時間が欲しい。
3 The man prefers to get there by train.	**3** 男性はそこへ電車で行きたいと思っている。
④ There is construction on the highway.	**4** 幹線道路で建設工事がある。

解説 ▶ 女性と男性が結婚式の会場への行き方について相談している場面。女性が最初の発言で「**幹線道路で建設工事があるみたいよ**」と言い，男性の「迂回する必要がありそうかな？」に対し，女性が2回目の発言で「**私たちが通れるいくつかの別のルートがあるわ**」と答えているので，**4** が正解。男性は2回目の発言で電車で行くことを提案したが，女性に反対され，それを受け入れているので，**3** は誤り。

重要語句 □ construction（⑧ 建設工事）　□ highway（⑧ 幹線道路）　□ take a detour（熟 迂回する）
□ alternate（形 別の，代わりの）　□ sandwich（動 ～をはさむ）

☐ **(8)** スクリプト / 和訳

Did you notice the abandoned car on the way to work?	仕事に来る途中で，あの廃車に気づいたかい？
I didn't, I was absorbed in the news. On the radio they were talking about new hybrid engine technologies. It was really interesting!	いいえ，気づかなかったわ，ニュースに熱中していたから。ラジオで，新しいハイブリッド・エンジン技術について話していたの。本当に面白かったわ！
That car looked like it had been manufactured in 1940s. It was ancient.	あの車は 1940 年代に製造されたように見えた。大昔の車だよ。
You must be exaggerating, it couldn't have been that old.	あなたはきっと大げさに言いすぎているわ，そんなに古いはずがないでしょう。
No really, it was in terrible shape. It looked like a bank robber left it on the side of the highway decades ago. It should be relocated to a transportation museum.	いや，実際ひどい状態だったよ。何十年も前に銀行強盗が幹線道路のわきに捨てたみたいだった。交通博物館へ移されてもいいくらいだ。
Well, at least the engine wasn't running — those old vehicles really pollute the environment.	でも少なくともエンジンは動いていなかったでしょ，そんな古い車は環境をひどく汚染するのよ。

What is the current status of the car?

1 It is being recalled for polluting the environment.

2 It is currently heading into town for work.

③ It is broken down on the side of the road.

4 It is being equipped with a new hybrid engine.

車は現在どんな状態か。

1 環境を汚染するため回収されているところだ。

2 仕事のために現在街へ向かっている。

3 道路のわきで壊れている。

4 新しいハイブリッド・エンジンを装備されているところだ。

解説 ▶ 男性が，仕事に来る途中で見つけた廃車について女性に話している場面。男性が 3 回目の発言で廃車について，「**実際ひどい状態だったよ**」「**何十年も前に銀行強盗が幹線道路のわきに捨てたみたいだった**」と述べているので **3** が正解。ハイブリッド・エンジンは女性が聴いていたラジオの中の話なので **4** は誤り。

重要語句 ☐ be absorbed in ～ (熟 ～に熱中して) ☐ exaggerate (動 大げさに言う)
☐ relocate (動 ～を移転させる) ☐ recall (動 (不良品)を回収する)

青文字=放送される英文(スクリプト)　赤文字=正解・語義

▨▨=男性　▨▨=女性

□(**9**)　スクリプト / 和訳

You always have the whitest smile in your photos! What's your secret?	写真の中であなたはいつも真っ白な歯の笑顔ね！　秘訣は何？
I brush three times a day and floss after every meal.	1日に3回歯を磨いて，毎食後に糸ようじで掃除するんだ。
Come on, you've got to be kidding. I do that, too, and my teeth don't shine nearly as brightly.	なによ，冗談でしょう。私もそうしているけど，私の歯はあなたほどとうてい輝かないわ。
Haha, OK. I buy special strips that I stick to my teeth for an hour every day. They're not too expensive, either.	はは，そうだね。僕は，毎日1時間歯に貼りつける，特別な細長い切れを買っているんだ。それはあまり値段も高くないよ。
Do you need a prescription?	処方箋が必要？
No, but you should probably talk to your dentist to see what all of your options are.	いいや，でも歯医者と相談してどんな選択肢があるか全部確かめる方がたぶんいいだろうね。

What does the man suggest to the woman?

1 To brush her teeth three times a day.
2 To floss after every meal.
3 To get a special prescription.
④ To consult with her dentist.

男性は女性に何を提案しているか。

1 1日に3回歯を磨くこと。
2 毎食後に糸ようじで掃除すること。
3 特別な処方箋をもらうこと。
4 歯医者に相談すること。

【解説】▶女性が男性に，歯を白く保つ方法について尋ねている場面。男性が最後の発言で**女性に歯医者と相談することを勧めている**ので，**4** が正解。女性は3回目の発言で「処方箋が必要？」と男性に尋ね，男性はそれを否定しているので，**3** は誤り。

【重要語句】□ floss（⑩ 糸ようじで掃除する）　□ strip（⑧ 細長い切れ）　□ stick（⑩ ～を貼りつける）
　　　　　□ prescription（⑧ 処方箋）　□ consult with ～（⑩ ～に相談する）

□(**10**) スクリプト / 和訳

There's some leftover Chinese food from last night in the fridge if you want.	君が欲しければ冷蔵庫の中に昨晩の残りの中華料理がいくらかあるよ。
You're not going to have dinner with me?	あなたは私と夕食を食べないの？
My coworkers and I went to an all-you-can-eat place for lunch today, so I'm still pretty full. I'm going to hold off for a couple more hours, I think.	今日の昼食に同僚と食べ放題の場所へ行ったから，僕はまだかなりお腹がいっぱいなんだ。あと 2，3 時間は遅らせようと思う。
Well, I'm not really in the mood for leftovers. Why don't I throw together some pasta, and you can chop up a fruit salad?	えーと，私はあまり残り物を食べる気分じゃないわ。私がパスタを手早くつくって，あなたはフルーツサラダを細かく切るのはどうかしら？
Maybe in an hour? I think I can work up an appetite by then.	1 時間後くらいかな？　それまでにはお腹をすかせておけるだろう。

What is the woman going to do?

① Cook pasta.
2 Go to an all-you-can-eat restaurant.
3 Chop up a fruit salad.
4 Eat leftover Chinese food.

女性は何をするつもりか。

1 パスタをつくる。
2 食べ放題のレストランへ行く。
3 フルーツサラダを細かく切る。
4 残り物の中華料理を食べる。

解説▶女性と男性が今日の夕食について話している場面。女性が最後の発言で**パスタをつくる**ことを提案して男性が応じているので，**1** が正解。同じく女性の最後の発言より，女性は残り物を食べる気はなく，フルーツサラダを細かく切るのは男性であることがわかる。したがって，**3** と **4** はいずれも誤り。

Lesson 17

重要語句 □ leftover（⑱ 残りの）　□ all-you-can-eat（⑱ 食べ放題の）　□ hold off（⑲ 遅らせる）
□ throw together ~（⑲（食事など）を手早くつくる）　□ chop up ~（⑲ ~を細かく切る）
□ work up an appetite（⑲ お腹をすかせておく，食欲を増進させる）

SCORE	CHECK YOUR LEVEL
╱50点 (10問×各5点)	0〜30点 ➡ *Work harder!* 31〜40点 ➡ *OK!* 41〜50点 ➡ *Way to go!*

LISTENING

Lesson 18
問題
Questions

◀)) 音声 ▶ **L&R_LV5_18-Q**

🕐 所要時間 ▶ **8** 分

✔ 目標得点 ▶ **30** /40点

DATE

▶英文を聞き，その最後にある質問に対して最も適切なものを **1**，**2**，**3**，**4** の中から１つ選びなさい。

[A] （ **1** ） **1** It required that English be used for all air communication.

2 It suggested that communication was important for air safety.

3 It recommended that English be used for all air communication.

4 It examined crash reports to discover how important communication is. ①②③④

（ **2** ） **1** They might speak too loudly.

2 They might speak too quickly.

3 They might be impatient with non-native speakers.

4 They might use uncommon phrases. ①②③④

[B] （ **1** ） **1** It was very expensive.

2 Problems with public transportation made travel difficult.

3 The new mayor was too inexperienced.

4 It was too unsafe. ①②③④

（ **2** ） **1** He understood the habits of criminals.

2 He thought people could change if they saw their own behavior.

3 He had tried the plan in other dangerous cities.

4 He thought it would bring international attention to Bogota.

[**C**] (**1**) **1** Decaf coffee does not contain caffeine.
2 Decaf coffee contains less caffeine than regular coffee.
3 Caffeine is a chemical substance that gives people energy.
4 Decaf coffee is also called decaffeinated coffee.

(**2**) **1** It has a stronger flavor than dark coffee.
2 It contains less caffeine than decaf coffee.
3 It often contains more caffeine than dark coffee.
4 It is made by the same method as dark coffee.

[**D**] (**1**) **1** Dressing pets in a variety of clothes.
2 Decorating pets to look like different animals.
3 Dyeing a pet's hair the same color as its owner's.
4 Taking a pet to a salon meant for people.

Lesson **18**

(**2**) **1** Some of them last for several days.
2 Groomers are given a time limit of 40 hours.
3 Groomers must use tools provided at the event.
4 There are two different kinds of events.

Answers & Explanations ☞

Lesson 18
解答・解説
Answers & Explanations

青文字＝放送される英文（スクリプト）　赤文字＝正解・語義

□ [A] スクリプト / 和訳

The Official Language of the Air

As air travel became more common around the world in the late 1940s and early 1950s, the International Civil Aviation Organization realized that universal communication between pilots and air traffic controllers would be essential to the safety of everyone. And so, in 1951, they recommended that English be the standard language for all air communication around the world. While it was only a recommendation, most of the world complied.

Unfortunately, during the following decades, there were many deadly airline crashes caused, at least in part, by failures in communication. Some pilots used non-standard words and phrases, or their accents were too thick to be understood clearly. Even native English speakers could cause problems by speaking too quickly, being impatient with non-native speakers, or using uncommon phrases. And so, as of March 5, 2008, all pilots and air traffic controllers around the world must pass an English proficiency test, one designed specifically for airline industry professionals.

空の公用語

❶ 1940 年代後半から 1950 年代初期に飛行機旅行が世界中でより一般的になるにつれて，パイロットと航空管制官とのユニバーサル通信がすべての人の安全にとって不可欠だと国際民間航空機関は気づいた。そこで 1951 年に，同機関は英語を世界中のすべての航空通信の標準語とするよう推奨した。それは推奨にすぎなかったが，世界中のほとんどの国々が従った。
❷ 不幸なことに，その後の数十年間で多くの致命的な飛行機の墜落事故があり，少なくともその一部は通信の失敗が原因だった。パイロットの中には，非標準的な語句を使う者や，訛りが強すぎて相手が明確に理解できない者がいた。英語を母語とする人であっても，速く話しすぎたり，英語を母語としない人にいらついたり，珍しい表現を使ったりして問題を起こしえた。そうした理由から，2008 年 3 月 5 日以降，世界中の全パイロットと航空管制官は，航空業界のプロ用に特別につくられた英語運用能力試験に合格しなければならない。

重要語句　□ air traffic controller（⑧ 航空（交通）管制官）　□ comply（⑩ 従う）　□ crash（⑧ 墜落）
□ thick（⑱（訛りが）強い）　□ be impatient with ～（⑲ ～にいらつく，怒る）
□ as of ～（⑲ ～以降，～現在）　□ English proficiency test（⑧ 英語運用能力試験）

□（1）　スクリプト／和訳

What did the International Civil Aviation Organization do in 1951?	1951 年に，国際民間航空機関は何をしたか。
1 It required that English be used for all air communication.	**1** 英語がすべての航空通信に使われることを要求した。
2 It suggested that communication was important for air safety.	**2** 通信が空の安全のために重要であることを示唆した。
③ It recommended that English be used for all air communication.	**3** 英語がすべての航空通信に使われることを推奨した。
4 It examined crash reports to discover how important communication is.	**4** 通信の重要性を知るために墜落事故の報告書を調査した。

解説 ▶ 第 1 段落の第 2 文に in 1951, they recommended that English be the standard language ... around the world と説明されており，**英語を世界中のすべての航空通信の標準語とすることを推奨した**とわかるので，**3** が正解。1951 年の時点では推奨しただけであり，要求まではしていないため，**1** は誤り。

□（2）　スクリプト／和訳

Which of the following is NOT a reason a native English speaker would need to take an airline industry English test?	英語を母語とする人が航空業界の英語試験を受けねばならない理由ではないのは，次のうちどれか。
① They might speak too loudly.	**1** 大きすぎる声で話すことがある。
2 They might speak too quickly.	**2** 早口で話しすぎることがある。
3 They might be impatient with non-native speakers.	**3** 英語を母語としない人に対していらつくことがある。
4 They might use uncommon phrases.	**4** 珍しい表現を使うことがある。

解説 ▶ 2 は第 2 段落第 3 文の speaking too quickly「速く話しすぎ」，**3** は being impatient with non-native speakers「英語を母語としない人にいらつく」，**4** は using uncommon phrases「珍しい表現を使う」に一致する。**1** の内容は説明されていないので，これが正解。

Lesson 18
解答・解説
Answers & Explanations

□ [B] スクリプト / 和訳

A Humorous Solution to a Serious Problem

Twenty years ago, the South American city of Bogota, Colombia, was an extremely dangerous place. In fact, many official organizations advised tourists to completely avoid the area because of widespread crime of all kinds. But when the new Mayor, Antanas Mockus, entered office in 1995, he had a unique idea to deal with the problem: he fired hundreds of police officers and replaced them with clowns.

Mockus, who was previously a theater teacher and philosopher, believed that if people's behavior was mirrored back to them, it could change their perspective and thus their behavior. He instructed the clowns to make fun of people who crossed the street illegally and to playfully copy the behavior of anyone breaking the law. Clowns also applauded and congratulated citizens who crossed the street using the crosswalks. This program, along with several of his other creative initiatives, led to a major reduction in violent crime over the next ten years.

ある深刻な問題のユーモアのある解決策

❶ 20 年前，南アメリカのコロンビアにあるボゴタ市は極めて危険な場所だった。実際に多くの公的機関は，あらゆる種類の犯罪が蔓延しているため，その地域には絶対に近寄らないよう旅行者に忠告した。しかし 1995 年に新市長のアンタナス・モッカスが就任したとき，彼にはその問題に対処するユニークなアイデアがあった。彼は何百人もの警官を解雇し，彼らの代わりに道化師たちを後任とした。

❷ 以前は演劇の指導者であり哲学者であったモッカスは，こう信じた。もし人々のふるまいが彼らに向けて正確に映し出されたならば，彼らの物事に対する見方を変え，それゆえに行動を変えることができるだろうと。彼は違法に通りを横断する人々をからかい，法を破るすべての人々の行動を面白おかしくまねるように道化師たちに指示した。また道化師たちは，横断歩道を使って通りを横断する市民に拍手を送って祝福した。この計画は彼のほかの独創的な構想のいくつかとともに，その後の 10 年間における凶悪犯罪の大幅な減少につながった。

重要語句 □ clown（⑧ 道化師，ピエロ）　□ perspective（⑧〔物事に対する〕見方）
□ playfully（⑩ 面白おかしく，ふざけて）　□ applaud（⑩ 〜に拍手を送る）
□ crosswalk（⑧〔米〕横断歩道）　□ initiative（⑧ 構想，計画）

□(1) スクリプト / 和訳

Why did officials tell travelers not to spend time in Bogota?

当局が旅行者にボゴタで時を過ごさないよう言ったのはなぜか。

1 It was very expensive.

2 Problems with public transportation made travel difficult.

3 The new mayor was too inexperienced.

④ It was too unsafe.

1 費用が非常に高かった。

2 公共交通機関の問題で旅行が難しかった。

3 新市長があまりにも経験不足だった。

4 危険すぎた。

解説 ▶ 第1段落の最初の文に city of Bogota, Colombia, was an extremely dangerous place「コロンビアにあるボゴタ市は極めて危険な場所だった」とある。また、第1段落第2文より、多くの公的機関が、あらゆる種類の犯罪が蔓延しているという理由で、旅行者にボゴタへ近寄らないよう忠告していたことがわかる。よって、**4**が正解。

重要語句 □ inexperienced (形 経験不足の)

□(2) スクリプト / 和訳

Why did Mayor Mockus believe his plan might be successful?

モッカス市長はなぜ自分の計画が成功するかもしれないと思ったか。

1 He understood the habits of criminals.

② He thought people could change if they saw their own behavior.

3 He had tried the plan in other dangerous cities.

4 He thought it would bring international attention to Bogota.

1 彼は犯罪者の習性を理解していた。

2 人々が自分自身の行動を見れば変わりうると彼は思った。

3 彼は別の危険な都市でその計画を試していた。

4 その計画によってボゴタは国際的に注目されると彼は考えた。

解説 ▶ モッカスは、第2段落の最初の文の if people's behavior was ... thus their behavior「もし人々のふるまいが彼らに向けて正確に映し出されたならば、彼らの物事に対する見方を変え、それゆえに行動を変えることができるだろう」という考えをもとに、道化師を採用し、ボゴタ市の治安を良くするための独創的なアイデアを実行していたと考えられるので、**2**が正解。

Lesson
18

☐ [**C**] スクリプト / 和訳

Tips for Coffee Lovers

Tired people often drink coffee to help them wake up. The chemical substance in coffee that gives people energy is called caffeine. Many people know about caffeine, but there are a few common misconceptions about caffeine and coffee. One of these misconceptions is that decaffeinated coffee, also known as "decaf," does not have any caffeine in it. In fact, the amount of caffeine in decaf coffee has only been reduced and not eliminated. Decaf coffee has considerably less caffeine than regular coffee, but it still has caffeine.

Another common misconception about caffeine has to do with light and dark coffee. Dark coffee has a much stronger flavor, so many people believe that it contains more caffeine than light coffee. This, too, is not necessarily the case. In fact, light coffee often has more caffeine than dark coffee. The amount of caffeine in coffee depends on how the drink was made and not its flavor.

コーヒー愛好家への助言

❶ 疲れている人は，目覚めの助けとなるようにしばしばコーヒーを飲む。コーヒーに含まれている，人々にエネルギーを与える化学物質は，カフェインと呼ばれる。多くの人々はカフェインについて知っているが，カフェインとコーヒーに関するいくつかのありがちな誤解がある。これらの誤解の1つは，デカフェという名でも知られるノンカフェインのコーヒーには，カフェインが全く含まれないということである。実際のところ，デカフェコーヒーは，カフェインの量が減らされているだけであり，取り除かれてはいない。デカフェコーヒーは，普通のコーヒーよりかなり少ないカフェインではあるが，それでもカフェインを含んでいる。

❷ カフェインに関するもう1つのありがちな誤解は，薄いコーヒーと濃いコーヒーに関係している。濃いコーヒーの方がずっと濃い味なので，薄いコーヒーより多くのカフェインを含んでいると多くの人は信じている。これもまた，実情は必ずしもそうとは限らない。実際には，薄いコーヒーはしばしば濃いコーヒーより多くのカフェインを含む。コーヒー中のカフェインの量は，味ではなくコーヒーのつくり方に左右されるのである。

重要語句 ☐ misconception（⑧ 誤解）　☐ decaffeinated（⑱ ノンカフェインの）

☐ eliminate（⑩ 〜を取り除く）　☐ considerably（⑩ かなり）

☐ not necessarily the case（⑲ 必ずしもそうとは限らない）

☐（1） スクリプト／和訳

Which of the following statements about caffeine is false?

① Decaf coffee does not contain caffeine.

2 Decaf coffee contains less caffeine than regular coffee.

3 Caffeine is a chemical substance that gives people energy.

4 Decaf coffee is also called decaffeinated coffee.

カフェインに関する次の文のうち誤りはどれか。

1 デカフェコーヒーはカフェインを含んでいない。

2 デカフェコーヒーは普通のコーヒーよりも少ないカフェインを含む。

3 カフェインは人々にエネルギーを与える化学物質である。

4 デカフェコーヒーはノンカフェインのコーヒーとも呼ばれる。

解説▶第1段落第5文に the amount of caffeine in decaf coffee has only been reduced and not eliminated「デカフェコーヒーは，カフェインの量が減らされているだけであり，取り除かれてはいない」と説明されており，decaf coffee はカフェインを含んでいることがわかるので，**1** が正解。

☐（2） スクリプト／和訳

What is one thing we learn about light coffee?

1 It has a stronger flavor than dark coffee.

2 It contains less caffeine than decaf coffee.

③ It often contains more caffeine than dark coffee.

4 It is made by the same method as dark coffee.

薄いコーヒーについてわかることは何か。

1 濃いコーヒーよりも味が濃い。

2 デカフェコーヒーよりも少ないカフェインを含む。

3 しばしば濃いコーヒーよりも多くのカフェインを含む。

4 濃いコーヒーと同じ方法でつくられる。

解説▶第2段落第4文に light coffee often has more caffeine than dark coffee「薄いコーヒーはしばしば濃いコーヒーより多くのカフェインを含む」と説明されているので，**3** が正解。第2段落第2文に Dark coffee has a much stronger flavor「濃いコーヒーの方がずっと濃い味」と述べられているので，**1** は誤り。

Lesson
18

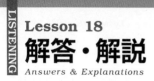

LISTENING

Lesson 18
解答・解説
Answers & Explanations

青文字＝放送される英文（スクリプト）　赤文字＝正解・語義

□ [**D**] スクリプト / 和訳

Creative Grooming

Many pet owners enjoy dressing their pets in different clothes. Some people take their cats and dogs to salons for haircuts. Others, however, enjoy giving their pets extreme appearance changes. They cut, style, and color their cats' and dogs' fur to look like completely different animals or fantastic creatures. Special groomers can make normal cats look like small tigers, pandas, or even dragons. Decorating pets in this way is popular in Russia and China, and it is called "creative grooming."

In the U.S., creative grooming competitions are gaining popularity. In some competitions, groomers use their tools to transform pets into artwork during an event that typically lasts around two hours. In others, owners bring their pets to the competition already styled. As some styling can take as long as 40 hours broken up into short sessions over many days, pets at these events tend to look even more fantastic.

クリエイティブグルーミング [独創的な手入れ]

❶ 多くのペットの飼い主は，ペットに様々な服を着せるのを楽しむ。ネコやイヌを毛のカットのためにサロンへ連れていく人もいる。また一方，自分のペットの外見を極端に変えることを楽しんでいる人もいる。彼らはネコやイヌの毛を切り，スタイルを整え，染めて，完全に違う動物や不思議な生き物のような外見にする。特殊なトリマーは，普通のネコを小さなトラ，パンダ，あるいは竜にさえ見せることができる。このようにしてペットを装飾するのはロシアと中国で人気が高く，「クリエイティブグルーミング」と呼ばれている。

❷ アメリカでは，クリエイティブグルーミングのコンテストが好評を博している。いくつかのコンテストでは，トリマーが彼らの道具を使って，通常 2 時間ほど続くイベントの間にペットを芸術作品に変える。他方では，飼い主がすでにスタイルが整えられたペットをコンテストに連れてくる。短い時間に区切って何日間もかけることで，（合計）40 時間もの時間を費やせるスタイリングもあるので，これらのイベントのペットは，さらにより素敵に見えやすい。

重要語句　□ grooming（⊛ 手入れ，（動物の）毛づくろい）

□(1)　スクリプト / 和訳

What is one example of creative grooming?

| クリエイティブグルーミングの例の1つは何か。

1 Dressing pets in a variety of clothes.

②Decorating pets to look like different animals.

3 Dyeing a pet's hair the same color as its owner's.

4 Taking a pet to a salon meant for people.

| 1　ペットに様々な服を着せること。
| 2　違う動物に見えるようペットを装飾すること。
| 3　ペットの毛を飼い主の毛と同じ色に染めること。
| 4　ペットをヒト用の店に連れていくこと。

解説▶第1段落第3文以降の内容から考えて，**2**が正解。特に第4～5文で「彼らはネコやイヌの毛を切り，スタイルを整え，染めて，**完全に違う動物や不思議な生き物のような外見にする。**特殊なトリマーは，普通のネコを小さなトラ，パンダ，あるいは竜にさえ見せることができる」と説明されており，第1段落の最後の文でそれは「クリエイティブグルーミング」と呼ばれていると述べられている。ほかの選択肢の内容はクリエイティブグルーミングとして説明されていないので誤り。

□(2)　スクリプト / 和訳

Which of the following is true about creative grooming competitions?

| クリエイティブグルーミングのコンテストについて正しいものは次のうちどれか。

1 Some of them last for several days.

2 Groomers are given a time limit of 40 hours.

3 Groomers must use tools provided at the event.

④There are two different kinds of events.

| 1　それらのいくつかは数日間続く。
| 2　トリマーは40時間の制限時間を与えられる。
| 3　トリマーはイベントで与えられた道具を使わなければならない。
| 4　2種類の異なるイベントがある。

解説▶第2段落第2～3文で，「いくつかのコンテストでは，トリマーが彼らの道具を使って，通常2時間ほど続くイベントの間にペットを芸術作品に変える。他方では，飼い主がすでにスタイルが整えられたペットをコンテストに連れてくる」と説明されているので，コンテストには2種類あるとわかり，**4**が正解。**1**について，数日続くのはコンテストではなく，ペットに行う事前のスタイリングなので，誤り。

Lesson
18

SCORE	CHECK YOUR LEVEL
╱40点 (8問×各5点)	0～20点 ➡ *Work harder!* 21～30点 ➡ *OK!* 31～40点 ➡ *Way to go!*

LISTENING

Lesson 19

問題

Questions

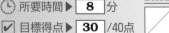
音声 ▶ L&R_LV5_19-Q

所要時間 ▶ **8** 分

✓ 目標得点 ▶ **30** /40点

DATE

▶英文を聞き，その最後にある質問に対して最も適切なものを **1**，**2**，**3**，**4** の中から 1 つ選びなさい。

[A]（ **1** ）
1 Experts thought the ideal conditions were too rare.
2 No one could hit the top speeds necessary.
3 Running shoes weren't advanced enough.
4 People thought the human body wasn't capable of it.

① ② ③ ④

（ **2** ）
1 The cold air temperature.
2 The wet track surface.
3 The pressure from other runners.
4 The crowd cheering him on.

① ② ③ ④

[B]（ **1** ）
1 The airplane was extremely light.
2 The airplane had a small engine on board.
3 The airplane had an electronic navigation system.
4 Bryan Allen trained hard to be able to power the airplane.

① ② ③ ④

（ **2** ）
1 Allen didn't bring enough water.
2 The wind started getting stronger.
3 The wind blew Allen off course and he got lost.
4 Allen was flying too low to be able to go quickly.

① ② ③ ④

[C] (1) **1** It is the highest place in Argentina.
2 Local people have a different name for it.
3 It was the inspiration for a famous work of art.
4 Women in this area make skirts nearby.

①②③④

(2) **1** Geologists have marked it according to different time periods.
2 The rocks changed colors over the span of millions of years.
3 Each of the seven colors is made of a different type of rock.
4 The white rocks cause light to reflect off of different materials.

①②③④

[D] (1) **1** Modern bicycles are powered using pedals.
2 Drais' bike had one more break than modern bicycles.
3 People sat closer to the ground on Drais' bike.
4 The Draisine was more popular in the West.

①②③④

(2) **1** Bicycles were too expensive for most people.
2 It cost too much to make the roads smoother.
3 Bicycles were both unsafe and uncomfortable.
4 Gear technology had not yet been invented. ①②③④

Lesson 19
解答・解説
Answers & Explanations

青文字=放送される英文(スクリプト)　赤文字=正解・語義

□ [A] スクリプト / 和訳

The Man Who Broke the Four-Minute Barrier

Until 1954, no one had run a mile in less than four minutes. Many people believed it to be impossible and that the human body would collapse under the pressure. British runner Roger Bannister thought otherwise, and aspiring to shave the necessary seconds off his time, he trained intensely, shattering record after record. Far from impossible, he was convinced the four-minute mile was within reach.

Experts thought that to break the four-minute barrier, the running conditions would need to be perfect: a comfortable air temperature, the right track surface, and a large crowd cheering the runner on. On May 6, 1954, Roger Bannister had anything but those sought-after conditions. It was cold, the track was wet, and the crowd was thin. However, Roger knew there were other runners nipping at his heels who were also trying to break the barrier. He wanted to be the first, so he pushed himself to the limit, and ultimately clocked in at 3 minutes, 59.4 seconds. He had broken the barrier by less than a second!

4分の壁を破った男

❶ 1954年まで，誰も1マイルを4分未満で走れなかった。多くの人々はそれを不可能であると信じ，人の体はその圧力をかけられると故障するだろうと思っていた。英国の走者ロジャー・バニスターはそうは思わず，走行時間から必要な秒数を縮めることを熱望して熱心に練習し，次々に記録を打ち破った。不可能どころか，1マイルを4分で走るのは目前だと彼は確信した。
❷ 専門家は，4分の壁を破るためには，快適な気温，適切な走路面，走者を応援する大勢の観客といった走行条件が完璧でなければならないだろうと考えた。1954年5月6日のロジャー・バニスターを取り巻く条件は，決してそのような求められているものではなかった。気温は低く，走路は濡れており，観客は少なかった。しかしロジャーは，自分と同様に壁を破ろうとすぐそばまで追い上げてきているほかの走者たちがいることを知っていた。彼は一番になりたかったので限界まで自分を追い込み，最終的に3分59.4秒を記録した。彼は1秒未満の差で壁を破ったのだった！

重要語句　□ mile（⑧ マイル（陸上距離の単位で1マイル＝約1.609km)）　□ collapse（⑩ 崩壊する）
□ shatter record（⑧ 記録を打ち破る［塗り替える］）　□ within reach（⑲ すぐ近くにある）
□ anything but ～（⑲ 決して～ではない）　□ sought-after（⑱ 需要のある，人気の）
□ nip at someone's heels（⑲ すぐそばまで追い上げる）
□ clock（⑩ ～のタイムを記録［測定］する，（記録）を達成する）

□（1）　スクリプト / 和訳

Why was the four-minute mile considered impossible?

1　Experts thought the ideal conditions were too rare.
2　No one could hit the top speeds necessary.
3　Running shoes weren't advanced enough.
④　People thought the human body wasn't capable of it.

１マイルを４分で走るのが不可能だと考えられていたのはなぜか。

1　理想的な条件は非常に珍しいと専門家たちは考えた。
2　誰も必要な最高時速に達することができなかった。
3　ランニングシューズが十分に進歩していなかった。
4　人の体ではできないと人々は考えた。

解説▶第１段落第２文に the human body would collapse under the pressure「人の体はその圧力をかけられると故障するだろう」と説明されており，１マイルを４分で走ることは人の体では不可能だと考えられていたことがわかるので，**4** が正解。

重要語句　□ ideal（⊛ 理想的な）

□（2）　スクリプト / 和訳

Which of the following most helped Roger break the four-minute barrier?

1　The cold air temperature.
2　The wet track surface.
③　The pressure from other runners.
4　The crowd cheering him on.

ロジャーが４分の壁を破るのに最も役立ったのは次のうちどれか。

1　低い気温。
2　濡れた走路面。
3　ほかの走者たちからのプレッシャー。
4　彼を応援する観客。

解説▶第２段落の第４〜５文より，ロジャーは，ほかの走者も同様に壁を破ろうとすぐそばまで追い上げてきていることを知っていて，その中で自分は一番になりたいと思い，限界まで自分を追いこんだことがわかる。よって，**3** が正解。ほかの選択肢は第２段落の第３文までの内容で，その日の走行条件が壁を破るのに望ましいものからかけ離れていたことが述べられているため，いずれも誤り。

Lesson
19

□ **[B]** スクリプト / 和訳

The Flight of the Gossamer Albatross

On June 12, 1979, an airplane called the *Gossamer Albatross* became the first human-powered aircraft to fly across the English Channel, a distance of 22.2 miles. Unlike most airplanes, the *Albatross* had no engine on board to power it. Instead, it was powered by a man named Bryan Allen, a pilot and bicycle rider. The *Albatross* was designed to be very light, weighing in at only 71 pounds. This meant that Allen could propel the aircraft forward using pedal-power alone.

Early in the morning on June 12, Allen took off from the English coast, pedaling into calm winds. Unfortunately, the wind picked up, slowing down his pace. As a result, the crossing took much longer than anticipated, and Allen's water supply ran out. Despite the setbacks, Allen reached France in less than three hours. That whole time, he flew at an average of just five feet above the water.

ゴッサマー・アルバトロスの飛行

❶ 1979 年 6 月 12 日，ゴッサマー・アルバトロスという名の飛行機が，22.2 マイルの距離を飛んでイギリス海峡を横断した最初の人力飛行機となった。ほとんどの飛行機と違って，アルバトロスは動力を生むエンジンを全く乗せていなかった。代わりの動力は，パイロット兼自転車乗りのブライアン・アレンという名の男性によるものだった。アルバトロスは，非常に軽くなるよう設計されており，重量はわずか 71 ポンドだった。このためアレンは，ペダルの動力だけを使って飛行機を進ませることができた。

❷ 6 月 12 日の早朝に，アレンはイギリスの海岸から離陸し，穏やかな風の中にペダルを踏んで進んだ。不運にも風が強くなり，彼の速度を落とした。その結果，横断には予想よりはるかに長い時間がかかり，アレンの飲み水は尽きてしまった。後退はあったが，アレンは 3 時間未満でフランスに到着した。その間ずっと，彼は水面上わずか平均 5 フィートの高さを飛行した。

重要語句　□ human-powered (彫 人力の)　□ propel ～ forward (働 ～を前進させる)
　　　　　□ pick up (働 (風などが) 強くなる)　□ setback (名 後退，妨げ)

□(1) スクリプト / 和訳

What design feature allowed the *Gossamer Albatross* to succeed?

ゴッサマー・アルバトロスの成功を可能にした設計の特徴は何か。

1. The airplane was extremely light.
2. The airplane had a small engine on board.
3. The airplane had an electronic navigation system.
4. Bryan Allen trained hard to be able to power the airplane.

（①に丸）

1　その飛行機は極めて軽かった。
2　その飛行機は小さなエンジンを乗せていた。
3　その飛行機には電子航法システムがあった。
4　ブライアン・アレンは，猛練習によって飛行機の動力を供給できた。

解説 ▶ 第1段落第4文で The *Albatross* was designed to be very light 「アルバトロスは，非常に軽くなるよう設計されていた」と述べられているので，**1** が正解。第1段落第2文より，アルバトロスはエンジンを全く乗せていなかったことがわかるので，**2** は誤り。

重要語句　□ electronic navigation system（⊛ 電子航法システム）

□(2) スクリプト / 和訳

Why did the crossing take longer than planned?

横断するのに計画したよりも長い時間がかかったのはなぜか。

1. Allen didn't bring enough water.
2. The wind started getting stronger.
3. The wind blew Allen off course and he got lost.
4. Allen was flying too low to be able to go quickly.

（②に丸）

1　アレンは十分な飲み水を持っていなかった。
2　風が強くなり始めた。
3　風がアレンを針路から吹き飛ばし，彼は迷子になった。
4　アレンは低く飛行しすぎていて速く進めなかった。

解説 ▶ 第2段落第2文で the wind picked up, slowing down his pace 「風が強くなり，彼の速度を落とした」と述べられているので，**2** が正解。第2段落第3文より，途中で飲み水が尽きてしまったことがわかるが，これは横断するのに時間がかかった結果であり，原因ではない。したがって **1** は誤り。

Lesson
19

□ [C] スクリプト / 和訳

The Hill of Seven Colors

There are many natural wonders on Earth, and each is majestic in its own way. One of Earth's true works of art is the Hill of Seven Colors. This hill is located in the mountains of Argentina, and as its name suggests, the hill looks as if it were painted with seven different colors. Local people call it the Hill of Seven Skirts because the colors make the hill look similar to the long skirts worn by many women in the area.

The Hill of Seven Colors is a particularly attractive location for geologists because the seven colors on the hill are seven different kinds of rocks. Each type of rock was created during a different time period, thus providing geologists with an abundance of material for analysis. The white rocks were discovered to be the oldest, and scientists estimate that they were created around 400 million years ago. The brown rocks are the youngest, at only 1 to 2 million years old.

七色の丘

❶ 地球上には多くの自然の奇観があり，それぞれそれなりに壮大である。地球の真の芸術作品の1つは，七色の丘である。この丘はアルゼンチンの山中にあり，その名前が示すように，まるで7色の異なる色で塗られているように見える。丘はその色によってその地域で多くの女性がはく長いスカートに似て見えるため，地元の人々はそれを七つのスカートの丘と呼ぶ。
❷ 丘の7色は異なる7つの種類の岩石であるため，七色の丘は地質学者にとって特に魅力的な場所である。それぞれの種類の岩は異なる時代に生まれ，そのため地質学者に分析のための豊富な題材を提供した。白い岩石が最も古いことが発見されており，科学者はそれらが約4億年前に生まれたと推定している。茶色の岩石が最も新しく，わずか 100 ～ 200 万年前のものである。

重要語句 □ wonder（⑧（自然界などの）奇観，驚嘆すべきもの［人，出来事］）　□ majestic（⑱ 壮大な）
□ in its own way（⑲ それなりに）　□ work of art（⑧ 芸術作品）　□ geologist（⑧ 地質学者）
□ an abundance of ～（⑲ 豊富な～）

□**(1)** スクリプト / 和訳

According to the passage, which of the following is true about the Hill of Seven Colors?

1 It is the highest place in Argentina.
② Local people have a different name for it.
3 It was the inspiration for a famous work of art.
4 Women in this area make skirts nearby.

本文によると，七色の丘について正しいのは次のうちどれか。

1 アルゼンチンで最も高い場所である。
2 地元の人々はそれについて異なる名前をもっている。
3 それは有名な芸術作品へのひらめきを鼓舞するものであった。
4 この地域の女性はすぐ近くでスカートをつくる。

解説▶ 第1段落の第2文から，本文は「七色の丘」について述べた文章であるとわかるが，第1段落の最後の文で Local people call it the Hill of Seven Skirts「地元の人々はそれを七つのスカートの丘と呼ぶ」と説明されているので，**2** が正解。同じ文から，その地域では多くの女性がその丘に似ているスカートをはいているとわかるが，つくっているかどうかは述べられていないため，**4** は誤り。

□**(2)** スクリプト / 和訳

Why does the hill appear to have seven colors?

1 Geologists have marked it according to different time periods.
2 The rocks changed colors over the span of millions of years.
③ Each of the seven colors is made of a different type of rock.
4 The white rocks cause light to reflect off different materials.

その丘はなぜ7色であるかのように見えるのか。

1 地質学者がそれぞれの時代に応じて，それに印をつけてきた。
2 岩石が何百万年もの期間をかけて，色を変えた。
3 7色のそれぞれが，異なる種類の岩石からできている。
4 白い岩石が光を異なる物質に反射させる。

解説▶ 第2段落の最初の文に the seven colors on the hill are seven different kinds of rocks「丘の7色は異なる7つの種類の岩石である」と説明されているので，**3** が正解。

Lesson
19

□ [D] スクリプト / 和訳

The Bicycle Picks Up Speed

In 1817, a German named Karl Drais built what most people consider to be the first bicycle. Unlike bicycles of today, it had no pedals and no chain powering the rear wheel. It had a wheel in the back with a brake and a wheel in front that could steer. The rider sat in the middle and pushed the bicycle along with their feet. The Draisine, as it came to be known, sold in the thousands across Western Europe and North America, achieving moderate popularity.

Engineers around the world worked to improve Drais' design. Reports vary as to who built the first pedal-powered bicycle, but the first commercially successful one was designed in France in 1863. The ride was dangerous and uncomfortable, a situation not helped by the rough roads of the time. Engineers continued refining their designs. The first modern bicycle with a chain-powered rear wheel was introduced in 1885. With steering, safety, comfort, and speed, sales exploded in the 1890s, and global productivity shifted up a gear.

自転車は速度を増す

❶ 1817 年，カール・ドライスという名のドイツ人が，ほとんどの人が最初の自転車だと考えるものをつくった。今日の自転車と違って，それにはペダルがなく，後輪を動かすチェーンもなかった。その自転車は，後ろにブレーキのある車輪を，前には進める車輪をもっていた。乗り手は中央に座り，足で蹴って自転車を進めた。それがドライジーネとして知られるようになると西ヨーロッパと北アメリカで数千台売れ，ほどほどの人気を得た。

❷ 世界中の技術者がドライスの設計の改良に取り組んだ。誰が最初にペダルで動く自転車をつくったかについては諸説があるが，最初に商業的に成功したものは 1863 年にフランスで設計された。ドライブは危険で心地悪く，その状況は当時の悪路によってよくならなかった。技術者は設計を改良し続けた。チェーンで動く後輪を持つ最初の現代的な自転車は，1885 年に導入された。操作性，安全性，快適さ，および速度によって，売り上げは 1890 年代に爆発的に増え，全世界の生産性が加速した。

重要語句　□ rear wheel （⑧ 後輪）　□ steer （⑩ ［船や車が］進む）
　　　　　□ push ～ along （⑲ ～を押して進める）　□ rough road （⑧ 悪路，でこぼこ道）
　　　　　□ refine （⑩ ～を改良する）　□ shift up a gear （⑲ 速度を上げる）

Lesson 19 問題→解答・解説

(1) スクリプト / 和訳

What was the major difference between modern bicycles and Drais' original design?

1 Modern bicycles are powered using pedals.
2 Drais' bike had one more break than modern bicycles.
3 People sat closer to the ground on Drais' bike.
4 The Draisine was more popular in the West.

現代の自転車とドライスによる元の設計の主な違いは何だったか。

1 現代の自転車はペダルを使って動力が供給される。
2 ドライスの自転車は現代の自転車よりも1つ多くのブレーキがあった。
3 ドライスの自転車では，人々が地面により近い位置に座った。
4 ドライジーネは西洋でより人気だった。

解説▶ 第1段落第2文で，ドライスのつくった自転車について，Unlike bicycles of today, it had no pedals と述べられ，第4文に The rider sat in the middle and pushed the bicycle along with their feet「乗り手は中央に座り，足で蹴って自転車を進めた」と述べられているので，**1** が正解。

(2) スクリプト / 和訳

Why didn't bicycle sales achieve major success until the 1890s?

1 Bicycles were too expensive for most people.
2 It cost too much to make the roads smoother.
3 Bicycles were both unsafe and uncomfortable.
4 Gear technology had not yet been invented.

自転車販売が1890年代まで大成功を収めなかったのはなぜか。

1 自転車はほとんどの人々にとって高すぎた。
2 道路をより滑らかにするには費用がかかりすぎた。
3 自転車は危険であり，心地良くもなかった。
4 変速ギアの技術がまだ発明されていなかった。

解説▶ ペダルで動く自転車しかなかった頃の状況として，第2段落第3文に The ride was dangerous and uncomfortable「ドライブは危険で心地悪く」と述べられており，第2段落第4～6文から，技術者が設計を改良し続けた結果，チェーンつきの自転車が導入され，1890年代に売り上げが爆発的に増えたとわかるので，**3** が正解。それよりも前の内容に注目するとよい。

Lesson 19

SCORE	CHECK YOUR LEVEL
/40点 (8問×各5点)	0～20点 ➡ *Work harder!* 21～30点 ➡ *OK!* 31～40点 ➡ *Way to go!*

259

▶英文を聞き，その最後にある質問に対して最も適切なものを **1**，**2**，**3**，**4** の中から１つ選びなさい。

(**1**) *Situation* : You are planning a trip to the UK and want a tour that includes Scotland. You can afford up to $3,000 including airfare. Your travel agent tells you the following.

Question : Which tour should you choose?

1   Best of the UK.

2   Green UK.

3   UK Landscapes.

4   England and Scotland Highlights.   ①②③④

(**2**) *Situation* : You are on a plane that will land in Boston and hear the following announcement. You are going to Los Angeles via Las Vegas.

Question : Which gate should you go to?

1   Gate 2.

2   Gate 3.

3   Gate 8.

4   Gate 9.   ①②③④

(**3**) *Situation* : You purchased a refrigerator 14 months ago, with an extended three-year warranty. The refrigerator is making strange noises. You call the manufacturer and hear the following message.

Question : What should you do?

1   Send it back to the company.
2   Schedule a repair visit.
3   Contact the store you bought it at.
4   Talk to an operator.   ①②③④

(**4**) *Situation* : You want to rent an apartment close to public transportation for the lowest possible price. You receive the following voice mail from a real estate agent.

Question : Which apartment building should you visit?

1   Stanton Heights.
2   Clinton Towers.
3   East Glen Apartments.
4   Pine Terrace.   ①②③④ **Lesson**
20

Answers & Explanations ☞

□(1)　スクリプト / 和訳

Situation: You are planning a trip to the UK and want a tour that includes Scotland. You can afford up to $3,000 including airfare. Your travel agent tells you the following.

The Best of the UK tour includes all the major cities in England, Scotland, and Wales. It costs just under $3,000, but you'll have to arrange your own airline tickets. Another popular option is Green UK tour for just $2,200 including airfare. It takes you to England and Ireland. A third option is the UK Landscapes tour. It takes you to some of the most beautiful scenery in England and Scotland. It's a steal for just $2,800. You won't find another tour like that with airfare included. Finally, there's England and Scotland Highlights, which takes you to the most popular attractions for just $3,200.

状況：あなたはイギリスへの旅行を計画しており，スコットランドに行けるような旅行をしたいと考えています。あなたは航空運賃も含めて 3,000 ドルまで使う余裕があります。旅行代理店の社員は次のように言います。

「ベスト オブ ザ UK ツアー」は，イングランド，スコットランド，ウェールズのすべての主要都市を含むものです。料金は 3,000 ドルに届かないくらいですが，飛行機のチケットは自分で手配しなければならないでしょう。もう 1 つの人気な選択肢は「グリーン UK ツアー」で，航空運賃も含めてたった 2,200 ドルです。それによってあなたはイングランドとアイルランドに行くことができます。3 つ目の選択肢は「UK ランドスケープ ツアー」です。それによってあなたは，イングランドとスコットランドの最も美しい景色のうちのいくつかを見ることができます。それはたった 2,800 ドルとお買い得です。航空運賃を含めたこのようなツアーはもうほかに見つけられないでしょう。最後に，「イングランド アンド スコットランド ハイライツ」という，たった 3,200 ドルで最も人気のある観光名所に行くことができるものもあります。

重要語句　□ **afford** (動 ～に対する (金銭的・時間的) 余裕がある)

□ **arrange** (動 ～を手配する，準備する)　□ **option** (名 選択 (肢))　□ **airfare** (名 航空運賃)
□ **scenery** (名 風景，景色)　□ **steal** (名 格安品，掘り出し物)　□ **attraction** (名 観光名所)

262

Which tour should you choose?

1　The Best of the UK.
2　Green UK.
③　UK Landscapes.
4　England and Scotland Highlights.

あなたはどのツアーを選ぶべきか。

1　ベスト オブ ザ UK。
2　グリーン UK。
3　UK ランドスケープス。
4　イングランド アンド スコットランド ハイライツ。

解説 ▶ 4種類のツアーが提案されており，その中から状況に合ったツアーを選ぶ問題。第1文と第5～6文，第9文より，「ベスト オブ ザ UK ツアー」と「UK ランドスケープス ツアー」と「イングランド アンド スコットランド ハイライツ」がツアーの行程にスコットランドを含んでいることがわかる。しかし第2文より，「ベスト オブ ザ UK ツアー」の場合は 3,000 ドル近くのツアー代を払ったうえに，自分で飛行機のチケットを手配しなければならないとわかる。すると予算である 3,000 ドルを超えてしまうので，**1** は誤り。「イングランド アンド スコットランド ハイライツ」も 3,200 ドルかかるので，**4** も誤り。「UK ランドスケープス ツアー」は航空運賃を含めて 2,800 ドルなので，**3** が正解。

Lesson
20

□**（2）**　スクリプト / 和訳

Situation: You are on a plane that will land in Boston and hear the following announcement. You are going to Los Angeles via Las Vegas.

Good evening, passengers. We will be landing on schedule in about 20 minutes, and the following information is for anyone with a connecting flight. The Red Wing Airline flight to Miami will depart from Gate 3, and the Stanton Airlines flight to Toronto is leaving from Gate 8. Anyone traveling to Los Angeles with a connecting flight through Las Vegas should proceed to Gate 9. The Epsilon Airlines direct flight to Los Angeles departs from Gate 2. We hope you have enjoyed traveling with Eagle Airlines today.

状況：あなたはボストンに着陸する飛行機に乗っており，次のようなアナウンスを聞きます。あなたはラスベガス経由でロサンゼルスに向かっています。

こんばんは，乗客の皆様。私たちは定刻どおりおよそ 20 分後に着陸する予定で，このあとのお知らせは飛行機の乗り継ぎをする方へ向けたものです。マイアミ行きのレッドウィング航空便は 3 ゲートから飛び立ちます。そしてトロント行きのスタントン航空便は 8 ゲートから出発します。ラスベガスで乗り継ぎをしてロサンゼルスへ向かう方は 9 ゲートに進んでください。イプシロン航空のロサンゼルスへの直行便は 2 ゲートから出発します。皆様が本日のイーグル航空での旅を楽しんでいることを願います。

重要語句　□ land（動 着陸する，上陸する）　□ proceed（動（〜の方へ）前進する，進む）

Which gate should you go to?	あなたはどのゲートへ向かうべきか。
1 Gate 2.	**1** 2ゲート。
2 Gate 3.	**2** 3ゲート。
3 Gate 8.	**3** 8ゲート。
④ Gate 9.	**4** 9ゲート。

解説▶飛行機でのアナウンスを聞き，自分が次に向かうべきゲートを判断する問題。第4文より，9ゲートから出発する航空便がラスベガスを経由してロサンゼルスに行くので**4**が正解。第5文より，2ゲートから出発するのは，ロサンゼルスへの直行便なので**1**は誤り。

Lesson
20

Lesson 20
解答・解説
Answers & Explanations

□（**3**）　スクリプト／和訳

Situation: You purchased a refrigerator 14 months ago, with an extended three-year warranty. The refrigerator is making strange noises. You call the manufacturer and hear the following message.

Thank you for calling Apex Appliances' service department. If you purchased your product in the last two weeks and would like to exchange or return it, please press 1 now. If you have had your product for 12 months or less, please press 2 to arrange a repair visit. Customers with other warranties should contact the place of purchase. For other inquiries, please stay on the line and an operator will assist you.

状況：あなたは 14 ヵ月前に 3 年間の延長保証がついた冷蔵庫を購入しました。冷蔵庫が異様な音を立てています。あなたが製造業者に電話をかけると，次のメッセージが聞こえます。

エイペックス電化製品のサービス部にお電話いただき，ありがとうございます。過去 2 週間に製品を購入し，交換または返品を希望される場合は，今すぐ 1 を押してください。購入してから 12 ヵ月以内の製品をお持ちの場合は，2 を押して修理訪問を手配してください。そのほかの保証をお持ちのお客様は，購入先にお問い合わせください。ほかのお問い合わせにつきましては，電話を切らないでおいてください。オペレーターがお手伝いします。

重要語句　□ warranty（⊛ 保証，保証書）　□ manufacturer（⊛ 製造業者，メーカー，製作者）
　　　　　□ arrange（⊛ ～を手配する，準備する）　□ inquiry（⊛ 問い合わせ，質問）

What should you do?

1 Send it back to the company.
2 Schedule a repair visit.
(3) Contact the store you bought it at.
4 Talk to an operator.

あなたはどうするべきか。

1 それを会社に送り返す。
2 修理訪問の予定を立てる。
3 それを購入した店に問い合わせる。
4 オペレーターと話す。

解説▶電話のメッセージを聞き，次に取るべき行動を判断する問題。すでに冷蔵庫を購入してから 14 ヵ月経過しており，第 2 文にある交換や返品，第 3 文にある修理訪問を手配することはできないので，**1**，**2** は誤り。第 4 文に「そのほかの保証をお持ちのお客様は，購入先にお問い合わせください」と述べられており，購入した冷蔵庫には 3 年間の延長保証がついているので，**3** が正解。

Lesson
20

□(4) スクリプト / 和訳

> Situation: You want to rent an apartment close to public transportation for the lowest possible price. You receive the following voice mail from a real estate agent.

This is Jan calling from Byron Real Estate. Stanton Heights has spacious apartments for $2,000 a month. They're about 10 minutes from Westview Station. Clinton Towers has a bus stop right in front of it, and it's priced at $2,100. If you had a car, then I'd strongly recommend East Glen Apartments, which are near a huge park and cost just $1,700 monthly. Another option would be Pine Terrace. It's within walking distance of the subway and costs $1,900. Please call me if you'd like to arrange a visit to any of these buildings.

> 状況：あなたは公共交通機関に近いアパートを最低価格で借りたいと考えています。あなたは不動産業者から次のボイスメールを受けとります。

こちらはバイロン不動産のジャンです。スタントンハイツには，1ヵ月2,000ドルの広々としたお部屋がございます。そこはウェストビュー駅から約10分です。クリントンタワーズは真正面にバス停があり，価格は2,100ドルです。車をお持ちの場合は，巨大な公園の近くにあり，月額わずか1,700ドルのイーストグレンアパートを強くお勧めします。もう1つの選択肢は，パインテラスです。地下鉄の徒歩圏内にあり，料金は1,900ドルです。これらの建物のいずれかの見学を手配したい場合は，お電話ください。

重要語句　□ real estate（⊗ 不動産）　□ spacious（⑯ 広々とした）

Which apartment building should you visit?	どのアパートを訪問するべきか。
1　Stanton Heights.	**1**　スタントンハイツ。
2　Clinton Towers.	**2**　クリントンタワーズ。
3　East Glen Apartments.	**3**　イーストグレンアパート。
④　Pine Terrace.	**4**　パインテラス。

解説▶不動産業者から4つの賃貸アパートを提案され，その中から自分の状況に合ったものを選ぶ問題。**3**の「イーストグレンアパート」は，第5文より月額1,700ドルと最も安いが，「車をお持ちの場合は」と説明されていることから**公共交通機関からは離れている**と推測できるので誤り。そのほかのアパートはすべて徒歩圏内に公共交通機関が存在し，第6～7文より「**パインテラス**」がその中で**最も家賃が安い**ので，**4**が正解。

Lesson
20

SCORE	CHECK YOUR LEVEL
╱40点 （4問×各10点）	0～20点 ➡ *Work harder!* 21～30点 ➡ *OK!* 31～40点 ➡ *Way to go!*

Q 英検や TOEFL でどのくらいの成績を取れば 無理なく英語圏で生活できますか？

A 「4技能試験において，具体的にどの程度の成績を取れば英語圏でも問題なく生活できますか」とよく聞かれます。しかし残念ながら，試験で良い点数が取れたからといって，英語圏で無理なく生活できるというわけではありません。

　4技能試験は，あくまでも**英語を使うための基礎力をはかるツール**です。英語を話したり，書いたりするための十分な素地があるかを判断することしかできません。英語圏を含む様々な国で，実際に人と対面して話せるか，英語を使って仕事ができるかというのは，もう1つ上の段階の話になってきます。

　例えば，スピーキングテストで高得点が取れるなら，それは簡単な応答が難なくこなせるということを示します。自分の考えを論理的に話せるようになったということかもしれません。しかし，実際に他人とコミュニケーションを取るにあたって，それは基礎的な技術にすぎないのです。うまくコミュニケーションを取るには，相手の主張をよく聞いてその人の気持ちを慮る，対立している2人を仲裁する，ジョークをはさみながら相手の心に入り込んでいくといったスキルが必要なのです。これは，試験勉強をするだけで身につくような能力ではなく，ある程度の場数を踏んで初めてできることです。

　もちろん，スピーキングテストで求められる能力はコミュニケーションにおいて非常に大切です。一方で，テストというのは円滑なコミュニケーションへの単なる入口にすぎません。そのため，**テストで高得点を取れることが，英語圏の国で問題なく生活できることに直結はしない**のです。

　皆さんは4技能試験を使ってはかれる能力とはかれない能力があることを知り，それらを混同しないようにしましょう。もちろん，**試験で求められる基礎的な能力が身につけば，上の段階に行くまでの敷居がぐっと低くなります**から，試験の勉強にもしっかりと励んでくださいね。

MEMO

MEMO

MEMO

MEMO

MEMO

MEMO

MEMO

【本書の音声】
東進 WEB 書店の本書ページから，無料でダウンロード [ストリーミング] できます。

▼東進 WEB 書店
www.toshin.com/books

▼パスワード (ログイン時に要入力)
r27s12Mn

レベル別問題集シリーズ

英語 L&R レベル別問題集⑤ 上級編

発行日：2021年　2月27日 初版発行

総合監修：安河内哲也　Andrew Robbins
発行者：永瀬昭幸

編集担当：河合桃子
発行所：株式会社ナガセ
　　　　〒180-0003 東京都武蔵野市吉祥寺南町1-29-2
　　　　出版事業部(東進ブックス)
　　　　TEL:0422-70-7456　FAX:0422-70-7457
　　　　URL:http://www.toshin.com/books(東進WEB書店)
　　　　※本書を含む東進ブックスの最新情報は、東進WEB書店をご覧ください。

英文校閲：Nick Norton
本文イラスト：丸子博史
校正協力：太田萌　清水梨愛　西岡美都　松下未歩
音声収録：財団法人英語教育協議会 (ELEC)
音声出演：Anya Floris　Guy Perryman　Jennifer Okano
　　　　　木村史明　水月優希
DTP・印刷・製本：中央精版印刷株式会社

東進の合格の秘訣が次ページに

合格の秘訣1 全国屈指の実力講師陣

東進の実力講師陣 数多くのベストセラー参考書を執筆!!

東進ハイスクール・ 東進衛星予備校では、 そうそうたる講師陣が君を熱く指導する!

本気で実力をつけたいと思うなら、やはり根本から理解させてくれる一流講師の授業を受けることが大切です。東進の講師は、日本全国から選りすぐられた大学受験のプロフェッショナル。何万人もの受験生を志望校合格へ導いてきたエキスパート達です。

英語

日本を代表する英語の伝道師。ベストセラーも多数。

安河内 哲也 先生
[英語]

予備校界のカリスマ。抱腹絶倒の名講義を見逃すな。

今井 宏 先生
[英語]

「スーパー速読法」で難解な長文問題の速読即解を可能にする「予備校界の達人」!

渡辺 勝彦 先生
[英語]

雑誌『TIME』やベストセラーの翻訳も手掛け、英語界でその名を馳せる実力講師。

宮崎 尊 先生
[英語]

情熱あふれる授業で、知らず知らずのうちに英語が得意教科に!

大岩 秀樹 先生
[英語]

数学

数学を本質から理解できる本格派講義の完成度は群を抜く。

志田 晶 先生
[数学]

「ワカル」を「デキル」に変える新しい数学は、君の思考力を刺激し、数学のイメージを覆す!

松田 聡平 先生
[数学]

付録 **1**

国語

東大・難関大志望者から絶大なる信頼を得る本質の指導を追究。

栗原 隆 先生
[古文]

ビジュアル解説で古文を簡単明快に解き明かす実力講師。

富井 健二 先生
[古文]

縦横無尽な知識に裏打ちされた立体的な授業に、グングン引き込まれる！

三羽 邦美 先生
[古文・漢文]

幅広い教養と明解な具体例を駆使した緩急自在の講義。漢文が身近になる！

寺師 貴憲 先生
[漢文]

小論文指導の第一人者。著書『頭がいい人、悪い人の話し方』は250万部突破！

樋口 裕一 先生
[小論文]

文章で自分を表現できれば、受験も人生も成功できますよ。「笑顔と努力」で合格を！

石関 直子 先生
[小論文]

理科

丁寧で色彩豊かな板書と詳しい講義で生徒を惹きつける。

宮内 舞子 先生
[物理]

化学現象の基本を疑い化学全体を見通す"伝説の講義"

鎌田 真彰 先生
[化学]

全国の受験生が絶賛するその授業は、わかりやすさそのもの！

田部 眞哉 先生
[生物]

地歴公民

入試頻出事項に的を絞った「表解板書」は圧倒的な信頼を得る。

金谷 俊一郎 先生
[日本史]

つねに生徒と同じ目線に立って、入試問題に対する的確な思考法を教えてくれる。

井之上 勇 先生
[日本史]

"受験世界史に荒巻あり"といわれる超実力人気講師。

荒巻 豊志 先生
[世界史]

世界史を「暗記」科目だなんて言わせない。正しく理解すれば必ず伸びることを一緒に体感しよう。

加藤 和樹 先生
[世界史]

わかりやすい図解と統計の説明に定評。

山岡 信幸 先生
[地理]

政治と経済のメカニズムを論理的に解明しながら、入試頻出ポイントを明確に示す。

清水 雅博 先生
[公民]

合格の秘訣2 革新的な学習システム

東進には、第一志望合格に必要なすべての要素を満たし、抜群の合格実績を生み出す学習システムがあります。

映像による授業を駆使した最先端の勉強法

高速学習

一人ひとりの
レベル・目標にぴったりの授業

東進はすべての授業を映像化しています。その数およそ1万種類。これらの授業を個別に受講できるので、一人ひとりのレベル・目標に合った学習が可能です。1.5倍速受講ができるほか自宅のパソコンからも受講できるので、今までにない効率的な学習が実現します。

1年分の授業を
最短2週間から1カ月で受講

従来の予備校は、毎週1回の授業。一方、東進の高速学習なら毎日受講することができます。だから、1年分の授業も最短2週間から1カ月程度で修了可能。先取り学習や苦手科目の克服、勉強と部活との両立も実現できます。

現役合格者の声

東京大学 理科一類
大竹 隆翔くん
東京都 私立 海城高校卒

東進の授業は映像なので、自分で必要と感じた科目を選んで、自分のスケジュールに合わせて授業が受けられます。部活や学校のない時に集中的に授業を進めることができ、主体的に勉強に向き合うことができました。

先取りカリキュラム（数学の例）

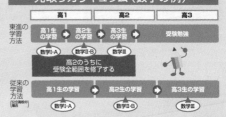

目標まで一歩ずつ確実に

スモールステップ・パーフェクトマスター

自分にぴったりのレベルから学べる
習ったことを確実に身につける

高校入門から超東大までの12段階から自分に合ったレベルを選ぶことが可能です。「簡単すぎる」「難しすぎる」といったことがなく、志望校へ最短距離で進みます。
授業後すぐに確認テストを行い内容が身についたかを確認し、合格したら次の授業に進むので、わからない部分を残すことはありません。短期集中で徹底理解をくり返し、学力を高めます。

現役合格者の声

早稲田大学 文化構想学部
加畑 恵さん
石川県立 金沢二水高校卒

高1の春休みに、東進に入学しました。東進の授業の後には必ず「確認テスト」があります。その場ですぐに授業の理解を確認することができました。憧れの大学に入ることができて本当に嬉しいです。

パーフェクトマスターのしくみ

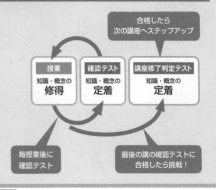

付録 3

徹底的に学力の土台を固める

高速マスター
基礎力養成講座

高速マスター基礎力養成講座は「知識」と「トレーニング」の両面から、効率的に短期間で基礎学力を徹底的に身につけるための講座です。文法事項や重要事項を単元別・分野別にひとつずつ完成させていくことができます。インターネットを介してオンラインで利用できるため、校舎だけでなく、自宅のパソコンやスマートフォンアプリで学習することも可能です。

現役合格者の声

慶應義塾大学 理工学部
畔上 亮真くん
神奈川県立 横浜翠嵐高校卒

おススメは「高速マスター基礎力養成講座」です。通学やちょっとした移動時間でもスマホで英単語などを勉強でき、スキマ時間を活用する習慣をつけられました。大学では自分の夢の基盤となることを学びたいです。

東進公式スマートフォンアプリ

▌東進式マスター登場！
（英単語／英熟語／英文法／基本例文）

スマートフォンアプリでスキ間時間も徹底活用！

1）スモールステップ・パーフェクトマスター！
頻出度（重要度）の高い英単語から始め、1つのSTEP（計100語）を完全修得すると次のSTAGEに進めるようになります。

2）自分の英単語力が一目でわかる！
トップ画面に「修得語数・修得率」をメーター表示。自分が今何語修得しているのか、どこを優先的に学習すべきなのか一目でわかります。

3）「覚えていない単語」だけを集中攻略できる！
未修得の単語、または「My単語（自分でチェック登録した単語）」だけをテストする出題設定が可能です。
すでに覚えている単語を何度も学習するような無駄を省き、効率良く単語力を高めることができます。

「共通テスト対応英単語1800」2018年共通テスト試行調査カバー率99.4%

君の合格力を徹底的に高める

志望校対策

第一志望校突破のために、志望校対策にどこよりもこだわり、合格力を徹底的に極める質・量ともに抜群の学習システムを提供します。従来からの「過去問演習講座」に加え、AIを活用した「志望校別単元ジャンル演習講座」が開講。東進が持つ大学受験に関するビッグデータをもとに、個別対応の演習プログラムを実現しました。限られた時間の中で、君の得点力を最大化します。

現役合格者の声

山形大学 医学部医学科
平間 三結さん
宮城県仙台二華高校卒

受験前の「過去問演習講座」では10年分の過去問演習の結果が記録でき、また「志望校別単元ジャンル演習講座」ではAIが分析した自分の弱点を重点的に学習できるので、とても役立ちました。

大学受験に必須の演習

▌過去問演習講座

1. 最大10年分の徹底演習
2. 厳正な採点、添削指導
3. 5日以内のスピード返却
4. 再添削指導で着実に得点力強化
5. 実力講師陣による解説授業

東進×AIでかつてない志望校対策

▌志望校別単元ジャンル演習講座

過去問演習講座の実施状況や、東進模試の結果など、東進で活用したすべての学習履歴をAIが総合的に分析。学習の優先順位をつけ、志望校別に「必勝必達演習セット」として十分な演習問題を提供します。問題は東進が分析した、大学入試問題の膨大なデータベースから提供されます。苦手を克服し、一人ひとりに適切な志望校対策を実現する日本初の学習システムです。

志望校合格に向けた最後の切り札

▌第一志望校対策演習講座

第一志望校の総合演習に特化し、大学が求める解答力を身につけていきます。対応大学は校舎にお問い合わせください。

合格の秘訣3 東進ドットコム

ここでしか見られない受験と教育の情報が満載！
大学受験のポータルサイト 東進 🔍検索

www.toshin.com

スマートフォン版も充実！

東進ブックスのインターネット書店

東進WEB書店

ベストセラー参考書から夢ふくらむ人生の参考書まで

　学習参考書から語学・一般書までベストセラー＆ロングセラーの書籍情報がもりだくさん！　あなたの「学び」をバックアップするインターネット書店です。検索機能もグンと充実。さらに、一部書籍では立ち読みも可能。探し求める1冊に、きっと出会えます。